# RESOURCE ALLOCATION AND ECONOMIC POLICY

*Also by Michael Allingham*

EQUILIBRIUM AND DISEQUILIBRIUM
GENERAL EQUILIBRIUM

*Also by M. L. Burstein*

MONEY
ECONOMIC THEORY: EQUILIBRIUM AND CHANGE
STUDIES IN THE DEMAND FOR DURABLE GOODS (*co-author*)

# RESOURCE ALLOCATION AND ECONOMIC POLICY

*Edited by*

MICHAEL ALLINGHAM

AND

M. L. BURSTEIN

*First published 1976 by*
THE MACMILLAN PRESS LTD
*London and Basingstoke*
*Associated companies in New York*
*Dublin Melbourne Johannesburg and Madras*

ISBN 978-1-349-02675-3     ISBN 978-1-349-02673-9 (eBook)
DOI 10.1007/978-1-349-02673-9

This book is for Mavis Cole

# Contents

*Preface*                                                                ix

*Notes on the Contributors*                                              xi

### PART I: RESOURCE ALLOCATION

Introduction                                                              3
1   Price Adjustment   *Michael Allingham*                                5
2   A Reconsideration of the Theory of Inflation   *Robert W.*
    *Clower*                                                             14
3   Paternalism and Prices   *G. C. Archibald* and *David Donaldson*     26
4   The Changing Economics of Education   *Z. Griliches*                 35
5   Mathematical Programming in Long-term Planning — Hungary
    *P. Bod*                                                             44
6   Interactions Between Planned and Market Economies —
    Hungary   *M. M. Tardos*                                            52
7   Economic Theory and Political Strategy — Cambodia
    *M. L. Burstein*                                                    61
8   Aid in a System of Taxes and Prices — Cambodia   *W. F.*
    *Beazer*                                                            72

### PART II: ECONOMIC POLICY

*Section 1: Petroleum Economics*

Introduction                                                            87
9   Public Investment in Energy Production under Price
    Uncertainty   *Michael Kennedy*                                     89
10  The Vertical Integration of Oil Firms   *Michael E. Canes*         103
11  The Macroeconomic Effects of the Higher Oil Price
    *J. R. Sargent*                                                    121
12  Conflict and Co-operation in an Era of High Oil Prices
    *Michael Jefferson*                                                136

*Section 2: Financial Economics*

Introduction                                                           151
13  Monetary Policy, the Stock Market and the Real Economy: A
    Keynesian Conspectus   *M. L. Burstein*                            153

14 Equity Values in Periods of Inflation  *Henry C. Wallich and
    Norman E. Mains*                                               164
15 'Keynesian' and 'Monetarist' Indicators of the United Kingdom
    Economy  *Gordon T. Pepper and Geoffrey E. Wood*               182
16 Money and Inflation: Some International Comparisons
    *Richard T. Selden*                                            199
17 Economic Foundations of Stock Market Regulation  *Irwin
    Friend*                                                        225

    *Index of Persons*                                             245
    *Index of Subjects*                                            249

# Preface

This volume contains the proceedings of a conference sponsored by the University College at Buckingham and the Institute of Economic Affairs, and held in London in June 1975. The editors, on behalf of the authors, who must be considered the real proprietors of the book, gratefully acknowledge the support of the College and the Institute which made the conference possible.

MA
*London*

MB
*Suffolk*

*August* 1975

# Notes on the Contributors

*Michael Allingham* teaches at the London School of Economics, and has previously taught at Edinburgh, Essex, Northwestern, Pennsylvania and Bristol Universities.

*G. C. Archibald* is Professor of Economics at the University of British Columbia. Prior to that he taught at the London School of Economics and the University of Essex, and edited the *Canadian Journal of Economics* in 1973–4.

*W. F. Beazer* teaches at the University of Virginia, and has done development work for IDA, the US DoD (AID), and other agencies.

*P. Bod* works at the Mathematical Institute of the Hungarian Academy of Sciences in Budapest, and has written extensively on multi-sectional planning.

*M. L. Burstein* taught in the United States and Canada, as well as at Warwick, before supervising the establishment of the School of Economics at Buckingham.

*Michael Canes* taught at Rochester University before joining the research staff of the American Petroleum Institute.

*Robert Clower* is Professor of Economics at the University of California, Los Angeles, and Editor of *Economic Inquiry,* the journal of the Western Economic Association.

*David Donaldson* is Associate Professor of Economics at the University of British Columbia. He took his B.A. in Mathematics at the University of Toronto in 1960 and his Ph.D. in Economics at Stanford University in 1966. His previous publications are in welfare economics.

*Irwin Friend* is director of the Rodney L. White Center of the Wharton School, University of Pennsylvania, and an authority on the analysis of securities markets and their regulatory processes.

*Z. Grilliches* is Professor of Economics at Harvard University, and has previously taught at Chicago. He was president of the Econometric Society in 1975.

*Michael Jefferson* is an economist with Shell International, and has worked widely in petroleum economics.

*Michael Kennedy* teaches at Texas University, and has published important research in the economics of the world petroleum economy.

*Norman Mains* studied at Colorado and Warwick Universities and was engaged in research on the securities industry before joining the staff of the Board of Governors of the Federal Reserve Board.

*Gordon Pepper* is a partner in Greenwell & Co., and a leading authority on British monetary economics, having pioneered in applying flow-of-funds analysis to British statistics.

*J. R. Sargent* taught at Oxford and Warwick, and has been an adviser to the British Treasury. He is now Group Adviser to the Midland Bank.

*Richard Selden* taught at Cornell and Columbia Universities before becoming chairman of the economics department at the University of Virginia. He is an authority on monetary velocity.

*M. M. Tardos* has worked in the Hungarian Planning Office, dealing with long- and medium-term planning, and is now a research officer in the Institute for Economic and Market Research, Budapest, and a member of several state committees.

*Henry Wallich* became a member of the Board of Governors of the Federal Reserve System after a teaching career at Yale. Earlier he was on the staff of the New York Federal Reserve Bank.

*Geoffrey Wood* taught at Warwick, before moving to the City University. He also participates in the preparation of Greenwell & Co's bulletins on monetary economics.

RESOURCE ALLOCATION AND ECONOMIC POLICY

# Part I
# Resource Allocation

# Introduction

Resource allocation is economics, and broadly speaking economics is resource allocation. Thus the eight chapters comprising Part I do not attempt to cover or even indicate the whole scope of the subject. Instead, they aim to illuminate certain important topics within the area. In most of these contributions theory and applications are essentially interwoven, yet in a loose sense one can identify the first four as predominantly theoretical and the last four as predominantly applied — if only in that they relate to specific rather than abstract economies.

Where resources are to be allocated through a price mechanism it is important that prices adjust in line with the underlying preferences and resources of the economy. Yet, in contrast with the established theory on the possibility and optimality of price systems as resource allocation mechanisms, the theory of price adjustment is yet to be given a sound axiomatic basis. This is considered in Chapter 1, where a price adjustment process which is completely explained by the independent optimising behaviour of individual agents is derived, and shown to be more stable than the traditional Walrasian process. In a monetary economy a particularly important facet of price adjustment is inflation. Since inflation is irrelevant in the Walrasian system, where excess demands are homogeneous of degree zero in prices, its investigation requires a wider perspective. This is provided, in the form of general process analysis, by Clower in Chapter 2.

One of the cases in which the price system may be an inefficient resource allocation mechanism is that of interdependent preferences. Under general interdependence the concept of optimality is difficult to define satisfactorily, and this is particularly true if the dependence is paternalistic. In Chapter 3 Archibald and Donaldson define such paternalism, and show that, under a suitable reinterpretation, the classical theorems of welfare economics continue to hold if the interdependence of preferences is of any form other than the paternalistic. One of the areas in which interdependence, possibly paternalistic, might be expected to exist is education, but interdependence is but one of the many problems of resource allocation here. The whole field is examined in Chapter 4 by Griliches, who concentrates on the changing nature of this single yet pervasive market.

It is important to remember that the general problem of resource allocation applies just as much to planned and to developing economies as to developed market economies. Chapters 5 and 6 discuss a particular planned economy — Hungary. In such an economy some long-term outlook is essential for the efficient intertemporal allocation of resources. Bod presents a mathematical programming model of such a process, which emphasizes the essentially flexible nature of all useful long-term plans, and provides an array of potentially optimal development paths rather than some unique best path. This planning process takes the form of an iterative dialogue between the centre and the sectors, but is open in that the adjustment mechanism of the iterative procedure will be specified only in the light of actual experience. Tardos examines the important links between the planned economy and market economies, and shows that greater flexi‑ bility is required in the planned economy if resources are to be allocated efficiently during periods of change in the market economies, and particularly during periods of inflation.

The developing economy of Cambodia during the period 1974—5 provides a most valuable example of an essentially pure-exchange economy; the final pair of contributions, Chapters 7 and 8, analyse this example. Burstein shows how economic theory can fruitfully be brought to bear on the complex and practical resource allocation problems of such a situation, and suggests solutions — solutions which were in fact in the process of being implemented when a change of regime took place. These involve a forced-loan scheme, which is shown to have optimal effects on the inflation—budget—foreign exchange nexus at the centre of the problem. Beazer concentrates more on the foreign exchange side of this nexus, and examines the relation between this and the aid received by the economy. When such aid is large, a system of taxes and subsidies must be devised if the price system is to remain an efficient resource allocation mechanism.

# 1 Price Adjustment

MICHAEL ALLINGHAM

## 1. Introduction

The purpose of this paper is to formulate how an economy adjusts itself
if it is not in equilibrium, and to examine whether such adjustment will
tend to bring the economy to equilibrium. Since we require the (decentralised) economy to adjust itself, this must be through the independent
optimising behaviour of the individual agents in the economy, rather than
through some *deus ex machina*, such as an 'auctioneer'. To do this it is
useful to reinterpret the concept of an equilibrium: as a state from which
there is no movement. This immediately identifies the natural movement
property of the economy; it is the stability of this which we examine.

The original approach to the stability problem was that of Walras
(1954), which was based on the *tatonnement*. This had two artificial aspects: the device of recontract, whereby none of the agents' declared
actions were in fact consummated if such joint consumption were not
feasible; and the external or imaginary 'auctioneer', who arbitrarily adjusted prices in response to market forces. The first generalisations of this,
stemming from that of Negishi (1961), avoided only the first of these, but
did not indicate who changed prices. Later approaches, stemming from
that of Fisher (1972), attempt to avoid the second artificiality and charge
specific agents with the setting of prices, but effectively remove only this
one stage, for the price-setting agents, as the auctioneer, act in an arbitrary
non-optimising manner. The present paper, on the other hand, retains
recontract, but allows individual agents to change prices in an optimising
way. Thus the paper may be seen as an analysis of the dynamic properties
of the concept of equilibrium presented in an earlier paper (Allingham,
1974). Alternatively, as will become apparent, it may be interpeted as an
analysis of the stability of perfect monopoly, viewed as the opposite polar
case to the Walrasian one of perfect competition. The analysis here, however, is concerned with the rationale underlying the adjustment process
and the comparison of the stability of this with the stability of the Walrasian *tatonnement* process, rather than with sufficient conditions for stability
in an absolute sense. These latter conditions have been examined elsewhere
(Allingham, 1975).

After this introduction the specific economy to be considered is discussed at an informal level, in Section 2, then formalised in Section 3. The relevant static properties of this economy are discussed and compared with those of the Walrasian economy in Section 4. Section 5 contains the main stability analysis, and shows that the economy considered is in some sense more stable than the corresponding Walrasian economy. Finally, the correspondence principle in this framework is investigated in Section 6, where it is shown that if a commodity becomes more competitive, then its price is likely to fall. An Appendix proves a minor lemma used in Section 5.

## 2. Specific Economy

We first discuss the nature of the economy we present at an informal level. This is a pure-exchange economy, but of course one that differs somewhat from the standard Walrasian economy; only these differences are discussed.

The basic difference is that commodities are distinguished by ownership, as well as in the usual way. By itself this needs no justification at a formal level, for it includes the Walrasian neglect of ownership as a special case, but in conjunction with a strict convexity of preferences assumption (which rules out perfect substitutes) it does require some explanation. Intuitively this may be relevant for two reasons: firstly, sellers, and therefore their commodities, may have location; and secondly, the quality of a commodity may be imperfectly known and judged in part on the reputation of its seller (together with risk-aversion this would provide some argument for strict convexity).

Because of this it is possible to consider individual agents, specifically sellers, as quoting prices. If prices are to change at all, they must be quoted by either buyers or sellers. Various considerations suggest sellers: firstly, sellers naturally know the market since they own the supply and are faced with the demand; secondly, this is more efficient informationally, in that it requires only one, rather than $n - 1$, prices for each commodity; thirdly, there are $n - 1$ potential buyers but only one seller so that market power (in a loose sense) will typically rest with the seller; and fourthly, this is generally observable. Since all transactions are for credit, rather than barter, the seller is well defined.

Formally, then, the economy is characterised by perfect monopoly. This should be interpreted as the opposite polar case to the Walrasian characterisation of perfect competition. Neither case applies exactly to real economies, but both may have implications for these.

In order for sellers to quote prices in an optimising manner they must have some expectation of the market demand which will result. Most generally, these expectations might depend on the existing state of the economy and on all preceding states, but here we consider expectations which depend only on the existing state. The basic reason for this is that we shall be considering sufficient conditions for stability of the economy, and comparing these with the corresponding conditions for the stability of the corresponding Walrasian economy; it is therefore of interest to consider only some minimal information system, since we would expect more information to lead to more efficient adjustments, and also one which is comparable with that of the Walrasian economy. More specific justifications might also lead to this: for example, agents may have point priors (for example on the *slopes* of the demand curves), so they would need only the latest indication of the *positions* of the demand curves; alternatively, it may be that the cost of taking account of the past were prohibitive.

Given, then, that the agent takes account only of the existing environment and does not learn, we must specify how his expectations depend on this. In so doing we shall consider the only aspects of the environment that the agent may take account of as those naturally known to him, namely the price system and the market demands for his commodities. It is then helpful to consider him as taking the *position* of his demand curve as given by this information, so we need specify only the believed *slope*. Here we shall assume that this is constant, that is, depends neither on the own nor on other prices. Again, the basic justification for this simple form is that it is simple, and that a more sophisticated estimate might be expected to lead to more efficient adjustments. (For ease of comparison with the simplest Walrasian economy we assume that there is one commodity whose price is always fixed, and all other prices are in terms of this numeraire; it is then the believed slope in numeraire price which is constant.)

Specifically, then, each agent first chooses prices for his commodities so as to maximise his expected income, that is, the product of these prices with the implied expected demands, subject of course to expected demands not exceeding endowments. This generates a complete price vector. Each agent then chooses a consumption, namely that which is preference-maximal subject to its cost at these prices not exceeding this expected income.

Since the change in expected demand does not depend on the prices of other commodities, the agent will choose the price of each of his commodities to maximise the expected revenue from that commodity. This means that without loss of generality we may consider each agent as being endowed with only one commodity; since ownership-distinction means that no two agents are endowed with the same commodity, we may then identify commodities with agents.

## 3. The model

There are $n$ consumers, or commodities, labelled by $i = 1, \ldots, n$, commodity $n$ being the numeraire, with price fixed at unity. The following discussion is to be understood as applying to non-numeraire commodities; the changes required for the numeraire are left to the reader. Consumer $i$ chooses a price $p_i = 0$ for his commodity and a consumption $x^i = (x^i_1, \ldots, x^i_n)$

$\in R_+^n$, so a state of the economy is given by the array $(p_1, \ldots, p_n,$ $x^1, \ldots x^n) = (p, x^1, \ldots, x^n)$. Specifically, given the existing state $(p(t-1),$ $x^1(t-1), \ldots, x^n(t-1))$, consumer $i$ first chooses $p_i(t)$ to maximise his expected revenue $p_i(t)\, \hat{x}_i(t)$ where $\hat{x}_i(t)$ is his expected demand, given by

$$\hat{x}_i(t) = x_i(t-1) - a_i(p_i(t) - p_i(t-1)) \tag{1}$$

Here $x^i = \Sigma_j x^j_i$ is aggregate demand and $a_i = -d\hat{x}_i/dp_i > 0$ is his belief of the (downward) slope of the aggregate demand curve for his commodity. Together this generates a new price vector $p(t)$. Consumer $i$ then chooses $x^i(t)$ to be $\pi_i$-maximal, where $\pi_i$ is his preference relation over the space of his consumptions (which relation is assumed to be continuous, strictly convex, and strictly monotone).

Consumer $i$ is endowed with one unit (by choice of units) of commodity $i$ and no other commodity. His choice of $p_i(t)$ is constrained by the requirement that expected demand not exceed his endowment, that is, by $\hat{x}_i(t) \leq 1$. (The non-negativity of $\hat{x}_i$ does not require mention, as it is clear that any effectively chosen $\hat{x}_i$ will be positive, as will any chosen $p_i$.) His choice of $x^i(t)$ is constrained by the requirement that its cost equal his expected income, that is,

$$p(t)\, x^i(t) = p_i(t)\, \hat{x}_i(t)$$

(Because of monotonacity there is no increase of generality in replacing this equality by a weak inequality.)

The solution to consumer $i$'s price choice problem is

$$p_i(t) = \max \left\{ \tfrac{1}{2}(x_i(t-1)/a_i + p_i(t-1)), (x_i(t-1) - 1)/a_i + p_i(t-1) \right\} \tag{2}$$

which with (1) gives

$$\hat{x}_i(t) = \min \left\{ a_i p_i(t), 1 \right\}$$

His consumption choice is therefore given by

$$x^i(t) \text{ is } \pi_i\text{- maximal on}$$

$$\left\{ x^i \in R_+^n \,|\, p(t)\, x^i = \min \left\{ a_i p_i(t)^2, p_i(t) \right\} \right\}$$

It should be clear that there exists a unique solution to each of these problems. It should also be clear that we may write $x^i(t)$ as a function of $p(t)$, say $x^i(p)$, and that this function is continuous. To see this continuity, one need consider only the fixed income demand function $z^i$, defined by

$$z^i(p, c_i) \text{ is } \pi_i\text{-maximal on}$$

$$\left\{ z^i \in R_+^n \,|\, pz^i = c_i \right\} \tag{3}$$

which, as is well known, is continuous (for $c_i > 0$), and note that

$$c_i = \min \left\{ a_i p_i^2, p_i \right\}$$

is continuous in $p$ (and that $p > 0$ implies $c_i > 0$).

Because of this continuity it is clear that we need consider only the stability of the price subsystem, $p(t)$. The dynamics of this are given directly from the individual agents' price choices (2), that is,

$$p_i(t) - p_i(t-1) = \begin{cases} \frac{1}{2}(x_i(t-1)/a_i - p_i(t-1)) \\ \qquad\qquad\qquad\qquad \text{if } p_i(t-1) \lesseqgtr 1/a_i \\ (x_i(t-1) - 1)/a_i \end{cases} \quad (4)$$

Note that, from (2), $p_i(t)$ is a function of $x_i(t-1)$ and $p_i(t-1)$, so that as $x_i(t-1)$ is a function of $p(t-1)$ we have $p_i(t) - p_i(t-1)$ as a function of $p(t-1)$, as required. Also note from (2) that when $p_i(t-1) = 1/a_i$ we have

$$\tfrac{1}{2}(x_i(t-1)/a_i - p_i(t-1)) = (x_i(t-1) - 1)/a_i$$

so that, since $x^i(p)$ is continuous, this adjustment function is continuous.

Instead of investigating the discrete process (4) we shall, as is usual, consider its continuous analogue, that is, from now on omitting time arguments,

$$\dot{p}_i = f_i(p) = \begin{cases} \frac{1}{2}(x_i(p)/a_i - p_i) \\ \qquad\qquad\qquad \text{if } p_i \lesseqgtr 1/a_i \\ (x_i(p) - 1)/a_i \end{cases}$$

$$(i < n),\ p_n \equiv 1,\ \text{where } x_i = \Sigma_j x_i^j \qquad\qquad (5)$$

and $x^j(p)$ is $\pi_j$-maximal on

$$\left\{ x^j \in R_+^n \,|\, px^j = \min\left\{ a_j p_j^2,\, p_j \right\} \right\}$$

This system will be the basis of our stability analysis; since its dynamics are determined in a natural way by the characteristics of the individual agents (with no auctioneer), or since it is characterised by monopoly, we shall refer to this as the *natural*, or monopolistic, system.

## 4. Static Properties

It is of interest to compare the natural system (5) with the Walrasian *auctioneer*, or competitive, system. For the same underlying preferences and endowments this, in its basic numeraire form, is

$$\dot{p}_i = g_i(p) = y_i(p) - 1$$

$$(i < n),\ p_n \equiv 1,\ \text{where } y_i = \Sigma_j y_i^j \qquad\qquad (6)$$

and $y^j(p)$ is $\pi_j$-maximal on

$$\left\{ y^j \in R_+^n \,|\, py^j = p_j \right\}$$

The function $y$ is the competitive aggregate demand function; this may be taken to characterise the economy (that is, the underlying preferences and resources), so we shall refer to the economy having some property if this function has the property. Clearly any preferences and endowments correspond to some demand function, and in fact the converse is also true (see Debreu, 1974, main theorem). It is well known that $y$ is continuous, as therefore is $g$, and that $g$ satisfies the (strong) Walras law, $pg(p) \equiv 0$. This means that if $g_i = 0$ for each $i < n$, then $g_n = 0$, which provides a justification for considering the numeraire system with $p_n$ fixed. Of course any numeraire system is trivially homogeneous of degree zero in absolute prices.

The function $x$ in (4) is the natural aggregate demand function, which we have noted is continuous; it follows that $f$ is continuous. However, $f$ does not satisfy the strong Walras law, though it does satisfy a weak Walras law: $qf(p) \equiv 0$ for some given $q_i = q_i(p_i) > 0$. To see this, write

$$R(p) = \{i|p_i \lesseqgtr 1/a_i\}, S(p) = \{i|p_i > 1/a_i\}$$

Then adding the individuals' budget constraints in (5) and rearranging gives

$$\sum_R 2a_i p_i \, (\tfrac{1}{2}(x_i/a_i - p_i)) + \sum_S a_i p_i ((x_i - 1)/a_i) = 0$$

which is simply $qf(p) = 0$ where $q_i = 2a_i p_i$ if $i \in R$ and $q_i = a_i p_i$ if $i \in S$. Of course, this is sufficient for each $f_i = 0$, $i < n$, to imply $f_n = 0$, and therefore to justify keeping $p_n$ fixed.

In the case where $x$ and $y$ are differentiable we may compare their derivatives. To do this it is helpful to define the (aggregate) price and (individual) income effects in the fixed income demand function (3), that is

$$\alpha_{ij} = \sum_k \partial z_i^k/\partial p_j \quad \beta_i^j = \partial z_i^j/\partial c_i \tag{7}$$

Then the derivatives of the functions $y$ and $x$ may be written

$$\partial y_i/\partial p_j = y_{ij} = \alpha_{ij} + \beta_i^j$$

$$\partial x_i/\partial p_j = x_{ij} = \begin{cases} \alpha_{ij} + 2p\beta_i^j \\ \qquad\qquad\quad \text{if } p_i \lesseqgtr 1/a_i \\ \alpha_{ij} + \beta_i^j \end{cases}$$

Now $\beta_i^j$ is an individual effect, where $\alpha_{ij}$ is an aggregate effect, so for a large economy, that is, one with many consumers, we might expect the former to be small relative to the latter. (Although reasonable, this is not ensured merely by having many agents, since the boundary case where $x_{ij} = 0$ is possible with any number of agents.)

Finally, we note an alternative interpretation of the natural system (5) which makes this more comparable with the Walrasian system (6) where the price changes are proportional to excess demands (since $g_i = y_i - 1$). This interprets expected demand $\hat{x}$ as expected sales or equivalently supply, so that $x - \hat{x}$ is excess demand. Then using (1) and (2) we may write the relevant part of (5) as

$$
\dot{p}_i = \begin{cases} \frac{1}{2}(x_i - \hat{x}_i)/a_i \\ \\ (x_i - \hat{x}_i)/a_i \end{cases} \quad \text{if } p_i \lessgtr 1/a_i
$$

so that price changes are proportional to excess demands at least in certain ranges.

## 5. Stability

We are now able to compare the stability of the natural and Walrasian processes $f$ and $g$, and show that in some sense the natural process is the 'more stable'.

Of course this will not apply without restriction, since although, as we shall see, the stability of the (non-numeraire) Jacobian of $g(p)$ evaluated where $g(p) = 0$ implies that of $f(p)$ evaluated where $g(p) = 0$, it does not imply this evaluated where $f(p) = 0$. This does not apply if the economy $y$ is linear, at least as an approximation or in the relevant range, but even then the natural system may not be the more stable because of the different effective speeds of adjustment (or equivalently choice of units) in the two systems ($a_i$ in the natural and unity in the auctioneer). It is clear then that we can consider only linear economies, and must compare the more basic properties of stability for any choice of units, or $D$-stability. Note that the ($D$-)stability of a linear numeraire system satisfying a weak Walras law is equivalent to the ($D$-) stability of its Jacobian.

The matrix $A$ is $D$-*stable* if $DA$ is a stable matrix for any (positive) diagonal matrix $D$. Arrow and McManus (1958) have shown that a sufficient condition for this is that $A = CBC^{-1}$ where $C$ is some diagonal matrix and $B$ is either negative quasi-definite or Hicksian (that is, each $(-1)^k B^k \geqq 0$ with some non-zero, where $B^k$ is a $k$-order principal minor of $B$) (corollary to Theorem 2, and using the equivalence of stability and Hicksian stability for gross substitutes matrices). They also suggest that this condition may be necessary (footnote 8). Accordingly, we define the matrix $A$ to be *strongly D-stable* if it satisfies this condition.

It is clear that if $B$ is negative quasi-definite, then so is $B - E$ where $E$ is a (non-negative) diagonal matrix. In fact an equivalent result applies if $B$ is Hicksian; a lemma showing this is given in the Appendix.

It was shown in Section 5 that if $y$ is linear (and large), then its (non-numeraire) Jacobian $Y$ approximates the Jacobian $X$ of $x$. Since it follows from (5) that

$$
f_{ij} = \begin{cases} \frac{1}{2}x_{ij}/a_i - \frac{1}{2}\delta_{ij} \\ \\ x_{ij}/a_i \end{cases} \quad \text{if } p_i \lessgtr 1/a_i
$$

(where $\delta_{ij}$ is the Kronecker delta), this means that the Jacobian of $f$ may be written as $F = D(Y - E)$ where $D$ and $E$ are diagonal matrices with elements $d_{ii} = 1/2a_i$ and $e_{ii} = a_i$ if $p_i < 1/a_i$, but $d_{ii} = 1/a_i$ and $e_{ii} = 0$ if $p_i \geq 1/a_i$. The comparison of the $D$-stability of $f$ and $g$ is thus that of the matrices $D(Y - E)$ and $Y$, or equivalently $Y - E$ and $Y$ (as $D$ has positive diagonal).

Now if $Y$ is strongly $D$-stable, then $Y = CBC^{-1}$ where $C$ is diagonal and $B$ is negative quasi-definite or Hicksian; but then $B - E$ is negative quasi-definite or (using the lemma) Hicksian, so that

$$C(B - E)C^{-1} = CBC^{-1} - E = Y - E$$

is, by definition, strongly $D$-stable. However, the reverse implication does not hold, as may be seen from the case where $p_i < 1/a_i = 2$ for each $i$ and $E = -\frac{1}{4}I$, so that $Y = \frac{1}{4}I$ ($I$ being the unit matrix). We have then some comparison of stability.

> *Theorem 1.* If the economy $y$ of (6) is linear and large, then the strong $D$-stability of the auctioneer system (6) implies that of the natural system (5), but not conversely.

## 6. Correspondence Principle

Finally, it is worth considering whether the assumption of the stability of the natural process implies any new comparative statistical information. Of course it is clear that the usual results of the correspondence principle will continue to apply, for we are merely replacing a stable $g$ by a stable $f$. There is, however, one new aspect to be considered, that is, the effect of a change in some $a_i$. Now if $a_i$ increases, the seller of commodity $i$ believes that the effect of a change of his price on the demand for his commodity increases, or that the commodity becomes more competitive.

It is straightforward to investigate this effect, for if the economy is linear, then differentiating the equilibrium condition $f = 0$ of the system (5) and rearranging, we have

$$\frac{dp_i}{da_i} = \frac{\partial f_i}{\partial a_i} \frac{F_{ii}}{|F|}$$

where $\partial f_i/\partial a_i$ is given by (5) as

$$\left.\begin{array}{c} -x_i/2a_i^2 < 0 \\[2em] (x_i - 1)/a_i^2 = 0 \end{array}\right\} \quad \text{if } \overset{\cdot}{p_i} \lessgtr 1/a_i$$

Now if $F$ is $D$-stable it follows immediately from the Routh–Hurwitz criterion (see, for example, Gantmacher, 1959, Section 15.6.2) that $F_{ii}/|F| \lesseqgtr 0$, so that we have the result $dp_i/da_i \lesseqgtr 0$

*Theorem 2.* If the system $f$ of (5) is linear and $D$-stable, then an increase in the competitiveness of commodity $i$ (that is, of $a_i$) leads to a decrease, or no change, in its equilibrium (numeraire) price.

Of course the conclusion holds if the conditions apply to the underlying competitive economy $y$, or if $D$-stability is replaced by strong $D$-stability. The fact that an increase of $a_i$ has no effect on $p_i$ if $p_i > 1/a_i$ is not surprising, for in this case $\hat{x}_i = 1$, so that all of the commodity is sold and none held back for monopolistic reasons, so that the commodity is 'perfectly competitive' anyway.

## Appendix

*Lemma.* If the (square) matrix $B$ is Hicksian, then so is $B - E$ for any (non-negative) diagonal matrix $E$.

*Proof.* It is sufficient to show this where $e_{ii} = 1$ and $e_{ii} = 0 (i > 1)$. Now let $\bar{B} = B - E$ and $B^b$ be a typical $b$-order principal minor of $B$ with $\bar{B}^b$ the corresponding minor of $\bar{B}$, and suppose that

$$(-1)^b \bar{B}^b \geq (-1)^b B^b > 0 \qquad (*)$$

for $b = k$. Then if $B^{k+1}$ does not include $b_{ii}$ we have $\bar{B}^{k+1} = B^{k+1}$. If $B^{k+1}$ does include $b_{ii}$ we have $B^{k+1} = b_{ii}B^k + \Delta$ and $\bar{B}^{k+1} = (b_{ii} - 1)B^{-k} + \Delta$ (where $B^k$ are the appropriate $k$-order minors and $\Delta$ a term not including $b_{ii}$), so that, noting that $b_{ii} \leq 0$, we have $(-1)^{k+1}\bar{B}^{k+1} > (-1)^{k+1}B^{k+1}$. The induction thus shows that $(*)$ holds for $b = k + 1$ if it holds for $b = k$, and since it clearly holds for $b = 1$ it therefore holds in general.

## References

Allingham, M. G. (1974). 'Equilibrium and Stability', *Econometrica*, XL 27–41.
Allingham, M. G. (1975). 'Stability of Monopoly', *Econometrica*, XXII 705–16.
Arrow, K. J. and McManus, M. (1958). 'A Note on Dynamic Stability', *Econometrica*, XXVI 297–305.
Debreu, G. (1974). 'Excess Demand Functions', *Journal of Mathematical Economics*, I 1–10.
Fisher, F. M. (1972). 'On Stability Without an Auctioneer', *Review of Economic Studies*, XXXIX 1–16.
Gantmacher, F. R. (1959). *The Theory of Matrices* (New York: Chelsea Publishing Company).
Negishi, T. (1961). 'Monopolistic Competition and General Equilibrium', *Review of Economic Studies*, XXVIII 196–201.
Walras, L. (1954). *Elements of Pure Economics* (London: Allen & Unwin).

# 2 A Reconsideration of the Theory of Inflation

ROBERT W. CLOWER

Recent discussions of inflation are disturbingly reminiscent of similarly topical discussions of unemployment that preceded and followed publication of Keynes's *General Theory of Employment, Interest and Money* in 1936. Now, as then, traditionalists argue that the economy will work best if left to itself. Now, as then, a much larger group of puzzled or simple uncommitted economists question whether private ownership economies can work well without constant governmental prodding. Now, as then, a small but vocal group of radicals contends that such economies cannot work well under any circumstances. Now, as then, finally, debate tends to be carried on largely at cross-purposes because adherents to different camps are unable to agree upon a common framework of analysis as a basis for rational discussion of their differences.

What is disturbing about all this is the melancholy prospect that the outcome of the present inflation debate will be as inconclusive and intellectually unsatisfying as that of the earlier unemployment debate. A different outcome is hardly conceivable unless at some stage discussion is directed away from issues that turn ultimately on implicit differences in method and ideology and is focused instead on issues that are reducible to questions of logic or fact.

If such a redirection were feasible within the framework of presently established theory, surely it would already have taken place some time ago; for whatever else might be said about the Knave of Science, it cannot be claimed that its practitioners are naturally more quarrelsome than those of other disciplines. If this is granted, then what seems to be required is a restatement of established theory that will provide fresh perspective on the manner in which individual economic activities are co-ordinated — or might fail to be co-ordinated — in private ownership economies that bear a family resemblance to economies of actual record.

Anything more ambitious than an outline of such a restatement is out of the question here. The best that might be hoped for in a single paper is to motivate further work by showing that central aspects of a presently confused and controversial literature can be significantly clarified by following

14

a line of inquiry that, if not at all new, represents a clear departure from prevailing modes. Such is my purpose in the pages that follow.

## 1. Background

Inflation is generally acknowledged to be a monetary phenomenon in the trivial sense that the phenomenon manifests itself in a sustained and rapid rise in the general money price level (see Johnson, 1972, 1975). It is possible to quibble about the meaning of the terms 'sustained', 'rapid' and 'general money price level', but these are matters more of terminology than of substance. Serious difficulties arise only when we ask: precisely what forces govern movements in the general level of prices in an ongoing monetary exchange economy?

The theoretically most sophisticated way to approach this question is through general competitive analysis. Here one starts with an unambiguous body of formal knowledge about the circumstances in which the production and consumption plans of a set of individual economic agents will be compatible with associated plans to trade commodities among themselves at rates of exchange that are defined in terms of underlying conditions of taste and technology. Assuming that one of the commodities traded is an asset called 'money' that serves as a common unit of account, one can proceed to prove various theorems about the way in which money rates of exchange will vary in response to alternative postulated changes in underlying conditions. As Patinkin and others have shown, this approach yields – among other things – a modern version of the quantity theory that serves rigorously to validate classical propositions about the invariance of equilibrium values of real magnitudes (including rates of interest) with respect to changes in the nominal quantity of inconvertible paper currency (see, particularly, Patinkin, 1956; Archibald and Lipsey, 1958; Clower and Burstein, 1960). On the basis of common knowledge about the sluggish manner in which underlying conditions of taste and technology normally change, it is then natural to argue that rapid unidirectional movements in all (or most) money prices must be attributable primarily to exogenous changes in the nominal quantity of money.

As recent contributions to the micro-foundations of monetary theory have shown, this approach to the explanation of inflation raises as many questions as it answers (see, especially, Ostroy, 1973; Howitt, 1973; Ostroy and Starr, 1974). Strictly speaking, general competitive analysis, as presently formulated, is descriptive only of *virtual* economic systems; it deals with the formulation of production, consumption and trading plans but it is utterly silent about their execution. This being so, it is difficult to see how the theory can be considered to characterise any but stationary states of an ongoing economy, and even more difficult to see how the commodity designated as 'money' within the theory could be considered to play any role other than that of an analytical *deus ex machina* – a device introduced *ad hoc* into what would otherwise be described as a model of centrally co-ordinated multilateral barter to lend it superficial verisimilitude as a theory of decentralised monetary exchange. Appearances to the contrary notwithstanding, therefore, general competitive analysis — at least as presently formulated — is incapable of providing an intellectually satisfying explanation even of stylised inflationary processes. This is attributable not to any logical weakness in the theory, but rather to the fact that its premises are too special to permit the theory to deal explicitly with situations in which — as in real life — commodity trades normally can be carried out routinely at prevailing prices even though individual trading plans are mutually inconsistent. More concretely, the central flaw in established competitive analysis lies in its lack of an acceptable theory of exchange intermediation. The conventional artifice of a 'market authority' or 'auctioneer' serves only to obscure this flaw, not to correct it. The question then arises whether an approach less sophisticated than general competitive analysis might be fruitfully utilised to discuss the theory of inflation.

Unfortunately, the class of presently promising alternatives contains just two types of theory, both of which are essentially aggregative variants of general competitive analysis. I refer, of course, to what are commonly referred to as 'monetarist' and 'income—expenditure' theories. It would be possible to deal critically and at length with each of these types, but I doubt that such an exercise would add even marginally to present professional understanding of their shortcomings. Here just a few broad comments are in order.

From a formal point of view, the main difference between monetarist and income—expenditure models is that, in the former, attention is focused on the willingness of economic agents in the aggregate to hold existing money balances while, in the latter, attention is focused on the willingness of separate economic sectors (households, firms, etc.) to equate money expenditure with money income and so maintain existing sectoral money balances constant. Obviously this difference does not amount to a distinction. The two types of theory are distinguished at another level by rather different presumptions about the self-adjusting tendencies of the economic system, but in neither case do the theories furnish any basis for reasoned assessment of the probable factual validity of their maintained hypotheses. The monetarist position is quite clear on this: it rests explicitly on a 'black box' conception of the economic system — what comes out can be predicted only by what goes in. The income—expenditure position is less clear, but it appears to rest on what might be called a 'grab bag' view of the economic system — regardless of what goes in, almost anything might come out! Neither point of view is of any value for circumventing the difficulties associated with the central flaw in their parent theory — the lack of an acceptable theory of exchange intermediation. Where the parent theory is unambiguously silent, its offspring are noisily ambiguous. As far as our understanding of inflationary processes is concerned, there is nothing to choose between them.

## 2. General Process Analysis: A Sketch

In every advanced society the exchange activities of individual economic agents are co-ordinated by a relatively small subset of these same agents who act in a special capacity as brokers and auction agents or as outright dealers in commodities that are regularly produced, consumed or used by members of the community. Thus the arrangement and execution of trades is almost never an independent do-it-yourself affair; on the contrary, most exchange transactions take place within a highly structured framework of market institutions that has evolved gradually out of an interplay of political, social and technological factors with everyday economic forces of greed and competition.

The main outlines of contemporary market arrangements are much the same as those of much earlier times, suggesting that the forces underlying these arrangements have worked continuously and with great power throughout the course of recorded human history. Recent work has clarified the nature of some of these forces (see, particularly, Hicks, 1967; Clower, 1969; Perlman, 1971; Brunner and Meltzer, 1971; Chuchman, 1975; Jones, 1975. For example, it can be shown that market intermediaries — inventory-holding middlemen of various kinds — will find it profitable to operate in any community where fixed costs of trade associated with individual search and bargaining activities are sufficiently great. Similarly, it can be shown that trade specialisation will occur in situations where higher trading volume is accompanied by economies of scale in holding inventories. Monetary exchange — involving arrangements where at least one commodity is used as a common means of payment by virtually all trade intermediaries — can be accounted for in a similar manner, and it is then a fairly straightforward matter to explain the emergence of banks and other loan merchants, the development of trade credit arrangements, the creation of manufacturing concerns, and so on. These problems have been explored extensively elsewhere (for references see Clower, 1975), so I shall not dwell on them further here. For present purposes, it is more to the point to take the existence of prevailing institutions for granted so that attention is focused on the behavioural properties of intermediary economies rather than on their evolution.

Let us begin by considering the special case of a pure commodity—money economy in which each trade intermediary deals with just two goods — one of them the money commodity — and in which all trading is spot (cf. Howitt, 1974). The essential function of intermediaries is to reduce search and bargaining costs to primary agents by providing a 'ready market'. To perform that function, intermediaries must at all times hold inventories of both money and goods and must stand ready to buy and sell at stated prices in such quantities as prospective customers might desire. In a literal sense, prices are administered by intermediaries, while quantities are (within wide limits) administered by customers. In general, however, prices set by intermediaries must be varied from time to time to maintain control of trade inventories. Since customer arrival times are random from the point of view of intermediaries, trade volume over short intervals of time cannot significantly affect price decisions. Prices will tend to vary discontinuously and discretely in response to perceived gaps between desired holdings of goods and money and actual holdings as determined by the average volume of purchases and sales over more or less extended intervals of time.

In this kind of economy, equilibrium requires that prices be uniform among traders of any single good (provided we abstract from transport costs); that rates of return on trade inventories be equal to the rate of return on capital in general; that prices be such that the quantity produced and sold of each non-money commodity is equal, *on average*, to the quantity demanded for purchase and consumed; that each trader's average inventory holdings be constant; that the general money price level be such that net production of the money commodity is zero; and that the total existing stock of money be just equal to the amount demanded to hold for trade or other purposes.

This is already a fairly long list of requirements — and it is by no means complete. In particular, I have omitted all mention of requirements imposed on primary agents. In the situation considered, each primary agent will hold inventories of goods and money, and these must be maintained constant, on average, if equilibrium is to be maintained. In addition all the usual marginal conditions must hold, at least in a stochastic sense, since otherwise the realised trade volume of some intermediaries would vary over time. Obviously formal modelling even of this very special kind of intermediary economy is a complex affair. On the basis of the discussion so far, however, it is possible to say some things about the probable dynamics of motion in such a system — and that is the essential purpose of the present argument. Previously I have called this kind of exercise *general process analysis*. What follows is merely a sketch of ideas that are developed much more fully elsewhere (for example in Clower and Leijonhufvud, 1975, and Leijonhufvud, 1973).

To make matters as simple as possible, suppose that the money commodity — let us call it 'gold' for the time being — serves no purpose in the economy except as a means of payment and store of value. Suppose further that, starting from a state of full equilibrium, the stock of money in the economy proceeds to grow at a steady rate as a result of a technological innovation in gold mining. The first impact will be felt by traders who deal with gold producers; their inventories of goods will decline and their inventories of money will rise. To replenish their inventories, these traders will either purchase goods from other traders or increase prices paid to primary agents or both. One way and another, the effect of the increased money stock will spread gradually throughout the economy — but certainly not at an even pace. There will be long lags in the adjustment of some prices, delayed shifts in the mix of outputs produced by primary agents, changes in consumption patterns because of differing individual price and wealth elasticities of demand, and so on. Eventually, however, the economy will settle down to a steady rate of inflation — not with the same pattern of relative prices as before, or the same patterns of production and consumption, but with patterns that are nevertheless constant over time. One can then envisage a situation where merchants would increase their prices to cover costs, and gold miners produce more, yet obtain a lower standard of living. Price controls might be proposed, causing merchants to increase their prices even more in anticipation.

What actually might happen is that gold miners finally would quit working so hard, prices would stop rising, and after a year or two everyone would find himself in the same position as before, except that pockets and cash registers would contain larger average quantities of gold — and gold miners would have more leisure.

No modern economy is as simple as the one just considered. In real life, few intermediaries act simply as middlemen. Retail merchants set prices to customers but take prices from their suppliers who, in turn, set prices to merchants but take prices from their suppliers — and so on, down the line, until one reaches primary producers, auction markets for farm and fishery products, etc. Most sales occur not spot but future. Orders are placed by merchants on the expectation that price at time of delivery will be similar to price today, but actual transaction prices generally are determined by date of delivery rather than date of order. The great bulk of all payments are made initially in the form of book debits to trade accounts which are settled later with cash or bank transfers. Formal modelling of these and other complications, although possible in principle, poses tasks that are truly mind-boggling. Sooner or later, of course, such modelling must be carried out if we are ever to place ourselves in a position to predict with any accuracy the short-run future behaviour of any actual economy. Meanwhile, it seems purposeful to work out the details of simple models of the kind set out above — though my hunch is that the qualitative behaviour of even very complex systems will not differ significantly from that of the pure commodity—money economy as sketched above.

### 3. General Process Analysis: Further Discussion

The account of market structure and performance outlined above is very traditional. It is compatible not only with Marshall's ideas as set out in his *Industry and Trade* (Marshall, 1919, book 2, chaps. 5—8) but also with those of his classical predecessors — Smith, Ricardo, Senior and Mill. It also accords well with views expressed by Marshall's most famous contemporaries — Jevons, Walras, Edgeworth and Walker. Its relation to more recent work should be equally clear. It includes general competitive analysis as a limiting case that is approximately valid for analysing full equilibrium states of a general process economy. As for monetarist and income—expenditure models, these are subsumed in general process analysis under the heading of 'partial, *ad hoc* representations of temporary equilibrium states'.

To be sure, a theory that covers all possible cases may be so general as to be useless (cf. Samuelson, 1947, pp. 7—8). Just as surely, a theory that is grounded on nothing more substantial than intuitive reflection and mathematical convenience is almost certain to be useless regardless of the restrictiveness of its so-called empirical implications. To be worthwhile in any meaningful sense, a theory should be so formulated as to fall somewhere in between these two extremes. I think general process analysis satisfies this condition.

To begin with, it should be evident that, for all *full equilibrium* comparative statics experiments, the empirical implications of general process analysis are qualitatively identical with those of general competitive analysis and related theories. As for other types of comparative statics exercises (for example, 'temporary equilibrium' experiments of the sort that characterise standard IS—LM analysis), general competitive analysis yields ambiguous results, but for a perfectly sensible reason, namely, such experiments deal with *transient states* of a general process model and such states do not fall within the logical purview of comparative statics analysis. Some might regard this as a weakness of general process analysis, but it is more accurately regarded as an indictment of the intellectually shoddy comparative statics exercises that fill modern texts in macroeconomic theory. In this respect, general process analysis deserves to be regarded as a guard against wishful thinking rather than an obstacle to fruitful inquiry.

The strength of general process analysis as a background for empirical inquiry comes out most clearly, however, in dynamical applications. It is customary in standard theories to construct dynamic models in a strictly mechanical fashion so that price adjustments appear to be made by 'unseen forces' rather than by individual economic agents. Given this framework, it is usual to proceed as if the motions of the system were determined once and for all by given structural factors. In the nature of the case, the motions of any given model may be stable or unstable depending on the values assigned to specific parameters. From this it is but a short step to the conclusion that some economies will work well while others will work ill, and it is then difficult to overlook the possibility that the world in which we live has cast up systems that work poorly and stand in need of redesign.

General process analysis rests upon another conception of market organisation and leads to radically different conclusions. In the first place, price as well as quantity adjustments are explicitly associated with conscious decisions of individual economic agents. Market structure and performance characteristics are regarded not as preordained consequences of technical and structural factors but rather as unforeseen and unforeseeable evolutionary consequences of the interaction of behavioural and technological forces. On this view, unstable economic systems, although theoretically conceivable, are not practically viable. Systems that survive over long intervals of calendar time effectively declare themselves to be 'of stable type'. Indeed, an even stronger assertion is warranted: systems that survive need not have a structure that guarantees *asymptotic* stability (i.e. stability in the limit as time tends to infinity), but they must have a structure that guarantees *practical* stability (i.e. strict boundedness of motion over any finite interval of calendar time).

This discussion might be continued at length, but it has been carried far enough already to support the only conclusion that is strictly required for present purposes, namely, the conclusion that general process analysis is in no way less informative or restrictive than standard theories, given comparably restrictive underlying assumptions, but that it differs sharply from standard theories in making us clearly aware of areas of inquiry where additional empirical research is required before we can safely draw any conclusions at all from our theoretical models.

## 4. The Problem of Inflation

I began this paper by stressing the need for a common framework of analysis as a basis for rational assessment of the factual validity of alternative views about the nature and control of inflationary processes. I have outlined a framework — general process analysis — that seems to me to go some way towards meeting this need. It is not a framework that will appeal to everyone. It leaves too much open for discussion to appeal to doctrinaires, and it focuses too much attention on messy institutional details to appeal to those who like their theories neat. All the same, in what follows I shall try to show that the framework is of some value as a device for professional communication despite its obvious limitations for other more ambitious purposes.

For the sake of argument, let me begin by supposing that we have to deal with a fiat money economy that is described to a good first approximation by a general process model that defines an asymptotically stable equilibrium motion that is unique up to a proportional transformation of all variables that are denominated in units of money. This means that the classical (Ricardian) quantity theory of the long-run value of money is rigorously valid, i.e. the full equilibrium values of all real magnitudes are independent of the nominal value of the cash base. Other things being equal, it also means that the general money price level depends in the long run only on the cash base. It follows that, except on highly implausible assumptions (e.g. sustained retrogression in resources and technology), an ongoing inflation can always be halted by holding the cash base constant.

This conclusion no doubt will sound like the opening gun in a salute to monetarism. In fact it is nothing of the sort, for to accept the conclusion as a valid statement about the real world commits one to nothing except a belief in the proposition that observed economic events are amenable to prediction in terms of formal theoretical models — a proposition the validity of which is not presently at issue. More pointedly, although cash-base control is a necessary and sufficient condition for long-run control of the general money price level, such control does not imply stability of money prices or anything else in the short run. Of course, this conclusion is also part and parcel of contemporary monetarist thought. But it is a central tenet also of all income—expenditure theories. Up to this point, therefore, we have no grounds for argument.

Proceeding to potentially more contentious matters, let us add detail to our model by supposing that the economy contains a fractional reserve banking system whose deposit obligations are equivalent to cash as means for settling trade debts. Suppose also that trade intermediaries maintain book credit accounts with one another and with other economic agents and that debit entries to these accounts are equivalent to cash as a means of payment. Then the total quantity of money in the economy — which we define as cash outside banks plus deposits transferrable by cheque plus gross accounts payable — is an endogenous variable the value of which is determined by (among other things) the cash base, bank reserve ratios and prevailing payment and settlement practices.

In this kind of economy, just as in one where money consists solely of cash, the full equilibrium general money price level will depend (other things being equal) on the nominal level of the cash base. As before, moreover, cash-base control is not a sufficient condition for short-run stability of prices or related real magnitudes. We then come to the central question of modern inflation theory: is short-run stability in the cash base of minor significance for economic stability, or is rigid adherence to a rule of steady and moderate expansion in the cash base essential to avoid serious economic instability in both the short and the long run?

I have purposely stated this question to avoid direct confrontation either with the view that economic stability depends *solely* on 'spending', or with the view that economic stability depends *solely* on 'money'. Neither position is espoused in this extreme form by any but members of the lunatic fringe of professional economists, though many economists apparently would subscribe to weaker versions of each. As I see matters, however, the issue is not which, if either, of these two alternatives is best suited to guarantee economic stability, but rather whether economic stability is even a remote possibility in the absence of highly responsible cash-base control. The first of these questions is, I submit, undecidable on the basis of present factual and theoretical knowledge, but the second seems to me to admit of a tentative answer within the framework of general process analysis.

Given a model in which (as in real life) trade credit and demand deposits dominate cash as a means of payment, and in which (again as in real life) non-cash means of payment can expand or contract by substantial amounts to meet 'the needs of trade' even when the cash base is constant, it is implausible to suppose that increases in the cash base will in all circumstances induce immediate increases in other means of payment, or that decreases in the cash base will not sometimes induce a sharp reduction in other means of payment by producing a 'liquidity crisis'. Suppose that the model also includes a business sector that produces and uses large quantities of long-lived capital goods. For good measure, add to the model a non-bank financial sector that deals in all varieties of long- and short-term debt. In this kind of system, quite minor random shocks are capable of producing wide swings in production, employment, interest rates and prices, even if all trade debts are settled in cash. If the 'slippage' and 'whiplash' possibilities inherent in a permissive monetary environment are also taken into account, then the stage is set for Wicksellian cumulative processes that work in both directions.

Specifically, suppose that the monetary authority — which we may presume has complete command of the cash base — pursues a general policy of 'leaning against the wind'. If it does not lean hard at the outset of any upward cumulative movement (and how is it to distinguish between random and systematic movements?), the cash base will expand in response to bank demands for additional reserves to support new loans to permit business firms to settle newly contracted trade debts. Prices will rise, interest rates will lag, and the cumulative process will gather momentum. What I am describing is the kind of nightmare that percipient classics associated with the 'real bills' doctrine. The scenario is just as nightmarish if it starts with a downward movement in economic activity. As far as I can see, moreover, only the details of the nightmare are altered if we suppose that the monetary authority pursues no consistent policy but simply 'drifts'.

Of course it is entirely possible that the economy will behave very poorly even if the monetary authority keeps a tight rein on the cash base and thereby forces trade intermediaries and dealers in debts to keep a weather eye at all times on the relation between accounts payable and currently available means of settlement. It is also possible that cumulative movements could be avoided if the monetary authority pursued a consistent policy of 'resisting the wind', except that, in this as in any other situation that involves impossibly delicate judgements, it is difficult to imagine how such a policy could be carried out successfully in practice. However that might be, it seems clear that, other things (specifically, fiscal policy) being equal, any erratic policy stands a good chance of producing needlessly violent ups and downs, or needlessly extended periods of inflation and deflation, or some combination of any or all of these.

## 5. Conclusion

As happens on occasion, the space available for argument falls short of that required to complete it. The rest must be supplied by the reader's imagination — assisted by a few concluding assertions. Earlier I implicitly denied any personal commitment to monetarist doctrine. I now explicitly reaffirm that denial. But historical evidence, common sense, economic intuition and considerations related to the present argument have all combined to lead me to a qualified monetarist position. Specifically, though I would not subscribe to the proposition that all would be well if monetary authorities pursued a policy of steady and moderate expansion in the cash base, I am fully convinced that any other policy is bound to lead to folly in the form either of boom and bust or sustained inflation. Against this, it has been argued that every monetary economy has occasional need for a lender of last resort. That may be so, but this function need not and probably should not be joined with the more routine task of providing a cash base adequate to sustain *normal* settlement requirements.

A final remark and I am done. In Britain it is common even today to hear professional economists insist that monetary policy must be conducted with an eye to 'general credit' conditions rather than to movements in the case base, and also to hear that the proper way to cure inflation is to adopt an appropriate wages and incomes policy and to combine this with brutal fiscal measures. To my mind, such views reflect wilful retreat from reality (cf. Johnson, 1972, pp. 4—21). There is one and only one cure for the present British inflation: firm control of the cash base. To impose such control in present circumstances must inevitably produce heavy if temporary unemployment and other serious dislocations of economic life. Failure to impose such control will inevitably produce exactly the same problems and may well lead to disastrous social consequences as well. There is no need to state the moral, but there is great need to heed it.

### References

Archibald, G. C. and Lipsey, R. G. (1958). 'Value and Monetary Theory: A Critique of Lange and Patinkin', *Review of Economic Studies* (Oct.) pp. 1—22.

Brunner, K. and Meltzer, A. (1971). 'The Uses of Money: Money in the Theory of an Exchange Economy', *American Economic Review*, LXI (Mar.) 784—805.

Chuchman, G. (1975). 'A Model of the Evolution of Exchange Processes', University of Western Ontario, Money Workshop, revised version.

Clower, R. W. (1969). *Monetary Theory: Selected Readings* (Harmondsworth: Penguin Books).

Clower, R. W. (1975). 'Reflections on the Keynesian Perplex', *Zeitschrift fur National ökonomie* (July) pp. 1—24.

Clower, R. W. and Burstein, M. L. (1960). 'The Invariance of the Demand for Cash and Other Assets', *Review of Economic Studies*, XXVIII (Oct.) 32—6.

Clower, R. W. and Leijonhufvud, A. (1975). 'The Co-ordination of Economic Activities: A Keynesian Perspective', *American Economic Review (Proc.)* (May), pp. 182—188.

Hicks, J. R. (1967). *Critical Essays in Monetary Theory* (Oxford: Clarendon Press).

Howitt, P. W. (1973). 'Walras and Monetary Theory', *Western Economic Journal*, XI (Dec.) 487—99.

Howitt, P. W. (1974). 'Stability and the Quantity Theory', *Journal of Political Economy*, LXXXII (Jan—Feb.) 133—40.

Johnson, H. G. (1972). *Inflation and the Monetarist Controversy*, De Vries Lectures (Amsterdam: North-Holland).

Johnson, H. G. (1975). 'The Problem of Inflation', in *On Economics and Society: Selected Essays* (Chicago and London: Univ. of Chicago Press).

Jones, R. (1975). 'The Origin and Development of Media of Exchange', forthcoming in *Journal of Political Economy*.

Leijonhufvud, A. (1973). 'Effective Demand Failures', *Swedish Economic Journal*, LXXIII, 27–48.

Marshall, A. (1919). *Industry and Trade* (London: Macmillan).

Ostroy, J. (1973). 'The Informational Efficiency of Monetary Exchange', *American Economic Review*, LXIII (Sept.) 597–610.

Ostroy, J. and Starr, R. M. (1974). 'Money and the Decentralisation of Exchange', *Econometrica*, XLII (Nov.) 1093–1113.

Patinkin, D. (1956). *Money, Interest and Prices* (Evanston, Ill.: Row Peterson).

Perlman, M. (1971). 'The Roles of Money in the Economy and the Optimum Quantity of Money', *Economica*, XXXVIII (Aug.) 233–52.

Samuelson, P. A. (1947). *Foundations of Economic Analysis* (Cambridge, Mass.: Harvard Univ. Press).

# 3 Paternalism and Prices

## G. C. ARCHIBALD AND DAVID DONALDSON

### 1. Introduction

As everyone knows, there is a considerable body of formal economic theory that supports the traditional 'liberal' belief in the price mechanism as a method of allocating economic resources. Indeed, it has been shown (1) that all competitive equilibria are optimal and (2) that all optimal allocations are competitive equilibria (Arrow, 1951), where by an optimal allocation is meant one such that no one can be made better off without making someone else worse off. A simple interpretation gives the prima facie case for *laissez-faire:* individuals allowed to trade freely in competitive markets will exhaust the gains from trade.

There are two quite different sorts of difficulties to be considered. The first is now well known. It is that markets are themselves costly, and in some cases so costly that they do not exist and cannot reasonably be expected to exist. Thus, as a general rule, we cannot rely on competitive markets to generate an optimal allocation in the face of uncertainty, costly information, and a wide class of externality problems (see Arrow, 1971, esp. chaps. 4, 5 and 8; Nagatani, 1975).

The second difficulty is of a quite different sort. It is that, in proofs of the two theorems stated above, it is explicitly assumed (as it is implicitly assumed in traditional 'commonsense' arguments for *laissez-faire*) that all individuals satisfy the *axiom of selfishness.* This is the axiom that each individual's preference index depends solely on his own consumption, and is independent of the consumption, welfare or happiness of everyone else in society. There are reasons of quite different sorts for thinking that this is a very bad assumption.

The first is empirical. We may not all love all our neighbours, but it is a fact of common observation that many people have at least some concern for others. Indeed, many people entertain definite opinions about economic justice. As a positive description of the real world the axiom of selfishness is therefore inaccurate.

Secondly, a social arrangement cannot be defended easily if the defence requires the assumption that everyone is amoral. As Baier has written (1958, p. vii), 'a general acceptance of a system of merely self-interested reasons [for actions] would lead to conditions of life well described by Hobbes as

26

"poor, nasty, brutish, and short" '. People ought to be moral agents, and are, at least on occasion; and an argument for competitive markets that assumes that they are *never* moral agents cannot be a good one.

These conditions appear to us to afford compelling reasons for investigating the arguments for the price mechanism in a model in which the axiom of selfishness is *not* employed. We therefore have to investigate how 'extended preferences' may be appropriately characterised. (We are, of course, not the first to investigate extended preference systems. We shall try to make acknowledgement and reference where appropriate, but our first object is to make the present argument self-contained. Further, we omit all reference to the literature on 'Pareto-optimal redistribution', which is discussed in Archibald and Donaldson (1975). The most important discussion of extended preferences and welfare economics is in Winter (1969).)

## 2. Non-Paternalism

We now allow the preferences of individuals to be defined over all states of society. Individuals may therefore have preferences not only about their own consumption but about the distribution of 'income', the behaviour of others, or even the precise consumption bundles of others. It may be expected that if we admit *any* preferences, then little of general interest will emerge. The question that arises is, therefore, whether there are any restrictions on extended preferences which are either morally or practically useful to assume. We shall argue that there is indeed a strong moral argument for a restriction that we propose; and that it also has the practical use that, without it, the case for the competitive price mechanism cannot be made.

Our proposed restriction on preferences is that they satisfy what we call the *non-paternalist condition*. We give the mathematical formulation of this condition in Section 3 below. It is sufficient for the present to say that non-paternalist preferences satisfy the following condition: that, no matter how an individual judges the welfare of another, or what his judgement may be as to its adequacy — or excess — he respects the other's preferences in the sense that he does not (under ideal conditions) wish to interfere with the other's choice of his personal consumption bundle. Thus for an individual's preferences to be non-paternalist, his marginal rate of substitution between goods in the consumption bundle of any other individual must be that of the other.

It might appear that the informational requirements of this condition are excessive, if not indeed absurd. For the most part, we do not even know the names of fellow-members of the society we live in, let alone their tastes. To show that this information is not, in fact, required, we must anticipate the argument. It proves that an efficient allocation, in a society of individuals with interdependent but non-paternalist preferences, can almost always be supported by a vector of competitive prices (abstracting, of course, from problems of externality, etc.). Thus non-paternalists do not in fact need to know the tastes of others. The requirement of 'non-interference' is sufficient: given that the distribution is acceptable, they will be content that everyone exhausts the gains from trade at competitive prices.

In the remainder of this section we shall argue that the preferences (or at least acts) of individuals who are moral agents should satisfy the non-paternalist conditions. We shall then discuss some supposed exceptions.

It would appear that only extended preferences that satisfy our non-paternalist condition would be morally acceptable to the Mill of *On Liberty* (1859). In our mathematical formulation, we think we capture the spirit of *On Liberty* without the utilitarianism. (There are certain difficulties in Mill's utilitarianism, discussed by Brown (1972, 1973).) Instead, we appeal to a simple non-utilitarian principle. This is what Baier (1958, p. 202) calls 'the negative version of the . . . Golden Rule: Don't do unto others as you would not have them do unto you.' This is the rule of 'reversibility' (also required by Hare, 1963).

When sane, adult individuals decide what to do on rational grounds, it is necessary that they decide what they want for themselves, which must include the conditions under which they want interference from others. Since it is prima facie wrong to act non-reversibly, it is similarly wrong to interfere with others in ways that they do not want or have not agreed to. Thus paternalistic acts are prima facie wrong (the force of 'prima facie' here is that we do not propose that reversibility override other moral rules in cases of conflict). A common argument for non-paternalism is that the individual is the best judge of what is good for him. This may or may not be empirically true: Donaldson may be right that Archibald's smoking is bad for him. If our argument is accepted, we are independent of the empirically dubious argument about 'who knows best'.

We shall consider some examples, but we must first note that the proper treatment of children and the insane presents acute difficulties which we do not consider. Similarly, we do not discuss the proper treatment of drug addicts, i.e. persons whose 'tastes' have been changed a great deal by their consumption behaviour.

In a most searching discussion of the occasions on which paternalism might be justified, Rosemary Carter (1973) has proposed an example. Suppose that she has the flu, feels sick and miserable, and wishes only to be left alone. Suppose also that we, her friends, are anxious for her, and think that she should see the doctor. We put her shoes on her feet, thrust her coat upon her, urge her into the car, and drive her to her doctor's office. She presents good argument that this may be an exceptional case of justified paternalism. The essential point is that, for it to be justified, we must believe that she would, when her judgement was not impaired by fever, agree that she wanted to be looked after in this manner when she had the flu. If she was of the considered opinion that doctors were incompetent, or at least that they could offer no remedy for the flu that was not already available to her, our interference would be unwarranted.

This sort of apparent exception may be put down as 'while the balance of his mind was temporarily disturbed'. There is another sort, which we may ascribe to custom or convention: that is, to an individual's expectations about the conduct of others. Thus suppose that a man goes to the pub with some friends. At closing time, they conclude that he should not drive, and take away his car keys. This is apparently a paternalistic interference. It may, however, be consistent with the reversibility principle. If our man had not relied upon his friends behaving in this manner, he would probably have drunk less; and he doubtless accepts the obligation to reciprocal action. Expectations based on more formal contracts can, *a fortiori*, justify other acts which are at first sight paternalist.

There are, of course, borderline cases which we do not attempt to resolve. An individual who has slashed his wrists may be trying to call attention to himself, relying on the convention that we try to prevent suicide, in which case our emergency hospital treatment is not paternalistic, or he may genuinely wish to be dead, in which case our interference is unjustified (and probably ineffectual, since on a subsequent occasion he will doubtless manage better).

The above discussion uses the word *obligation* for the first time in this paper. We must consider the relationship between obligation and non-paternalism.

It is essential to our argument that, if A has an obligation to B, he has an obligation to discharge it in a non-paternalist manner. This obviously does not apply if the obligation arises in the sort of circumstances just considered, i.e. when interference is expected and at least implicitly assented to, or is justified by the temporary non-rationality of the affected individual.

If there is no obligation, matters are, of course, different. Consider a gift. By an obvious definitional rule, a gift cannot discharge an obligation. It is, therefore, morally permissible to give another person anything one wishes provided no harm is done.

We have to consider an important utilitarian argument. Suppose that Donaldson is made less happy than he otherwise would be because of Archibald's consumption of cigarettes. Suppose further that this is not due to the smoke in the room (a real externality), but due to Donaldson's concern for Archibald's health. In this case it is clearly morally permissible for Archibald to smoke less because of Donaldson's unhappiness. It is even conceivable that, if Donaldson's concern with Archibald's health is genuine, and he is being made seriously unhappy by Archibald's conduct, Archibald has some obligation in the matter. It is clear, however, that we cannot be put under obligations by the prejudices of cranks and meddlers. Indeed, paternalists often claim disutilities of the sort suffered by Donaldson to justify their inclination to meddle, and in practice it may be impossible to distinguish.

It is now convenient to distinguish between acts and preferences. Donaldson's paternalist preferences towards Archibald's smoking belong to the

subset of paternalist preferences that, in themselves, violate no moral rule.
It would, however, be undesirable for Donaldson to coerce Archibald,
either by a private act or through an institution. Thus, while individuals
may have paternalistic preferences towards others, what is important is that
they refrain from manipulating social arrangements to reflect them. If they
insist, we are fully justified in resisting.

## 3. Extended Preferences

We now specialise the argument to exchange. We consider preferences defined over ordinary goods and services only. These are not utilities in the
usual sense of the word but are extended to include political, religious and
moral judgements. They are therefore more closely akin to individuals' or-
derings of alternative states of society than to 'private' utility functions.

Let $X_{ij}$ be the $i$th individual's consumption of good $j$ and $X = (X_{11}, \ldots,$
$X_{ij}, \ldots, X_{nm})$ be the complete allocation of society's goods to all individuals. We assume first that each individual has a well-behaved ordering over
his own consumption $X_i = (X_{i1}, \ldots, X_{im})$, and that it can be represented
by the function $b^i(X_i)$. We further assume that he has preferences defined
over the entire allocation, and that this ordering may be represented by
$\phi^i = \phi^i(X)$. The non-paternalist condition is that each individual respect the
tastes of others, however he forms his judgement of their welfare, and whatever his opinion of the justice of the distribution. This requires that the
functions $\phi^i$ be weakly separable. Person $i$ is a non-paternalist if and only if
$\phi^i(X)$ can be written

$$\phi^i(X) = F^i(b^1(X_1), \ldots, b^i(X_1), \ldots, b^r(X_r), \ldots, b^n(X_n)) \qquad (1)$$

The form of $F^i$ reflects the distributional preferences of the $i$th individual;
$F^i_r$, if it exists, may be positive, negative or zero. From (1), we note that

$$\text{MRS}^i_{(rj)(rk)} = \frac{\phi^i_{(rj)}}{\phi^i_{(rk)}} = \frac{\phi^r_{(rj)}}{\phi^r_{(rk)}} = \text{MRS}^r_{(rj)(rk)} \qquad (2)$$

whenever these marginal rates of substitution are defined. $\phi^i_{(rk)} = \partial \phi^i / \partial X_{rk}$,
and $\phi^i_{(rj)}/\phi^i_{(rk)}$ is the $i$th individual's marginal rate of substitution between
goods $j$ and $k$ in the $r$th individual's consumption. Of course, $\phi^i_{(rj)}$ need not
be positive, just as $F^i_r$ need not be positive. If $\phi^i$ is not weakly separable,
then some element of $X$ must appear in more than one of the $b$'s. In this
case, (2) cannot be everywhere satisfied.

An immediate implication of (1) is, of course, that the $i$th individual's
marginal rate of substitution between goods in his own bundle is independent of the rest of the allocation. If we draw his indifference map in the
space of $X_i$ it will be invariant to changes in the allocation to others, although, of course, the $\phi$ index attached to each indifference curve will, in
general, be changed by changes in the allocation to others.

We note also that preferences in the form of (1) exclude Veblen, snob and bandwagon effects (see Leibenstein, 1950). This is a somewhat accidental by-product of our condition. We do not wish to argue that such preferences are immoral (although we might judge them to be misguided). It is, however, the case that they are inconsistent with the independence of marginal rates of substitution which is required by non-paternalism. Thus the requirement that an individual respects the tastes of others in turn requires that, in any case in which they had the knowledge, their preferences would must be invariant to the choices of others.

We may recall the argument above. In the 'real world' it is not necessary that individuals have all the knowledge implied in (1). What is necessary is that, he respect his own, in the sense that his marginal rates of substitution conform to (1).

We may now discuss 'harm' and see that some harm is legitimate while some is not. Consider a distributional preference indicated by $\phi^i(X)$. Suppose that, at some allocation $X$, $F_r^i$ is negative. This means that the $i$th individual believes that the $r$th individual should have less. If this is to be consistent with reversibility, the $i$th individual must agree that there is some $X$ at which he himself should have less. If he does not agree, then the negativity of $F_r^i$ must reflect some sort of malevolence, or at least 'unfairness'.

We must emphasise here that non-paternalist preferences may, but need not, satisfy the Pareto principle. The main difference between the conditions we propose on preferences and those of Winter (1969) are that we separate the non-paternalist condition from considerations of distributive justice, while he combined the non-paternalist condition and the Pareto principle into a single condition on preferences. Thus our condition is considerably weaker: non-paternalists may be strict egalitarians, or indifferent to wide ranges of the distribution; they may entertain strong opinions about the worthiness or 'desert' of certain individuals or classes of individuals; they may accept the Pareto principle or believe strongly that an increase in world G.N.P. that accrued entirely to a vulgar and ostentatious millionaire would be a social disaster.

An attempt to alter the distribution may, then, involve 'harm' to some, in a well-defined sense that is consistent with non-paternalism. Consider by contrast the harm done by a private paternalist act. Suppose that A has an obligation to help B by transferring goods to him, but that he is paternalist towards B. It is immediate that the bundle of goods he will wish to give B will have the following property: in general, there will be another bundle which will do B at least as much good (in terms of $b^B$, his preferences on his own consumption) while costing A less in terms of $b^A$. If A's obligation to B is fixed in terms of $b^B$, A will 'pay' for his paternalism in terms of $b^A$ (not, of course, in terms of $\phi^A$). If the obligation to B is fixed in terms of $b^A$, then B will be harmed by A's paternalism. We note that, if A were selfish, but were required to help B, he would do so in an efficient fashion (i.e. at least cost to himself).

Externalities present a problem which we note briefly. If a consumer—consumer externality exists (from individual $r$ to individual $i$, say), then $i$'s preferences cannot be written as in (1) above: the injurious consumption activity of $r$ will necessarily appear outside $b^r$. It seems that it might be easy to confuse preferences in the case of an externality with paternalistic interdependent preferences, but if confusion arose it could be readily removed by an extension of the notation, as the following example makes clear. Let $X_{AC}$ be Archibald's consumption of cigarettes, disliked by Donaldson. If Donaldson's dislike is paternalist, $X_{AC}$ will appear in $b^D$. If he merely dislikes having smoke blown in his face when Archibald and he are working together, the required term in $b^D$ is $X_{ACTP}$ where T and P are time and place indices, such that $X_{AC}$ appears only if it occurs at a time and place at which Donaldson is present.

## 4. Institutions

In the introduction above we referred to the two basic theorems of welfare economics, (1) that all competitive equilibria are Pareto optimal and (2) that all Pareto optima are competitive equilibria. If we drop the axiom of selfishness, without imposing any other restriction on preferences, both are false (in general). Many economists accept any preferences, however bizarre or repugnant to others, as having an equal claim to be reflected by social arrangements. In our view, only preferences that are morally acceptable ought to count. The restrictions proposed here on moral grounds are in fact required to sustain the efficiency argument for competitive markets.

The non-paternalist condition ensures the survival of theorem (2) as long as extreme malevolence is ruled out (see Archibald and Donaldson, 1975). This was shown for the first time by Winter (1969), albeit with a restriction on preferences that excluded some important views of distribution justice. The reason why (1) must go is simple: *a* competitive equilibrium corresponds to any arbitrary initial endowment, and may therefore be distributionally unacceptable to some, or indeed all, members of society. The reason why (2) survives may be explained intuitively: non-paternalists will always be able to exhaust the gains from trade in ordinary competitive markets (facing identical price vectors) because of the equality of marginal rates of substitution in each $\phi^i(X)$. As we have also pointed out (1975), it is immediate that Lerner—Lange socialism can generate optimal solutions for a society of non-paternalists, while competitive capitalism offers no such guarantee.

Casual observation suggests that the real world, even in 'liberal' societies, is characterised by the gratuitous profusion of offensively paternalist institutions, e.g. government intervention in behaviour with regard to sex, Sundays, saving, seat-belts, drink, drugs, housing and hospitals. Doubtless much of this intervention *is* paternalist, but we must remember the first sort of difficulty with *laissez-faire* mentioned in Section 1 above: market costs. To illustrate the difficulty, let us consider the legal requirement that motor-cyclists wear helmets.

The basic motivation is distributional: others do not wish to contribute to the costs of otherwise unnecessary medical attention for the foolhardy. The method, however, appears to be purely and unnecessarily paternalist. There is an obvious non-paternalist alternative, that motor-cyclists be offered two types of first-party insurance policy, the cheaper to be conditional on their signing an undertaking to wear helmets. The trouble is, how could we in fact enforce the undertaking? And what would we do with a bleeding cheat (i.e. one who had signed, left his helmet off, and crashed)? Reflection suggests that transactions costs, rather than paternalism, may justify the rest of us in requiring helmets rather than additional insurance.

The case for medicare in some form rests largely on similar considerations (see Arrow, 1971, chap. 8) as does that for 'social insurance' (see Donaldson, 1967).

When we take into account the problems of 'market failure' (costs of operating markets, non-existence of markets) it is clear that some simple judgements cannot be sustained. We list some implications:

(*a*) Non-paternalism does not entail unqualified approbation of *laissez-faire*.

(*b*) Interference with *laissez-faire* does not entail paternalism: there are other justifications.

(*c*) Paternalism necessarily entails interference with *laissez-faire*.

We shall consider (*c*) further below. As for (*a*) and (*b*), we have only to note that the non-paternalist will require that every departure from *laissez-faire* be justified in a fashion consistent with preferences given by (1), i.e. by an appeal to the costs of a market solution and the proposal of an alternative which satisfies the reversibility criterion.

Finally, consider a non-paternalist society. Either all individuals would have non-paternalist preferences or institutional arrangements would in no way reflect any paternalist preferences. Such a society would differ from our own, but in precisely what ways is, in part, an empirical question. The cases of sex and Sundays are reasonably obvious; those of helmets and seatbelts depend upon costs. (Housing policy, which doubtless reflects some mixture of paternalism with concern for income distribution, complicated by the presence of important externalities, is too important and large a subject for discussion here.) We may, however, usefully contrast a paternalist with a non-paternalist society, abstracting from the problem of market failure.

In a non-paternalist society there is a presumption in favour of market solutions (although not necessarily all those of competitive capitalism, and certainly not all those offered by contemporary capitalism). A paternalist society will allow a dominant group to impose institutions on all reflecting its preferences, whatever they may be. Since we cannot know them, we can say little about such a society, except that there will be no presumption in favour of ordinary competitive markets. On the contrary, efficiency will require that different individuals face different price vectors (or physical rations), and there is no knowing who will impose what prices on whom. There is a simple way of summarising the results of this paper. Anyone who wishes to maintain that there is a presumptive case for the price mechanism must *either* swallow the axiom of selfishness with all its Hobbesian difficulties and treat distribution as a wholly separate matter *or* swallow non-paternalist extended preferences, thus permitting institutions to reflect citizens' opinions about economic justice.

## Acknowledgements

For comments we are indebted to M. G. Allingham, Charles Blackorby, Rosemary Carter and R. I. Sikora.

## References

Archibald, G. C. and Donaldson, D. (1975). 'Non-Paternalism and the Basic Theorems of Welfare Economics', forthcoming in *Canadian Journal of Economics*.

Arrow, K. J. (1951). 'An Extension of the Basic Theorems of Welfare Economics', in *Proceedings of the Second Berkeley Symposium on Mathematical Statistics and Probability* (Berkeley: Univ. of California Press).

Arrow, K. J. (1971). *Essays in the Theory of Risk-Bearing* (Chicago: Markham Publishing Co.).

Baier, K. (1958). *The Moral Point of View: A Rational Basis of Ethics* (Ithaca, N.Y.: Cornell Univ. Press).

Brown, D. G. (1972). 'Mill on Liberty and Morality', *Philosophical Review*, LXXXI (2).

Brown, D. G. (1973). 'What is Mill's Principle of Utility?', *Canadian Journal of Philosophy*, III (1).

Carter, R. A. (1973). 'A Justification of Paternalism', unpublished M.A. thesis (Department of Philosophy, University of British Columbia).

Donaldson, D. (1967). 'On the Optimal Mix of Social Insurance Payments', in *Old Age Income Assurance*, Part III, Joint Committee Print 83–200 (Washington, D.C.: US Government Printing Office).

Hare, R. M. (1963). *Freedom and Reason* (London: Oxford Univ. Press).

Leibenstein, H. (1950). 'Bandwagon, Snob and Veblen Effects in the Theory of Consumers' Demand', *Quarterly Journal of Economics*, LXIV.

Mill, J. S. (1859). *On Liberty* (London: J. W. Parker & Son).

Nagatani, K. (1975). 'On a Theorem of Arrow', *Review of Economic Studies*, XLII(3).

Winter, S. (1969). 'A Simple Remark on the Second Optimality Theorem of Welfare Economics', *Journal of Economic Theory*, I (1).

# 4 The Changing Economics of Education

## Z. GRILICHES

We are currently at the end of a long historical boom in education as a high-growth and a high-payoff industry. We are also at a point at which the views of economists about education may be changing and are subject to significant intellectual attacks. It may be worthwhile therefore to review briefly from whence we have come and where we might be going.

I shall focus largely on the recent American experience, because I know it best. But it is also likely that rather similar developments have taken and will be taking place elsewhere. 'Knowledge is power' has been our advertising slogan as educators. 'Education' is an escape from darkness and lower-class status. As economists, we have to amend these slogans and to remind our listeners that only *scarce* knowledge is power, and that while education can lead a single individual out of one group into another, nothing can lift everyone above the average. Having said that, we should keep on trying to lift the average. It is still, I think, a worthwhile goal.

In the rest of this paper I discuss the trends in the changing scarcity of knowledge and some recent ideas about the sources of economic returns to private and social investments in education. Education also, of course, has important consumption aspects, but I shall not be dealing with that directly in this brief paper.

The post-Second World War era in the United States opened with an excess demand for schooling on the part of the cohort whose schooling was interrupted by army service and a rising appreciation of the potential economic importance of schooling as the result of the various technological and scientific changes induced and diffused by the war. The initial push was financed by governmental benefits provided to the returning war veterans and by the rising affluence of individuals and local governmental units as the result of the rapid economic growth and the concomitant expansion of the local tax base. In addition, and perhaps most importantly, these decisions and trends were validated by the rather high perceived and actually realised rates of return to high school completion and college attendance resulting from the post-war economic boom, low unemployment rates, and the smallness of the cohorts reaching the labour market for the first time.

35

Enrolments in higher education expanded rapidly and were about double pre-war levels by the early 1950s. The rate of growth in supply declined thereafter as the smaller cohorts of the depression-year children began to reach the colleges. While participation rates increased, total enrolments in higher educational institutions went up only by about 20 per cent between 1950 and 1960. Thus, even though a larger fraction of youths were going through higher educational systems in the 1950s, their absolute numbers were not rising very fast and did not impose much strain on the universities or on the absorptive capacities of the labour market.

But largely unnoticed, tremendous demographic changes were working their way through the age structure. The first waves of the post-Second World War baby boom, having reached the secondary schools in the mid- and late 1950s, started inundating the universities in the 1960s. Between 1960 and 1970 the number enrolled in higher educational institutions more than doubled, while expenditures on higher education more than tripled (as did graduate enrolments).

Very few other large industries were growing anywhere near the same rate as the educational system. Standing in the midst of this period of expansion one could begin to worry whether all this increase in the number of highly educated workers would not drive down their market price and the associated rate of return to higher education. But the superficial signs were all positive. Thus, one (cf. Griliches, 1970) could take the relative constancy of skill differentials and estimated rates of return to higher education through the 1950s and the 1960s as a sign that the demand for education may be very elastic, allowing one to hope that since the past expansions in the educated labour force had not reduced them, neither may the current and future expansions. But we had not done our homework carefully enough, not having noticed that the big demographic swings and the associated accelerator-like expansion in the demand for teachers had greatly distorted the observed data and made the persistence of such trends into the future quite unlikely. Neither did we realise that the big government-financed space/defence/R & D boom was something that may not last forever, or appreciate the fact that much of the impact of the growth in higher education on the labour force was delayed because of the large expansion in graduate education. It was not until 1968 that 'net' production of B.A.s (those entering the labour market rather than first continuing on to graduate school) began rising above its 1952 levels.

Unfortunately the fortuitous influences that kept up demand for the products of the higher education system and kept down its supply have run their course. The educational system has come close to reaching its equilibrium level of primary and secondary teachers for the next ten years or so. Given that most of the current stock of teachers is quite young, the gross-investment demand from this source will approach zero in the near future. At the college level some expansion is still projected, but it is unlikely to materialise as the current budget squeeze continues and the enrolment rates actually turn down (as they have been doing since 1969) in response to perceived market conditions. At the same time, for the next five years or so, an annual wave of about a million additional highly educated workers will be arriving at the doors of the full-time labour force. If the R & D boom does not get going again, if the economy does not start operating in high gear (low unemployment) again, and if the educational system does not move to some new highly intensive way of dealing with disadvantaged children, the outlook is rather bleak. Rates of return to education will fall, perhaps even sharply, and they have already started falling (see Freeman, 1976). This will lead to a new problem, a problem with which the United States has had little experience: the existence of a relatively large group of highly educated but underemployed and disappointed young people.

The expansion in education and the concomitant expansion in economics brought a renewed interest in the economics of education. The new wave of interest in the economics of education can be traced to the important works of Schultz (1960), Becker (1964) and Mincer (1958) and tagged by the label of 'human capital' theory. The important aspects of that theory are the view that education, in addition to its consumption (general culture) aspects, is an investment process during which resources are used, and that final consumption is forgone for the purpose of improving the productivity and marketability of labour and its skills.

The work of Becker, Mincer and their followers focused largely on elucidating all the relevant costs of this investment process, especially in the form of the cost of time (earnings forgone) of the students themselves, on the correct formulation of the decision rules for such investments (computing the relevant private and social rates of return correctly), and on the implications of this theory for the analysis of wage differentials across occupations and age categories (age—earnings profiles). In addition, the works of Schultz, Denison, Griliches and Jorgenson, among others, used this underlying framework to re-analyse aggregate growth data and concluded that the growth in the education of the labour force had been a major source of the observed productivity growth in the past and hence an important and major cog in the overall 'engine of growth.'

It is a fair criticism, I think, to note that almost all this work can be characterised as dominated by a 'supply' view. The emphasis was on the decision mechanism of individuals, to pursue or not to pursue additional education or training, and on the resultant returns of such decisions to individuals and to the economy at large. Implicitly it was assumed that human capital is very malleable and that the demand for it, in its various varieties, was highly elastic, and that therefore demand forces could be ignored, as a first approximation, or subsumed in some overall growth-trend terms.

Demand considerations were not entirely ignored by economists during these years, but that type of work, characterised almost derogatorily as the 'requirements' school, was not where the action was. It was only relatively recently, in the works of Freeman (1971) and others, that one can discern the beginnings of a synthesis in which demand forces are accorded a role which is not inferior to that of supply forces.

While this was not necessarily inherent in the human capital approach, the earlier work focused on education primarily as an investment in marketable skills and derived measures of returns to such investments from observed wage and income differentials across different schooling categories. From the beginning this has attracted a long list of critics, particularly from among those who do not believe that observed labour market outcomes in a capitalist economy can be taken as either measuring anything at all or as shedding light on productivity differences. Some of my own earlier work (1963, 1964, 1967) was an attempt to answer such critics by showing, successfully I think, that not only differences in wage rates but also actual differences in productivity (as measured by econometric estimates of production functions in agriculture and manufacturing) were related to differences in the schooling level of the labour force, across states, regions or enterprises. One does not have to rely on the logic of marginal productivity analysis alone to conclude that the past changes in average schooling levels contributed significantly to recent United States economic growth.

Several somewhat contradictory objections have been raised recently against this interpretation of the role of the expansion of schooling in American economic growth:

1. The role of schooling is overestimated when income differentials by schooling categories are used to estimate its effect because of the spurious correlation of schooling with ability and other variables.
2. Schooling is in fact rewarding to the individual, but the social return is much smaller (perhaps nil) than the private return—most of the observed returns being in effect transfers from one group to another. This is the implication of various 'screening' and 'signalling' theories of the payoff to schooling.
3. Schooling does pay off, but to the wrong people. It is a scarce social resource which is appropriated by the children of the ruling class to the detriment of the others.
4. None of the above, including schooling itself, matters.

(These positions are capsule caricatures which can be associated with (among others and at different times) (1) Denison (1964) and Bowles and Gintis (1973); (2) Taubman and Weles (1974), Spence (1974) and Arrow (1973); (3) Bowles and Gintis (1973); and (4) Jencks (1972).)

Much of my own work in recent years has been devoted to the ability problem and is fated to remain there quite a bit longer. The 'solution' of one problem discloses a new one and the analysis of a particular set of data raises more new questions than it settles. The issue of 'ability' bias in the estimates of returns to schooling was discussed in my survey paper (1970) where it was conjectured that it is not all that large. An intensive effort to estimate its actual magnitude culminated in the joint paper with Mason (1972) where it was shown that this source of bias is only on the order of 10—15 per cent as against the 40 per cent or more conjectured earlier by others. This conclusion has recently been supported by others (Hause, 1972; Solmon and Wachtel, 1972) and my own re-computations (1974) based on the newly available National Longitudinal Survey data.

Another way of attacking the 'ability bias' problem is to analyse jointly the returns to schooling of relatives, such as brothers, sisters or twins. Early work along these lines was done by Gorseline (1932). Chamberlain and I (1975) have recently re-analysed his data and concluded that they indicate very little bias from this source. Similarly my own analysis of more recent data on brothers from the N.L.S. tapes (in process) appears to confirm the impression that either there is very little bias from this source or that the relevant 'ability' concept has little to do with scores on such standard psychological tests as I.Q. or A.F.Q.T.

The issue as a whole is still in an unsatisfactory state. This is why I have kept on working on it. There is a sense in which we all believe that ability is quite important but we do not really know how to define or measure such 'ability'. Scholastic ability, as measured by I.Q. and similar type of tests, is important in seeing who gets how far in school, but does not seem to have much of an effect above and beyond its effect via schooling and hence results in little bias in the estimated effects of marginal changes in schooling levels.

The second major strand of criticism of recent human capital type work is that schooling does little more than sort individuals according to ability and that the resulting private returns to schooling overestimate significantly the rather meagre social returns from such an activity. There are two versions of this argument:

1. Schools do little but sorting. No additional 'real' human capital is embodied (augmented) during the schooling process itself.
2. Sorting itself is not particularly socially productive, it only exacerbates income inequality, and leads people to over-invest in activities such as schooling which are supposed to certify (signal) their potential abilities to ignorant employers.

There is a major important, though not all that novel, theoretical point contained in these criticisms. In a world of uncertainty in which information and the appearance of information has value, the private returns from the production and dissemination of information can easily exceed the social returns from the same activity. But the empirical import of such criticisms appears to me to be quite exaggerated.

Screening and signalling, like ability and motivation, are generalised concepts with few observable empirical counterparts that one could get one's teeth (or computers) into. If the returns to schooling were largely due to the informational content of the certificate and not to the process of schooling itself, one would expect that (1) cheaper ways of testing and certifying would be developed by employers and employees; (2) the returns to schooling would be lower among the self-employed versus wage and salary workers since, presumably, the self-employed would not pay themselves (or be able to collect) for a false signal (cf. Wolpin, 1974); and (3) the returns to schooling should decline with age as more experience is accumulated by employers about the 'true' worth of their employees and as the initial signal provided by schooling fades away into insignificance. None of these effects is observed in the data, leading one to question the empirical import of the 'schooling as a signal' hypothesis.

The issue of who gets schooling was not adequately considered in the earlier literature and the radical critics have rightfully, I think, focused their attention on the exaggerated hopes for egalitarianism that were implicit in some of the more extreme 'schooling is good for everything' positions. First, it is relatively easy to see that a general expansion in schooling need not result in any reduction in inequality. Second, the large public investments in schooling, like much of other governmental investment, were not as progressive as advertised. Much of the benefit of such subsidies redounded to the children of the middle classes and was dissipated in the induced rise of teacher salaries. Nevertheless, the critics seem to underestimate the amount of social mobility that did occur in the past and the opportunity provided by the schooling system for turn-over in the social class structure (see Blau and Duncan, 1967, on schooling as a source of social mobility in the United States), and the use of this route for social mobility by specifically disadvantaged ethnic groups such as Jews in the earlier part of this century and Blacks more recently (cf. Freeman, 1973). Nor do they give enough credit to schooling for the rise in the *average* standard of living in the economy as a whole and the concomitant driving-up of the price of human time, the one resource distributed relatively equally throughout our economic system.

Finally, there is the strand of criticism that takes the position that none of this can matter much, since little of the total observed inequality of incomes (say the variance in the logarithm of income or wages) can be accounted for by differences in schooling. At the individual level, detailed regression equations (income-generating functions) explain only between 30 and 50 per cent of the observed inequalities, and the partial role of schooling differences in such an accounting is much smaller (on the order of 10–15 per cent). There are a number of responses to be made to such criticisms. First, some of the more prominent studies claiming to have shown the importance of 'luck' and the negligible impact of schooling are marred by not taking adequate account of the rather large transitory variations in income at the individual level and ignoring age, life-cycle effects and on-the-job training differences as a source of *ex-post* but not *ex-ante* inequality. Second, in a recent analysis (1974) I show that, while schooling by itself does not account for a great deal of the observed variance in wages or income, additional schooling could be and had been used in the United States in the 1960s to overcome social class handicaps and to compensate for and eliminate some of the *systematic* sources of observed income inequality. The results of the data analysis and the estimated model can be summarised by asking what they imply for two youngsters who are one standard deviation apart on each of a list of family background variables *and* I.Q. The model predicts that they would find themselves, other things equal, about 0·75 and 0·4 of a standard deviation apart on schooling and wages, respectively, implying a rather strong regression towards the mean. Now, if the youngster with the lower family background and I.Q. managed somehow to acquire an extra four years of schooling (e.g. went on to and completed college), which would be equal to an additional 1·5 standard deviation units of schooling, it would essentially wipe out his original handicap. If, in fact, he had an equal I.Q. to start out with, he would need only about two more years of schooling to compensate him for his lower social class start.

It has been 'open season', recently, as far as education is concerned. From various sides it has been attacked either as a tool of the establishment or as a waste of money. From its zenith as the hope and glory of the American Dream and the main catalyst of the melting-pot it has dropped to the nadir of the imprisoner and brainwasher of our children and the perpetuator of the class structure. As most swings in American public opinion, this too was overdone. Schooling was probably not the panacea that some of the discoverers of human capital and the defenders of the educational establishment were careless enough to imply occasionally, nor is it as ineffective or even malicious a social force as is often asserted these days.

These attacks, which came in part as a response to the rising economic position of the educational industry and the rising rewards to the factors specialised in it, are unlikely to make a serious dent in our views as to what education is really about. Their intellectual foundations are weak and the empirical import of the various points actually scored is rather meagre. But while we beat off the attacks from within, the world outside is changing and with it the economic fortunes of the educational system.

The slowdown in population growth and possibly in economic growth may bring to an end an era of over two hundred years of rising importance of and rewards in education. The era was initiated by the 'enlightenment' period, fed by the rapid rise in population which started in the West in the eighteenth century and by the great burst in economic growth and technical change that ran through the nineteenth and twentieth centuries. With both population and economic growth slowing down and with the educational industry seriously over-expanded, we are in for hard times, at least for a while.

There are other changes that may be impinging on the scarcity value of knowledge. The technological revolution in communications and copying has reduced significantly the transmission costs of knowledge and made it even harder to appropriate. It has also increased significantly the flow of information (both relevant and irrelevant) that inundates employers, consumers, and public officials. Whether or not this will lower or raise the price of knowledge 'handlers', if not of knowledge 'possessors', is still an open question. It is also quite likely that part of the economic value of education arises out of its interaction with technical change. That is, better-educated entrepreneurs and managers use new technology quicker and current technology better, in the sense of allocating the available resources more optimally. This line of thought (due to Nelson and Phelps, 1966, and Welch, 1970) would imply that much of the returns to schooling would evaporate if there were no new information to process. Up to now these ideas have been tested only on agricultural data. If they are correct, as well they may be, and if we are approaching a no-growth era in the future, including a slowdown in the rate of economic and technical change, this too may contribute to a decline in the scarcity value of education.

One should not perhaps end on such a pessimistic note. It is quite likely that the pace of technical change will not decelerate significantly in the foreseeable future. New developments in biology and a renewal and expansion of space exploration could boost the demand again. On the other hand, the decline in outside pressures on the educational system may have blessings of its own. We might be able to do a better job on a smaller scale. Finally, the role played by the monks of the Middle Ages, who kept alive, transcribed and transmitted the meagre knowledge of the times, may, in the sum of things, have been no less important and valuable than the contribution of those who opened the new vistas to us in the past two centuries. There is still a great deal to digest, to transmit and to preserve.

### Acknowledgements

I am indebted to the National Science Foundation and the National Institute of Education for financial support to work on this and related topics, and to M. L. Burstein, R. B. Freeman and T. W. Schultz for comments on an earlier draft.

### References

Arrow, K. (1973). 'Higher Education as a Filter', *Journal of Public Economics*, II, 193–216.
Becker, G. S. (1964). *Human Capital* (New York: National Bureau of Economic Research).

Blan, P. M. and Duncan, O. D. (1967). *The American Occupational Structure* (New York: Wiley).

Bowles, S. and Gintis, H. (1973). 'I.Q. and the U.S. Class Structure', *Social Policy*, (Jan.–Feb.).

Chamberlain, G. and Griliches, Z. (1975). 'Unobservables with a Variance–Components Strucutre: Ability, Schooling and the Economic Success of Brothers', *International Economic Review*, XVI (2).

Denison, E. F. (1964). 'Measuring the Contribution of Education', in O.E.C.D., *The Residual Factor and Economic Growth* (Paris).

Freeman, R. B. (1971). *The Labor Market for College-Trained Manpower* (Cambridge, Mass.: Harvard Univ. Press).

Freeman, R. B. (1973). 'Changes in the Labor Market for Black Americans, 1948–72', *Brookings Papers on Economic Activity*, No. 1, pp. 67–132.

Freeman, R. B. (1975). 'The Declining Economic Value of Higher Education and the American Social System', Discussion Paper No. 421 (Cambridge, Mass.: Harvard Institute of Economic Research).

Gorseline, N. E. (1932). *The Effect of Schooling upon Income* (Bloomington: Indiana Univ. Press).

Griliches, Z. (1963). 'The Sources of Measured Productivity Growth: U.S. Agriculture, 1940–60', *Journal of Political Economy*, LXXI (4).

Griliches, Z. (1964). 'Research Expenditures, Education, and the Aggregate Agriculture Production Function', *American Economic Review*, LIV (6).

Griliches, Z. (1967). 'Production Functions in Manufacturing: Some Preliminary Results', in M. Brown (ed.), *The Theory and Empirical Analysis of Production*, Studies in Income and Wealth, vol. XXXI (New York: Columbia Univ. Press for National Bureau of Economic Research) pp. 275–90.

Griliches, Z. (1970). 'Notes on the Role of Education in Production Functions and Growth Accounting', in Lee Hansen (ed.), *Education and Income*, Studies in Income and Wealth, vol. XXXV (New York: National Bureau of Economic Research).

Griliches, Z. (1974). 'Wages and Earnings of Young Men', unpublished.

Griliches, Z. and Mason, W. (1972). 'Education, Income and Ability', *Journal of Political Economy*, LXXX (3), Part II.

Hause, J. C. (1972). 'Earnings Profiles: Ability and Schooling', *Journal of Political Economy*, LXXX (3), Part II.

Jencks, C. (1972). *Inequality* (New York: Basic Books).

Mincer, J. (1958). 'Investment in Human Capital and Personal Income Distribution', *Journal of Political Economy*, LXVI (4).

Nelson, P. R. and Phelps, E. S. (1966). 'Investment in Humans, Technological Diffusion, and Economic Growth', *American Economic Review*, LVI (2).

Schultz, T. W. (1960). 'Capital Formation by Education', *Journal of Political Economy*, LXVIII (6).

Solmon, L. C. and Wachtel, P. (1972). 'The Returns to Education Quality', in National Bureau of Economic Research, *2nd Annual Report*.

Spence, M. (1974). *Market Signalling* (Cambridge, Mass.: Harvard Univ. Press).

Taubman, P. and Wales, R. (1974). *Higher Education and Earnings* (New York: McGraw-Hill).

Welch, F. (1970). 'Education in Production', *Journal of Political Economy*, LXXVIII (1).

Wolpin, K. (1974). 'Education and Screening' (University of Chicago, unpublished).

# 5 Mathematical Programming in Long-term Planning —Hungary

P. BOD

This chapter discusses a mathematical programming model for the Hungarian long-term economy-wide plan, a model which is designed to serve very practical goals.

## 1. Background

It is well known that the Hungarian national economy is a centrally controlled socialist economy. Such an economy as a system requires a national economic plan as one of its subsystems. Such a plan includes all important sectors of the economy and all phases of the social reproduction process. No controlled economy can exist without systematic national economic planning; also, there are national economic plans in various uncontrolled economies.

The category planned or controlled economy reflects first of all a qualitative social property of the economy in question. The national economic plan in a country having a controlled economic system has to function in the framework of a general directive system which is developing historically but which is a well-defined given system at any point in time, and has a well-defined institutional background. National economic planning in a controlled economy is thus a real social activity, having given, mostly codified, rules and a specific organisation.

If one wants to use mathematical methods in this kind of planning to achieve a higher degree of rationality in economic thinking, one must formalise the existing, real planning process. Formal models which differ from the actual planning process are unable to improve the efficiency and reliability of the plan. The given system of the national economic plan represents the unique information basis for any applicable planning model. The parameters of models not related to the institutional information system of the national economic plan are hard to determine and it is extremely difficult to interpret the results obtained from such models in usual economic terms.

44

In Hungary, long-, medium- and short-term plans are drawn up. These three kinds of planning activity are closely related to each other, having at the same time their particular roles. Long-term plans have a horizon of 15–20 years, medium-term plans cover five years, while short-term planning covers one year.

The task of long-term economy-wide planning is to formulate in quantitative terms the economic policy of the socialist state for 15–20 years and to offer a systematic framework for the strategic plans of long-term economic development. The long-term national economic plan does not provide compulsory decisions for any field of economic activity; instead, it contains various possible development paths of the economy, and tries to compare their different social effects.

The control of the socialist economy necessitates such long-term plans because in the framework of the medium-term plan and in the course of managing the socialist economy one frequently encounters decisions which involve long-term consequences. These are, for example, decisions related to the training of manpower, to education in general, those aimed at developing infrastructure, and those related to environmental protection, energy supply, the food economy, the transport economy, and so forth.

To take such decisions we must be able to assess the long-term consequences of the different feasible variants. This is only possible if we are in a position to examine the alternatives of such decisions in the framework of a system simulating the whole movement of the economy with acceptable accuracy. This is provided by the long-term plan.

In a controlled economy the most important decisions concerning allocations are taken in the framework of the plans. Therefore, the long-term plan must comprise the elements of the main measures to be taken by the central power for creating the conditions of some desired economic development. At the same time, we are clearly aware that the development of the economy is not merely a function of the decisions by the central power. The internal and external circumstances of economic development have a certain movement of their own that hardly depends on the conscious decisions of the state. Between certain limits it is possible to prognosticate this own movement, but foresight is rather uncertain in this context. Therefore we conceive of long-term planning as a continuous activity, where we always try to look ahead to 15–20 years. But we do not imagine that the economy will actually develop by the end of the period in this way which we now predict. The horizon of 15–20 years is necessary to provide a rational framework for our present long-term decisions. In five years' time we shall have different ideas about the ways of development ten years later from those we have now on relations 15 years hence.

Every experience in economy-wide planning has pointed to the fact that it is impossible to survey and work out the detailed development possibilities of the various branches of the economy in a single central body of planning, such as the National Planning Office. In such a central institution the information necessary for making detailed decisions is unavailable. Therefore, the Hungarian long-term plan relies on long-term planning by the branches. This means that long-term economy-wide planning has a two-stage organization. In this organisation we can distinguish between a centre and several sub-centres.

The task of the centre is to represent overall social interests, while the sub-centres represent the various economic sectors. Long-term planning takes the form of a dialogue between the centre and the sub-centres.

This dialogue starts with the sub-centres, which draw up proposals, in several variants, for the development of their own sectors. In this work they mainly start from the analysis of their own possibilities and express in their proposals, quite naturally, their own sectoral interests. The sub-centres work out their proposals simultaneously, and independently of each other. In this stage the sectors have no exact idea about the development concepts of the other sectors and, of course, they cannot thus exactly know the size and pattern of social demand for their activities.

The sub-centres send in their proposals to the centre. The planning task to be performed by the centre consists in drawing up, from the sectoral proposals, balanced and, if possible, efficient paths for the economy as a whole. Thus the central planning has to co-ordinate, and to represent social interests and preferences. This means that the centre must decide whether there exists a consistent development conception for the entire economy, based on the sectoral proposals, and, if so, analyse and compare the different feasible development paths of the economy.

The model for the plan is related to the problems of how to allocate new productive capacities among the different branches and how to schedule the development of the different sectors among the sub-periods of the entire planning period. Formally, this is a multi-period mixed linear optimising model comprising aggregated sectoral activities with continuous and integer variables. However, in spite of the formally optimising nature of the model, we do not aim at determining a unique optimal long-term plan.

The heart of the model is the system of constraints. Mathematically, this is a system of inequalities, each feasible solution of which corresponds to a long-term balanced development strategy of the economy. The set of feasible solutions of the model is deliberately multi-dimensional. We consider the economy in the long run as a system with high degree of freedom, and assume that the society has many choices in determining its own economic goals.

Optimisation, as a technique, appears in the model so that, from among the set of feasible solutions, we examine primarily those which have extreme properties from the viewpoint of objective functions expressing various social preferences.

The model is thus a tool for making experiments, with the aid of which a large number of implementable economic development strategies can be generated by considering different assumptions about external circumstances and applying various preconditions as regards economic policy.

In the model, coefficients change from period to period; thus, strictly speaking, the model is not linear in its continuous part, but approximates the non-linear relationships relating to the period as a whole in a linear manner. The model also comprises coefficients which are treated as variables, that is, which have no numerically fixed values; the model itself determines the values of these parameters.

The basic philosophy of the model is such that it defines a certain sectoral consistency which must not be violated by the centre and for this reason the competence of the centre comes to be limited.

## 2. The Model

There are $T$ periods (in practice $T = 15$) and $n$ sectors (in practice $n = 31$), including non-productive ones (in practice 5). Every sector works out development variants. The development proposals of sector $j$ are $K_j^1, \ldots, K_j^{k(j)}$. The set $J$ of sectors is partitioned into two groups. In one $(J_1)$ the various development variants can be combined with each other. In the other $(J_2)$ the variants are mutually exclusive.

The development proposal of a given sector $K_j^l$ is represented in the model by a choice variable $\xi_j^l$. We have

$$0 \leq \xi_j^l \leq 1, \quad j \in J \tag{1}$$

and

$$\xi_j^l \in \{0, 1\}, \quad j \in J_2 \tag{2}$$

The sectors base their development proposals on three classes of variable. The first is the $K_j^l$, that is, the measures of all new capacities which will be established during the whole long-term period if the corresponding development variant materialises in its entirety, that is, if $\xi_j^l = 1$. The second is the $\kappa_j^l$, that is, $T$-vectors of the extents of the developments realised from period to period in the case of full implementation; note that $\Sigma_t \kappa_j^l(t) = K_j^l$. The third is the $b_j^l(t)$, that is, $n$-vectors of levels of capital inputs needed to produce in the sector $j$ and in period $t$ new capacities $\kappa_j^l(t)$ according to the development proposal $K_j^l$.

The capital input vectors of the sector $j$ constitute in each period an $n \times k(j)$ matrix $B_j^t = [b_j^1(t), \ldots, b_j^{k(j)}(t)]$, so for the whole economy we have the $n \times \Sigma_j k(j)$ investment matrix, for each period, $B^t = [B_1^t, \ldots, B_n^t]$.

Note that the elements of the investment matrices are not coefficients but volumes of assets engaged in period $t$ under the assumption that the corresponding sectoral proposal will be fully implemented.

The alternatives in the first group of sectors are supposed to be mixable and consequently the investment inputs are considered here to be proportional to the actual level of implementation. In the second group of sectors this question does not arise, for the alternatives there can be implemented here only fully or not at all.

Sectoral activities are carried on with the initial capacities existing at the beginning of the long-term plan period and with the capacities created as results of the development actions.

In period $t$ the sector $j$ performs activities $x_j^t$, a vector of $k(j)$ components. These components correspond to activities yielding the same output, but having different input patterns depending on which variant has created the corresponding capacity, so the total activity of the sector is $\sum_i x_j^t(i)$.

These activities with identical outputs are characterised by input coefficients differing by periods and elaborated in the course of the sectoral planning. These coefficients are the elements of the $n \times k(j)$ matrices $A_j^t = [a_j^1(t), \ldots, a_j^{k(j)}(t)]$, so for the economy as a whole we have the matrices $A^t = [A_1^t, \ldots, A_n^t]$.

The centre now has to choose from among the sectoral proposals, subject to

$$\sum_l \xi_j^l = 1 \tag{3}$$

These constraints assure the possibility of mixing the alternatives in the group of sectors $J_1$ and bring a unique choice in each sector with non-mixable proposals. The capital inputs and the related developments in capacities are determined by the choices and a new structure of capacities comes about for each sub-period, whence it is possible to determine the levels of the sectoral activities.

The centre cannot change the development proposals of the sectors but is free in deciding the activity levels. The centre may modify the activity levels planned by the sectors but has to do this on the basis of sectoral information about technological patterns.

We now introduce some notation. Firstly, we define the two vectors $X^t = [x_1^t, \ldots, x_n^t]$ and $\Xi = [\xi_1, \ldots, \xi_n]$, each of $\sum_j k(j)$ components. Secondly, we define the $n \times \sum_j k(j)$ operator

$$E = \begin{bmatrix} e_1 & & 0 \\ & \ddots & \\ 0 & & e_n \end{bmatrix}$$

where $e_j$ is the summation operator of $k(j)$ elements. Thirdly, from the vectors $\kappa_j^l$ we form the $\sum_j k(j)$-square diagonal matrix $H^t$, the first $k(1)$ diagonal elements of this being the vector $\kappa_1^1, \ldots, \kappa_1^{k(1)}$, and so forth.

Then the product $H^t \Xi$ gives the new capacities created during the period $t$. We shall assume that these new capacities are workable at the beginning of the period $t + 1$.

We also employ the following variables:

$y^t$   the
$z^t$   public consumption in period $t$
$s^t$   closing stock at the end of period $t$
$m^t$   net imports in period $t$.

With the notation introduced we can now formulate the system of balances expressing the most important internal relations of social reproduction:

$$s^{t-1} + EX^t = A^t X^t + B^t \Xi - m^t + y^t + z^t + s^t \tag{4}$$

We have thus a balance of the social product for each period of the plan. We also have the further constraints that, in each period, sectoral activities must not exceed the sum of starting capacities of the sectors and the capacities created in the preceding periods. Formally,

$$X^t = k_0 + \sum_{i=1}^{t-1} H^i \Xi \tag{5}$$

Thus in (1)–(5) we have the most important internal elements of the constraint system. The model also contains further constraints. These mainly concern primary resources which are not reproducible in the framework of the model and foreign trade activities.

We obtain in this way the set of the feasible solutions on which we try to optimise various functions expressing different social preferences. Let me illustrate how we do this by the example of consumption. One of the most important preferences in a socialist economy is the satisfaction of the society's material and cultural demands on the highest level possible and the continuous improvement of the quality of life. We introduce the following consumption function into the model in order to be able to implement this preference in the economic analyses to be performed:

$$y^t + z^t = \bar{f}^t + \lambda^t f^t$$

We maximise $\sum_t \alpha^t \lambda^t$ where $\alpha^t$ are coefficients expressing time-preference.

In the consumption function $\bar{f}^t$ denotes a basic consumption for the period $t$ the realisation of which is a feasibility condition of any programme. The second member of the right-hand side is an additional consumption, the weighted sum of which we wish to maximise.

The pattern of basic consumption is fixed by the vectors $\bar{f}^t$. We do not, however, fix the pattern of additional consumption definitely, but consider it be be unknown. We want the optimisation procedure to choose, together with the optimal programme, the structure of additional consumption that secures the greatest surplus possible. Of course, the pattern of additional consumption cannot be wholly optional. The vector describing the acceptable pattern of additional consumption can move only within certain limits. But we may safely assume that a closed convex set can be given, each point of which means an acceptable pattern of surplus consumption. In other words, while the pattern of basic consumption is fixed for every period, for the pattern of surplus consumption we give a domain of movement $F^t$ from which we choose on the basis of the optimality criterion defined in the objective function.

The task thus defined is therefore a generalised linear programming problem, with the difficulty that some of the variables are integer-valued. The generalised linear programming problem is that of choosing scalars $x_1, \ldots, x_n$ and vectors $P_1, \ldots, P_n$ to maximise $\Sigma_i c_i x_i$ (for some given $c_i$) subject to $\Sigma_i P_i x_i = b$ with the $x_i \geq 0$ and the $P_i \in M_i$, where the $M_i$ are given closed convex sets. It can be seen that the problem is reduced to a simple linear programming problem if every set $M_i$ consists of a single point.

In the generalised linear programming problem every variable is a continuous one. In this form the problem can be solved and its solution does not cause complicated situations provided the number of unknown coefficient vectors is not too high and the structure of the sets is not too complicated, for example if they are convex polyhedrons.

It is an open mathematical question how to solve such a problem when the variables, or some of them, are discrete. To overcome this difficulty, we solve our model in two phases. In the first phase we choose a feasible pattern of surplus consumption for each period and with these solve the mixed integer optimisation problem. Then we fix the values of the integer variables thus obtained, and then solve the problem, now comprising only continuous variables, as a generalised linear programming problem. The technique of generalised linear programming allows us to investigate alternatives in the light of the preferences expressed by the objective function, which used to be considered as given. Surplus consumption is only one of these exogenously planned alternatives. Others, given from outside the model, are the schedules of the sectoral developments. The planning centre has to revise these schedules from a macroeconomic point of view. We assume that a timetable for a long-term sectoral development plan determined by the planning authority can be modified within certain limits without risking the technical feasibility of the plan. That is, the corresponding $\kappa_j^i$ may be thought of as unknowns which may be determined in the central planning procedure. Note that a shift in the phasing of investments will affect the product balances; however, in the product balances we have used investment inputs of a fixed size and not per unit coefficients. Let us now consider the identity

$$B^t = B^t (H^t)^{-1} H^t = \bar{B}^t H^t$$

where $\bar{B}^t = B^t (H^t)^{-1}$. Using this we may transform the investment matrix into a matrix containing per unit coefficients. Thus in the product balances instead of $B^t \, \Xi$ there will appear $\bar{B}^t H^t \Xi$. This means that the effect of the changing of the $\kappa_j^l$ is felt, and thus that the decision variables will have unknown coefficients in the product balances.

Thus, in the second phase of solving the model, the patterns of additional consumption and the timetables of the sectors may undergo modifications. Consider this in the dialogue between the centre and the subcentres. The sub-centres have worked out development variants, and phased over time the necessary claims on investment and the resulting production possibilities. The centre has accepted all the development proposals and the per unit data of all continuous activities.

The centre did not consider as fixed from the outset which variant to accept from among those proposed by the sectors with non-mixable alternatives, what mixing it prefers for the sectors having mixable alternatives, and what the rate of development in the sectors should be. These are determined by the optimum solution. The levels of the activities to be performed by the sectors and the best pattern of surplus consumption also come from this.

From the viewpoint of the sectors, it is the latter which are the most important information from the solution of the model. In the initial sectoral planning the sectors mainly relied on their own ideas and interests. It will turn out in the course of solving the model whether it is possible to construct from the sectoral proposals, with the given rules, a plan that would be consistent on the economy-wide level. If the answer is yes, how do these consistent sectoral plans compare with the original ideas of the sectors? If there are major divergencies between the two, the sectors have to draw up new plan proposals, but now taking into account the results of the previous comprehensive economy-wide computations.

The model thus enables the development of a dialogue in the framework of which the sectors give development proposals to the centre and the centre in turn hands down balanced programmes for sectoral activities. Since sectoral planning has not yet been formalised, this dialogue cannot be seen as a formal system. Thus, for the time being, the problem of convergence cannot be investigated with mathematical tools. Nevertheless, we hope that we shall be able to generate consistent and efficient development strategies by this partially formalised dialogue between the centre and the sectors.

# 6 Interactions Between Planned and Market Economies —Hungary

## M. M. TARDOS

This chapter examines the problems of a centrally planned economy in its economic relations with capitalist economies, using the example of Hungary over the years 1973–5. The chapter commences with a discussion of the relations between the world market and the domestic economy in general, then examines the effects of the reform in Hungary on its foreign trade and the effects of capitalist inflation on the Hungarian economy. The effects of world market changes on the actual management of the Hungarian economy are then discussed, and some conclusions suggested.

### 1. The World Market and the Domestic Economy

It is apparent that any economy which does not have proper links between domestic and external prices cannot expect to make rational decisions in questions of foreign trade. This problem is particularly severe if we also have no unequivocal information on domestic costs either. Specifically, in socialist countries, the prices of the outside world do not present themselves directly, and costs can be perceived only indirectly and inaccurately. The reason for this is that planned economies attach extreme importance to setting plan targets under stable conditions, and to measuring the fulfilment of these targets. The stability of economic conditions, particularly domestic prices, may contradict two important conditions for successful economic management. Firstly, enterprises fail to appraise adequately the changes in their economic environment that were neglected or misjudged when this environment was planned, and consequently adapt themselves to these changes inefficiently, or not at all. Secondly, the stability of prices makes it impossible to follow properly changes in relative costs, and this makes it difficult for the central planners to determine the desirable production and development rates, and to determine how the country should join in the international division of labour.

In Hungary the planners tried to eliminate these contradictions through the economic reform of 1968, and by providing the preconditions for joining in the international division of labour. To attain these ends, among other things, the following major changes took place in the economic system. Firstly, control of enterprises by means of plan instructions was discontinued; secondly, measures were taken for world market prices and C.M.E.A. contractual prices to act directly on producing enterprises; and thirdly, the system of fixed producer prices was replaced by a system of maximum and free prices, and the discrepancy between producer prices and production costs was reduced.

The conditions of adjustment to changes in external market conditions improved substantially, mainly as a consequence of the above changes. The creators of the reform believed that efficient adjustment to changes in external conditions and stability in economic management were not contradictory at that time. This was because the late 1960s were years of balanced and steady world market circumstances. The rise of the world market price level was less than 0·5 per cent per year on average, and relative price changes were also slow. It was thus reasonable to hope that if the fixed elements of the price system were modified only every five years, this would not upset the relative harmony between the domestic and the world market price systems.

## 2. Foreign trade results of Hungary's economy after the reform

The changes in the system of economic control and management which took place in 1968 led to favourable economic results despite the inconsistencies. The readiness of enterprises to adjust themselves to market conditions improved appreciably and the choice of goods on the domestic market expanded.

Foreign trade also improved. Over the years 1967—72 socialist exports grew by 80 per cent and non-socialist exports by 98 per cent; this was substantially higher than the growth rate of the preceding five-year period. Growth of exports of industrial finished products could keep abreast with the general rate of development. The efficiency of exports also improved. The costs of earning one dollar amounted on the average to Ft 72 in 1968, but were reduced to Ft 64 by 1972. There was a similar, although somewhat smaller, improvement in the costs of earning a rouble: they decreased from Ft 47 to Ft 44.

A comparison of the costs of export- and import-substituting activities also showed an improvement of foreign trade efficiency. Although the production costs of exports continued to be below the costs of import substitution, export activity ensured the availability of industrial finished products which could not be manufactured at home. On the other hand, part of the improvement in the trade with non-socialist countries may have been the result of changes in the world market price proportions, for the non-socialist terms of trade improved by 9 per cent between 1968 and 1972.

### 3. Capitalist inflation and the Hungarian economy

The accelerating capitalist inflation took the Hungarian system of economic control by surprise. The problems were of dual origin: firstly, the economic system presupposed a quiet world market situation and was therefore not prepared for adaptation to rapidly changing conditions; and secondly, these changes were directly unfavourable for the Hungarian economy.

We first examine the effects of actual economic changes. The world market inflation made itself felt as early as the late 1960s. But the Hungarian terms of trade had not deteriorated until 1973. Thus the prices of Hungarian exports to the non-socialist market increased more quickly than those of imports. But in 1973–4 the rate of inflation accelerated, and further changes also acted adversely and directly on Hungarian foreign trade.

The high rate of import price increases was followed by the price increase of Hungarian exports at a moderate rate only. The price increase of imports, consisting of up to three-quarters of raw materials, amounted to 31 per cent in forint terms during two years, while the increase of export prices reached only 14 per cent.

The ratio of highly processed industrial finished products in Hungary's exports to non-socialist countries is hardly lower than in its imports. It was mainly the West European overproduction of meat that led to the deterioration of the terms of trade by 16 per cent in two years. During the period of the general rise in prices, the export prices of Hungarian animal products fell by 14 per cent on the average in 1974, with the export price of beef cattle by 20 per cent, while the possibilities of export decreased at the same time as a consequence of the import prohibitions of the Common Market. The other factor in this deterioration of the terms of trade was that Hungarian exporters were not able to raise their prices sufficiently on the capitalist markets. The explanation for this is partly historical. During the past ten years, changes in the West European markets were not properly recognised by Hungarian enterprises, and the period since 1968 was not long enough to bring about fundamental changes. As a consequence, the demand for exports was not strong enough to allow Hungary to follow the price rises of the capitalist market successfully. We cannot assess this with certainty, but it seems that this unfavourable situation is also due to the fact that the Hungarian enterprises had no incentive to make the most of the price rises, and were not forced to raise prices either. Also, the increasing costs of imports did not restrict consumption, because the budget acted as a cushion against price increases. We revert to a more detailed explanation of these factors later.

Hungary's difficulties were worsened by the desire of the socialist countries to keep pace with the rises of world market prices. Prices were raised in C.M.E.A. trade from the beginning of 1975. These new contractual prices, although they rose moderately compared with the increase in world market prices, are likely to result in an 8 per cent deterioration of the terms of trade in 1975. The changes in the C.M.E.A. contractual prices will certainly cause further losses to Hungary's economy in the coming years, since the price of the imported raw materials will further increase on the basis of the sliding price-calculation system accepted by the C.M.E.A. in 1975.

Hungary's situation will be rendered still more difficult by the slowing down of the growth rate of raw material imports from the C.M.E.A. countries. The increase in input coefficients from exports and import substitution already experienced in socialist trade may be interpreted as foretokening this situation. For the future we must also take into account that exports to the capitalist market, which are limited anyway, will be required to pay for raw materials.

All this will have the result that price changes are likely to consume at least one year's increment of the national income, and this will leave the national economy in serious difficulties.

The single most serious change in the capitalist economic situation was that connected with the oil crisis. The price of oil rose four- to fivefold on the world market in 1973—4. This rise was accompanied by an increase in the prices of other energy resources. The balance of payments of leading industrial countries are also seriously affected by these changes, but their costs changes are not as dramatic as in Hungary. The costs of energy rose since 1973 by about 70 per cent in the West (in dollars) which, considering the dollar inflation, is not a particularly rapid relative rise in energy costs.

In Hungary, on the other hand, this change is of a greater order of magnitude. In the late 1960s it seemed as if Hungary was able to meet her energy requirements from Soviet crude oil imports, at a price of 16 roubles per ton to a practically unlimited extent. This meant that the price of $10^9$ calories of energy was Ft 64. The price level of the other energy resources could have been calculated to keep the price of coal and the other primary energy below this level, since the calorific use-value of coal is lower than that of fuel oil. Yet, in fact, prices were not fixed in this way; the combined costs of the planned consumption of oil, coal and natural gas were taken as a basis, and divided among the energy resources. Thus the price of fuel oil became Ft 112 for $10^9$ calories.

Following the price changes on the world market, not only was the price of Soviet oil raised from 16 to 37 roubles (and this will be followed by a further price increase), but the growth rate of Soviet deliveries slowed down at the same time. The consequence is that the additional requirements of primary energy must be met from Near Eastern oil at an increased price. And Near Eastern oil, even if possible reductions of the world market price are taken into account, cannot be cheaper than $80—90 per ton delivered at the Hungarian frontier, which means a price around Ft 380 per $10^9$ calories, considering the revaluation of the forint, but may easily go as high as Ft 450. Nor will the natural gas coming from the Soviet Union be substantially cheaper if we take into account the investment costs. All this means that the price increase of energy imports would justify a fivefold increases compared with the price level of the 1960s, and a threefold increase compared with the actual price level. This, however, would require a fundamental structural reshaping of the domestic price system.

It may be concluded that, in general, world economic changes had an adverse effect on the small raw-material importing socialist countries, including Hungary. These changes resulted in an increase of the import requirements, especially of raw-material import requirements, from non-socialist countries, and exports will have difficulties in keeping abreast with these increased demands. It is questionable, too, whether these countries will be able to adjust themselves to the new conditions and revise their export development projects to take account of the demands of Western markets, a problem which appeared to be difficult even before. It is to be feared, therefore, that the industrial imports of these countries will increase, and therefore that their credit demands will grow at the same time.

The raw-material exporting socialist countries will be in a much more favourable position: their free foreign exchange revenues will be greater than before, and so it will be easier for them to satisfy their home demands for investment goods.

### 4. World market changes and the management of the Hungarian economy

As mentioned above, the stability of economic management, and of the economic units, played an important role in the stated social-political objectives of the Hungarian economic system. This general stability requires price stability which, in a period of world economic changes that affect Hungary's economy intensely, contradicts the requirement, stated at the time of the 1968 reform, that the economic units should perceive through the price system the changes of the external markets, and should adjust themselves to these changes.

The control system of a socialist economy, based on plan instructions, has at its disposal a clear-cut arsenal for handling such conflicts. Owing to the lack of an organic relationship between domestic and external prices, budget expenditures are increased by growing import subsidies paid to enterprises, but the possibility of a set-off is given by reducing export subsidies. These financial measures are less necessary if the state avails itself of the possibility to modify the exchange rate. Revaluation of the home currency, which is stable, or at least considerably less exposed to inflation than the free currencies, may at best result in an unchanged magnitude of budgetary expenditures. However, these external economic changes are concealed from the economic units; their possible adverse effects become manifest only in the reduction of the welfare expenditures of the budget, or in a shortage of commodities which results, instead of inflation, from budgetary overspending, with the given fixed-price system. All this has given rise to complex contradictions in Hungary. It had to be decided anew whether orientation of the enterprises or the stability of prices should be the principal economic policy objective. The relative stability of prices emerged victorious from this conflict.

As early as 1970, considerable changes had to be carried out in the economic system for the sake of price stability. When the economic reform had been introduced, stability was achieved through the financial bridges introduced for a temporary curbing of disturbances and by making these bridges permanent. However, while in 1968 the subsidies given to agricultural and food-industrial imports were compensated by the receipts of the metallurgical and machine-industrial import pools, in 1971—2 the direct import subsidies and the net expenditures of the import pools in financing the trade of fixed-price products amounted to more than 5 per cent of the value of total non-socialist imports. Although the forint was revalued several times, the amount of budgetary grants for setting off the increase of import prices grew considerably between 1971 and 1974. The sum paid through various channels for checking the increase of import prices reached almost 27 per cent of the value of non-socialist trade in 1974.

Although enterprise receipts per dollar of exports decreased because of devaluation, the direct receipts of enterprises from non-socialist exports increased, because the 66 per cent increase in export prices between 1968 and 1974 was accompanied by only a 38 per cent revaluation of the forint. This means that the forint was effectively devalued. Also, the subsidies to non-socialist exports were increased at the expense of the state budget. By 1974 these subsidies exceeded their 1968 value by 124 per cent while the volume of non-socialist exports grew by only 80 per cent. This increase was necessary because the inflationary effect of import prices infiltrated the home price system despite restrictive measures, and home inflation was further increased by the budgetary deficit: the rise of the forint producer price level was about 20 per cent between 1968 and 1974.

At the same time, one should note that the receipts of certain enterprises from capitalist inflation were regarded as excessive and, therefore, a special production tax was imposed on such receipts, whereby almost 40 per cent of export subsidies were collected from the enterprises. Consequently, the net state subsidisation of non-socialist exports grew by only 39 per cent, that is, to a considerably smaller extent than the increase of export volume. The actual production tax, and the possibility of imposing other taxes, restrained exports and set back the increase of export receipts.

Hungary's balance of payments with capitalist countries became particularly unfavourable in 1974 as a consequence. Import prices had risen by 35 per cent, but the volume of imports grew by about 18 per cent. The volume of non-socialist exports decreased by about 8 per cent, and this was not only due to the decrease in the exports of livestock and animal products.

It appears from all this that the situation developing in 1974 was characterised by a confusion of state regulations in which the profit-interested enterprises were no longer concerned with adjusting themselves to market impulses, but instead were interested in the successful outcome of negotiations with government agencies conducted incessantly over taxes and subsidies.

Why was the state forced into this jungle of economic regulations (financial bridges in Hungarian usage) which, in addition, increased the tension of the balance of payments with capitalist countries? Why did the government not let the forint, devalued in 1968, reach its equilibrium value? Following this, the government could have protected itself against inflation by a regular revaluation of the forint, thus letting changes in world market prices act on the home economy in accordance with the requirements stated at the time of the reform. It is difficult to answer these questions, but one thing seems clear: namely, that it cannot be justified to accept so many disadvantages just for the sake of a stable price.

Attempts to achieve relative stability of enterprises through a relative stability of prices are made a first-order political objective in the C.M.E.A. countries, and even in Hungary, which makes the greatest efforts of all to follow the trends in demand. There are various explanations for this.

Firstly, the central bodies cannot easily abandon their promises concerning the continuous improvement of living standards and the stabilisation of consumer prices. If there is a considerable change in consumer prices, a decrease in the living standards of a given social stratum may be avoided only if the effects of price increase are compensated by measures of price reduction or wage increases in excess of these effects. If producer prices change spontaneously, and these changes are felt in consumer prices, a set-off in the above sense cannot be ensured. It is on this account that, so far, there has not been a single socialist country whose government would have decided to permit free movement of the majority of consumer prices.

Secondly, periodic adjustment of consumer prices to the changes in costs or world market prices cannot be solved in harmony with the above requirements. In order that the measures for setting off price increases should compensate all strata sufficiently, even in the consumer's judgement, it would be necessary to effect considerable budgetary expenditures for which a coverage cannot be provided. This also explains why the alteration of the consumer price structure suggested in the plans is chronically postponed, or abandoned.

Thirdly, it is not easy to develop a producer price system that reflects the changing market conditions well, or to solve the covering from the budget of the price differences between producer and consumer prices. If producer prices fluctuate intensely, enterprise efforts and chance cannot be kept apart in the profit-and-loss accounts of enterprises. As a consequence, it is not possible to appraise the success of enterprise activities adequately, or to evaluate the results of enterprise management objectively. A centrally planned economy usually insists on such objective evaluation.

Besides this, the Hungarian economic system has linked the wage changes of the employed population to enterprise results. It was for this reason that the Hungarian economy was forced to aim at a steady increase of enterprise profits.

If, however, producer prices are stable and do not adjust themselves to the changing demand and supply situation of the world market, the enterprises cannot adjust to a changing world. This inability of keeping informed and adjusting enforces the maintenance or renewed consolidation of central control. And this tendency develops even if everybody accepts that a good foundation of central decisions can be ensured only by acceptably orientating prices, and even if the poor adaptability of the central decision system to rapid changes is known.

Hungarian practice tries to solve this contradiction by a staged adjustment of producer prices. In the course of such price adjustment is is difficult to carry out such a fundamental structural modification of price proportion as would be justified, for example, by the change in the costs of energy mentioned above, for a large increase of energy prices would entail a multiplier effect whose every consequence would have to be borne by the state.

A general defect of staged price adjustment is that it promotes enterprise clear-sightedness only belatedly and, therfore, sometimes not at all. The case of price changes carried into effect at the beginning of 1975 is typical in this respect. The world market price increases of many raw materials were misjudged in mid-1974, on the basis of the market prices of that time. The prices of textiles and other raw materials were fixed at a very high level. Following the fall in world market prices, the high fixed domestic prices rendered home production non-competitive on the foreign markets by the first half of 1975. Some of the emerged contradictions had to be averted by special budgetary measures. As a consequence of these measures, the control system became much more complicated and there emerged new obstacles to making enterprises interested in increasing their receipts.

## 5. Conclusions

Hungarian experience clearly shows that the small raw-material importing socialist countries, whose external economic relations are important not only with C.M.E.A. countries but also with non-socialist countries, have been placed in a particularly difficult situation by the rapid and profound world market price changes that took place from 1973 to 1975.

This experience gives rise to the especially difficult economic question of what sacrifices are justified to achieve the stability of enterprises. What is it expedient to do for the sake of a stable economic management? The position of Hungary's economy convinces us that in the circumstances of a rapidly changing world market situation, rational management is rendered more difficult by frequent state intervention. Therefore, for the sake of a more efficient joining in the international division of labour, the state should free the enterprises, and also the consumers, from the consequences of economic fluctuations to a moderate degree only. Even if we have no reason for placing trust in the optimal nature of market relations, the organic relation between enterprises and the market should not be disrupted by incessant interventions of the state. It is exactly on this account that a wider range of prices should be made free, and conditions should be provided for enterprises to be able to carry on management without special grants from the state budget: only prices can objectively show enterprises the trends in internal and external demand. Enterprises should then be made to adjust themselves to the changing conditions of the economy. Meanwhile, all means of the financial and fiscal policy, including an active exchange-rate policy, should be employed for keeping inflation within reasonable limits.

# 7 Economic Theory and Political Strategy—Cambodia

## M. L. BURSTEIN

The political-strategic factors requiring economic analysis concerned what all agreed would be a transition from the Lon Nol regime, the Khmer Republic, to a government which at the least would have substantial Khmers Rouges representation. A more humane transition to the most liberal of feasible regimes was the American objective, shared by a significant segment of Lon Nol's Cabinet. Monetary stabilisation, restoring confidence in the riel and bringing inflation under control, would, it was believed, importantly strengthen the Lon Nol regime.

This paper concerns a number of problems in economic theory which I encountered in Cambodia in November—December 1974 and which I continued to work on in 1975, specifically the theoretical foundations of a stabilisation programme. I believe that my analyses were correct so that, if the Mekong had not been closed in January 1975, imposing a lexicographic ordering upon the strategy space, a stabilised Khmer Republic economy would have comprised a valuable card for my clients. The validity of this paper is independent of any ideology, whether mine or the reader's.

The material of the paper is organised in the following way. Section 1 develops a quite formal framework of the Khmer inflationary process, rooted in the budget deficit. This framework is especially easy to set up because it is possible to work with a fixed *masse de biens* due to the very high proportion borne by aid-based goods to total available resources. Thus a $mv = p$ accounting relationship dominates. Section 2 flows from another oddity based on the exceptional importance of foreign aid to the Khmer Republic: since a major source of government revenue was based upon the sale of fungible aid-dollars, exchange depreciation could be viewed as an increase in the level of excise (indirect) taxes. Depreciation of the riel abetted fiscality. And since a significant portion of dollar sales was accomplished through a discriminating pricing scheme, it became interesting to study data with the idea of constructing an econometrically valid demand function for dollars. But the strong element of conjectural interdependence in the data-generating processes invalidated conventional inferences which might have been drawn. Section 3 concerns a project for an *emprunt obligatoire* (forced loan) belonging, of course, to the domain of direct taxation. The theory underlying its tactical implementation includes certain basic ideas of stock-flow analysis as well as the transfer problem.

It is most unlikely that specific analyses described here will have valid application in some other actual setting: all who have studied Cambodia between 1970 and 1975 agree that it was bizarre in any number of directions. The extent to which this paper can be exemplary will depend on the extent to which it spans a wide range of substantial economic theory and successfully focuses this theory on well-defined policy issues.

## 1. A Formal Framework of the Khmer Inflationary Process

It is useful to couch the analysis in terms of a controlling vector of inflation. In the simplified Khmer conditions the crucial ratio, determining the vector's slope, is that of the initial budgetary deficit to the initial money stock: $\alpha = D(0)/M(0)$. Taking *la masse de biens* as given and appropriately defining $p$, the monetary equation is

$$mv = p$$

$$\mathrm{d}m/m + \mathrm{d}v/v = \mathrm{d}p/p$$

One is quickly led up to the correct analysis of indirect taxation. It is easy to assert two propositions which in fact are contradictory:

(i) as a result of the new taxes, sellers working at minimum required rates of profit *à la* Ricardo will raise prices 1:1 with taxes;

(ii) the monetary equation, velocity given, will continue to hold, i.e. $mv^0 = p \cdot 1 = p$.

Since we have required, by hypothesis, that money supply be determined by the budgetary position, budget balance requires $\mathrm{d}m = \mathrm{d}p = 0$. But proposition (i) requires that $\mathrm{d}p > 0$ — thus the contradiction.

The contradiction contains an interesting implication. If the rate of profit is to remain intact, i.e. if $\mathrm{d}p = b$, where $b$ = the tax increment, the budget will not be balanced in, so to speak, the initial period of fiscal reform: fiscal discipline is to be relaxed to the extent that enough money is to be put into the system to sustain the 'permitted' price rise (determined by $b$); i.e. $v^0 \mathrm{d}m = b$, or $\mathrm{d}m = b/v^0$.

It follows from this equation that if the deficit rate at $\tau$ were 100 and velocity were 10, then for $m(\tau) = 100$, a long-run tax increase (via the excises) yielding 10 per cent of the initial money value of the national product would erase the deficit. For $v = 2$, 50 per cent would have to be extracted. In any case, veterans' bonuses and other kinds of compensatory transfers could be employed until the money supply were increased by

100. But the effect on the price level, whilst obeying the constraint that the rate of profit be kept intact, would be a monotonically decreasing function of the level of velocity. The higher is initial monetary velocity, the less formidable would be the political problem of raising excise taxes, always distinguishing between higher and rising prices.

Consider

$$y(t) \;\; = k_1 \qquad\qquad\qquad\qquad\qquad \text{for all } t$$

$$D(t) \;\; = D(0)e^{\alpha t}; \; p(t) = p(0)e^{\alpha t}; \; v(t) = k_2 \qquad \text{for all } t$$

The deficit accumulated on the interval $(a, b)$ = the increase in the money supply on that interval =

$$m(0) \int_a^b e^{\alpha t}$$

and

$$p(0) \int_a^b e^{\alpha t} =$$

the increase in $p$ on the interval = a measure of the increase in the cost of the budget theoretically accompanied by revenues indexed to the rate of inflation so that the real deficit is unchanged.

In the transition there is to be established an excise system capable of balancing the budget together with the compensatory remission earlier described, so that

$$p(t) \;\; = (1 + \gamma)p(\tau) \qquad\qquad\qquad\qquad t > \tau + \epsilon$$

$$m(t) \;\; = (1 + \gamma)m(\tau) \qquad\qquad\qquad\qquad t > \tau + \epsilon$$

$$D(t) \;\; = 0 \qquad\qquad\qquad\qquad\qquad\qquad t > \tau + \epsilon$$

$$\int_\tau^{\tau+\epsilon} D(t) \, dt = \gamma D(\tau) = \gamma D(0)e^{\alpha\tau} = b/m(\tau)v^0, \; 0 < \gamma < 1, \; D = F(t)$$

## 2. Fiscality of the Foreign-Exchange Regime

It is important to distinguish between a force leading to a once-over price increase (and likely henceforth to be deflationary) from a force leading to continuing excess demand. Now the properly inflationary consequences of exchange depreciation — over whatever interval exchange depreciation effects are not evaporated out — concern a persistent net increase in resource demands by exporters, together with a persistent net decrease in import demand.[1] In the Khmer Republic, c. 1974—5, the small export sector absorbed resources largely irrelevant to home goods production and, as the writ of the Lon Nol government became more and more confined to Phnom Penh, exportation became less and less significant. (We can ignore here the barter exchanges along the Thai frontier.) What about imports? It is obvious that, in a *laissez-faire* Khmer regime, exchange depreciation would lead to increased nominally valued demand for imports, measured in riels, so long as the point elasticity of expenditure (equal to the algebraic value of the point elasticity of demand plus unity) exceeded zero, i.e. so long as demand was inelastic. Depreciation would promote fiscality so long as import elasticity $<$ $|1|$ in a *laissez-faire* regime.

One reckons that import demand probably was inherently inelastic:

1. The bourgeoisie did not make serious choices, surely not at the margin, between home goods and imported goods for consumption.

2. Demand for dollars was a derived demand. Consider interest, storage and handling costs of imported components of Scotch whisky. Next consider how, at the high prevailing rate of price inflation, the proportion borne by the dollar-based element of final goods would fall by the time the goods reached their final point of sale. If, indeed, subsequent riel depreciation increased the value of this dollar component, the dollar purchaser would enjoy a capital gain. To the extent that such a gain could continuously be anticipated, demand price for dollars would continuously rise. Maximised riel proceeds of dollar sales would require persistent depreciation for this reason too.

More interestingly, there could be set up a Corporation able to accomplish at least two significant objectives: enhancement of latent price discrimination via multi-part tariffs, an obvious revenue-maximisation device; and diversion of resources into working-class consumption, desired by its allies and the I.M.F., if not by the Lon Nol government.[2] The Corporation may have supported the dollar so to speak, absorbing dollars not taken off the open market at an enhanced riel price per dollar and spending these dollars on working-class goods which, in the natural course of things, would be sold on loss-making terms, measured in riels (a purely bookkeeping loss).

An efficacity inequality can be established. Assume that an arbitrary increase in the riel rate (i.e. an arbitrary riel-depreciation increment) would lead to withdrawal of $Rx$ in acceptable bids while other bidders affected by the rise agreed to pay $R(0\cdot6)x$ more. (Under the controlling dollar-auction procedures successful bidders paid what they bid. So substantial discriminatory elements played out in the ongoing system. But keep in mind the conjecturally interdependent nexus in which all this took place: received bids supplied a biased basis for demand-function estimation. By the same token, the text just above rigorously must refer to an increase in the *cours minimum retenu* perceived as a leading instrumental variable. This increase is stipulated to be sufficient to eliminate substantial bid value hitherto deemed acceptable.) Next define the following terms:

$b$ = the average riel rate initially realised on the relevant foreign-exchange market; $b$ is a riel/dollar rate.

$c$ = the average rate ultimately realised by the Corporation; $c$ is a riel/dollar rate.

$z$ = the number of *dollars* not sold initially (i.e. *au dehors* the corporation) because of the rate change.

$T$ = the increased riel proceeds from bidders willing to pay the higher rates.

Pursuing the illustration, riel proceeds of total dollar sales would be kept intact if the $x/b$ dollars thus released could realise as little as $R(0\cdot4)x$: if the average realised revenues of the Corporation were as little as 40 per cent of the established rate, fiscality would be protected. The controlling formula for efficacity is

$$c/b \geq 1 - T/bz$$

where

$$bz - T \leq cz$$

Efficacity requires that the ratio of realisation rates exceed what might be called the *local inefficiency* factor on the foreign-exchange market.

Obviously merchants bid no more for dollars than the maximum amounts they were willing to pay.[3] It may be less obvious that such 'maximum amounts' were *not* independent of the bidding process: if I could be fairly sure that the *cours retenu* would become established at, say, $R3,000$ per dollar, then I could afford to bid, say, $R3,200$; certain quasi-rents adherent to my operation would assure profitability at $R3,200$, provided competing bidders' costs were thus established; a bid of $R3,200$ would prove disastrous for me if the average realised price were, say, $R2,000$.[4] Bidding data do not comprise a proper basis for demand-function estimation and indeed promote a distinct downward bias—certainly if, for example, it were assumed that the expectation of, say, the average realisation at date $\tau$ is that of date $\tau - 1$. Finally, unless the bidders were kept in strict isolation during the bidding process, orthodox theory would have trouble focusing on the situation: the contracting/recontracting process itself would here have to be interpreted as vitally affecting the underlying subjective estimates of profitabilities of alternative actions in the conjecturally interdependent context.

We are brought into the realm of game theory, especially if my conjec-

ture—I think well informed—that there was *au fond*, and perhaps despite
the appearance of things, a small number of bidders, say nine, in the market. It seems clear that any small capability of joint maximising behaviour
among the bidders for dollars (here merchants; capital outflow supposedly
was excluded from the market) would lead to average realisations for
dollar sales inferior to those obtainable in a truly competitive market. In
particular, if, as I have already suggested, final elasticities of demand were
decidedly low, it is possible that the disparity was quite massive. Recall
that the only important substitutional relationship for middle- and rich-class
consumers was between imported goods and accumulation of gold, jewellery
and foreign currency. But riel depreciation increased prices of the substitutes (measured in riels) 1:1 with those of imported goods. Also, keep in
mind that the Corporation would mop up unutilised dollars so that the
revenue-promotion effects of exchange depreciation would be greater
than would be suggested by elasticities of demand *per se*.

Section 2 is concluded with some brief further remarks about the conjectural characteristics of the structure of demand on the foreign-exchange
market. And in order to supply additional context we shall refer to another
of my proposed 'reforms', the conversion of the *cours minimum retenu*
into an instrumental variable rather in the manner of the rediscount rate
of the Federal Reserve Bank of New York. It was proposed to keep pushing up the *cours minimum reténu*, perhaps at first having to utilise the
Corporation rather heavily, so as to establish the firm intention of the
authorities to persist in riel depreciation. So expectational formation
could be conceived as being keyed to the C.M.R. It thus becomes useful
to define the time-path — expected or otherwise — of the C.M.R, $f(t)$. In
fact it is harmless to assume here that $f(t)$ becomes an instrument and
is announced by the authorities: $f^*(t)$. Among other things, the $j$th bid
for dollars at t = $\tau$, $d_\tau^j$, will depend upon $f^*(t)$, $d_\tau^j = F\{f^*(t)\}$. If $f(t)$
can be described in terms of certain parameters so that we can break out
of functionals, then $\partial d_\tau^j / \partial \alpha > 0$, where $\alpha$ might be the slope of a linearised
version of $f(t)$.

The ultimate fiscality potential of the foreign-exchange market was,
of course, rooted in final demand. Assume a correspondence between the
average realisation on the foreign-exchange market (in riels per dollar)
and the prices of imports to final users so that the revenue-maximisation
problem can be stated as

$$\max R = p_1 f(p_1) + p_2 g(p_2)$$

so that

$$g(p_2) \leq C - f(p_1)$$

$p_1 = \Phi$ (*cours minimum retenu*). The function is single-valued, continuous, etc., so that we can speak of setting $p_1$ as surrogate for the C.M.R.
$f(p_1)$ determines demand for dollars in the open market. $p_2$ is the real-

isation rate of the Corporation and $g(p_2)$ has obvious connotations. The fixed number of aid-dollars available is given by $C$. Be careful to note that the underlying functions cannot be estimated from foreign-exchange market data. Indeed, a key objective of the controller (comptroller) would be to discover the underlying functions and then simply declare $p_1^*$ and $p_2^*$ optimal relative to fiscality and relative to the 'true' underlying functions, thus smashing up tacit partial joint maximisation strategies flowing from the context of conjectural interdependence.

Upon forming the Lagrangian, etc., and upon stipulating for the purpose of this exposition that the constraint hold as an equality (in general, this would emphatically not be true in the solution; in general, some dollars would be disposed of for refugee purposes, etc., even under the cruel criterion of this section), the first-order conditions reduce to $MR_1/MR_2 = f'/g'$, i.e. to a requirement that the rate of transformation between marginal revenues be equal to that on the production surface, (so to speak, a fixed quantum of output is being distributed between two hermetically sealed markets).

## 3. L'emprunt Obligatoire

The analysis of Section 3 concerns a forced-loan scheme intended to lead to quite massive increases in government receipts over a short period as assets would have had to be sold or cash disgorged from hoards. Several intersections of economic theory and political strategy are close to its surface:

1. Stock-flow analysis supplies the root insight.
2. The mechanics of implementation involve a number of considerations leading back to the transfer problem.
3. Some problems of disaggregation of liquid asset holdings emerge. Does it matter for purposes of monetary-fiscal policy how $M$ initially is distributed between households?

The behaviour of some processes over, say, the time-interval $AB$ — say an interval of two years — depends not upon the cumulant of, say, taxes collected over the interval, but instead upon characteristics of the time-path of tax collections, measured in flow rates, over the interval: the behaviour of the process is a functional of the time-path of the control variable. In particular, if government receipts could be severely front-loaded so that unsustainably high flow rates were quickly achieved, then, for example, inflationary expectations might soon be crushed, perhaps inducing demand for increased monetary hoards (inflation being an obvious tax on money-fixed balances) so that some degree of budgetary imbalance would for some time be consistent with non-inflationary finance. At the least, time would have been bought, perhaps time in which to improve the terms of a negotiated settlement. I find a 'von Rundstedt' analogy to be attractive. Consider the Ardennes breakthrough of the winter of 1944—5. The limited German resources were sufficient to mount a strong attack for a short while — not long enough from their viewpoint, but long enough to make a very substantial impression.[5]

Important theoretical material for the forced-loan initiative is found in the literature about the transfer problem. Thus Keynes, Ohlin *et al.* wrote about the (in)feasibility of post-First World War reparation demands upon Germany. In the upshot it became clear that stock-flow theory controlled correct analysis of the transfer problem. If enough time were allowed, a very small stock of gold could switch back and forth between the defeated country, X, and the victor, Y, reducing X's debt to Y each time it flicked across the scanner, reflecting X's continuing balance-of-payments surplus vis-à-vis Y. On the other hand, if time were of the essence, it would become necessary to tear off what might be an infeasibly large chunk of some fungible stock, the most obvious example being gold. Thus it might have become necessary for the Government of the Khmer Republic (G.K.R.) to support a secondary market in various fungible assets, including *devisen.* Then the fiscal impact of the forced loan would be delayed: riels paid in which simply have been paid out by the G.K.R. to buy in assets merely complete a 'null' circuit. But once the import proceeds of the sales abroad of these assets (the dollars are sold for imported goods in the scenario) would have been put into Khmer markets, then deflationary pressure would be generated. And to the extent that the upshot would have found the Corporation bringing in working-class goods, there would have been involuntary aid from the richer to the poorer classes.

Several comments concerning disaggregation are called for. It might be thought that to the extent that 'idle' riels are sucked into *emprunts obligatoires,* no deflationary pressure would have been generated. But this would ignore the fact that the initial liquid balances were voluntarily accumulated; some sort of optimisation was occurring. So it can be assumed that there would follow efforts to rebuild liquidity. Still, these efforts would play out over some reach of time: for some time the velocity of the reduced money stock might exceed that of the initial stock, admittedly thus reducing the all-important thrust of the programme at impact.

Under the institutional arrangements I proposed there would have been a clear redistribution in the field of current consumption. The working classes would have been favoured so long as the forced loan centred on the middle and rich classes. Assigning as they would a smallish probability to the possibility of repayment and finding themselves suddenly illiquid, the *bourgeois* and *riches* would cut back demand prices for imported consumer goods as they attempted to rebuild liquidity and as they adjusted to their wealth loss. And if these events were to have been accompanied by continuing depreciation of the riel and by the Corporation's mopping-up of dollars whilst spending the proceeds on working-class goods, then the built-in consumption transfer would have become obvious. In fact the inflation rate was higher for working-class than for middle- and rich-class goods. A forced loan not directed in part against the working classes (I recommended that workers be impacted too) thus could lead to stabilisation of prices of middle-class goods but not of working-class goods, bringing out problems of disaggregation in money-stock-based theories of control.

The concluding case is nested in the essentially pure-exchange characteristics of the aggregate Khmer economy of the time. It suggests the possibility that a forced loan, unaccompanied by the Corporation and the manipulated *cours minimum retenu*, would lead to price stabilisation of bourgeois consumption but not of workers' consumption. Also the possibility that, despite what might have been a substantial reduction in the rate of monetary expansion (i.e. what might have been a substantial reduction in the budget deficit), the rate of inflation of working-class goods' prices might have been little changed, thus again trailing the disaggregation cape before the reader.

Assume that what can be taken as a fixed quantum of dollars — aid to be auctioned — simply continued to be bid for and absorbed by those merchants licensed to bid on the foreign-exchange market. Of course, the riel/dollar rate would have fallen relative to the rate which would have prevailed *sans* the forced loan. But also assume that the decline in the rate would not be great enough importantly to affect the proportion of goods imported for working-class consumption.[6] It follows that *bourgeois/riches* consumption would not have been affected. And the political effect could have been damaging: one would perhaps have observed unchanged *bourgeois/riches* consumptions of goods at stabilised price levels whilst workers remained in the same 'real' condition whilst experiencing unabated rates of price inflation.

True, *bourgeois/riches* wealth positions would have been eroded to the extent that the loans were treated as taxes. And the consumptions of their portfolios surely would have been distorted.

Under the stipulations of Section 3, the partitioned consumption set pertinent to the *bourgeois/riches* would have become cheaper vis-à-vis alternative policy actions; real values of their accumulations of financial assets and other stores of value would have been correspondingly enhanced. Thus the *bourgeois/riches* could have, in time, sustained their positions in all directions. The intertemporal consumption availabilities, ordered by class, have been fixed by hypothesis. The *bourgeois/riches* could — under the regime *contre* my proposals — rebuild the real value of their assets, expressed in terms of a consumption-good measure, simply by (indirectly) lowering their bids in the foreign-exchange market. True, their wealth, expressed in foreign measures, may thus have been permanently reduced under the assumption that the G.K.R. would devote the internationally fungible receipts incident to a forced loan to consumption-good purchases:

forced consumption! On the other hand, this assumption violates the 'purity' of the model, albeit in an interesting way. Instead of working with fixed foreign-exchange availability, the analysis has been shifted to that internationally fungible assets — not able again to be accumulated because of the loss of productivity of the economy as the Khmers Rouges tightened their grip — are extracted from the *bourgeois/riches* and then spent by the state (via its merchants) on consumption goods for those very classes. All this, would comprise one of the most bizarre examples of 'invariance versus variance' in the literature.

Under the regime I prescribed, the forced loan would have led to the following:

1. Deterioration of the asset/liquidity positions of the *bourgeois/ riches*, forcing them to retrench their planned consumptions.
2. A very heavy squeeze on Khmer financial markets as liquidations of riel assets were attempted.
3. Transfer of imported-good consumptions from the *bourgeois/ riches* to the workers as the Corporation picked up slack in demand at roughly the initially prescribed riel rate (if not a further depreciated rate).
4. The increased flow of goods on to markets frequented by workers would promote price stability of working-class goods.
5. Weakened demand for *bourgeois/riches* goods would promote price stability in that sector too.
6. Satisfaction of naive monetarist requisites what with the implicit sharp reduction in the rate of monetary expansion.

## Notes

1. It is true that foreign-exchange depreciation also makes one's assets cheaper in terms of foreign currencies. This is not directly important to the portfolio investor: he will be concerned with appreciation potential *cum* yield. But the discount can be significant for direct investors: cf. a car company considering alternative plant locations. To this extent, foreign-exchange depreciation will have inflationary impact effects: investment demands on resources will increase; higher asset prices will encourage incremental accumulation.

2. To the extent that depreciation would have discouraged capital outflow, resources would have been freed for, say, working-class consumption. This would not be important for the bourgeois-based Lon Nol regime, fully committed to a philosophy of 'a king in his castle, a peasant in his hovel'.

3. Remember that bids were accepted 'as bid'. If accepted bids were all taken in at the same price, then one would have an incentive to bid well over his demand price in order to secure acceptance, subject to the risk that the ultimately established price (if equal to or less than his bid) were not greater than his demand price (which, note, will partly depend upon the 'ultimately established price').

4. One is willing to pay a probable premium of ﷼200 per dollar in order to increase one's chances of securing his bid, noting that this action increases his exposure if the average yield (in terms of riels per dollar) is less than he expects it to be.

5. An important underlying point is that economies with simple structures of liquid asset holdings and *financement* (e.g. the Khmer economy) are easier to stabilise through conventional monetary-fiscal policy than are financially more complex economies. Khmer workers must largely constrain their spending to the time-profiles of their receipts. If Khmer firms were squeezed by banks, they could not obtain alternative credits. Sales of liquid assets, borrowings from non-banking financial intermediaries, borrowing abroad — evasive procedures open to American companies, for example — were mostly infeasible in the Khmer Republic: if Khmer companies became short of cash, they had to sell off inventories or abruptly reduce their demands for fresh stocks, at least if gold holdings and capital successfully transferred to Paris and Zürich were to be kept intact.

6. The rate would, under a *laissez-faire* regime, tend to fall because of shrunken *bourgeois/riches* demand for imported goods. Since capital transfers were *interdit*, the riel rate would not be pushed down by attempts to liquidate riel assets. On the other hand, Khmer asset markets would have become depressed in this very way, leading to a mixed bag of effects: demand would be all the more depressed, including demand for investment goods. However, animal spirits were so depressed by the siege conditions that investment, gross or net, could be ignored in 1974—5. Indeed, an important form of capital flight was based on using depreciation reserves to buy durable imported goods.

# 8 Aid in a System of Taxes and Prices—Cambodia

W. F. BEAZER

Between 1971 and 1975, United States aid became the dominant factor in nearly every aspect of the economic and political life of the Khmer Republic. The amount of aid and the policies governing its use determined the patterns and level of consumption of the people, the income distribution, the degree of inflation, and the amount of resources the government was able to acquire in its pursuit of objectives associated with the war. It also greatly influenced the internal political relationships of the Khmer ruling groups as well as relations between these groups and the United States Embassy.

The amount of aid given (both military and civilian) was large relative to the size of the Khmer economy and yet, in spite of the volume of aid, the country fell to a group of people who were initially dismissed as being virtually non-existent and who were not, until the very end, regarded with any great degree of seriousness by the majority of both the Khmer and Americans in Phnom Penh.

This chapter, however, will be devoted to but a few of the aspects of the role of aid in an aid-dominated economy. We shall be concerned only with civilian aid and its relationship to government expenditures, the money supply, inflation and the rate of exchange. As a result, there are numerous interesting questions that will be completely ignored or touched upon only peripherally.

We shall assume that the amount of civilian aid was determined by political considerations but that its main purpose was to make up income lost from war damage plus the opportunity cost associated with mobilisation to fight the war. When aid was first given in 1971 the explicit objective was to make up all the income loss. This dollar value was used as the basis for all future aid levels. As a result, no further explicit decisions about this objective were made, but it was clear that the ratio of aid to loss declined substantially over time.

In such a situation, it is the host government that must be the conduit through which the aid is channelled. The aid serves two basic purposes — to purchase resources with which to wage the war and to replace lost income for those whom the war has rendered unproductive without providing them with a new role. The major elements in these two categories were military pay and refugee support.

The aid represented real resources, but the Khmer government, for the most part, distributed its largesse in the form of money rather than kind. The aid-derived funds had to be commingled with any that the government acquired from other sources. This commingling meant that, although there might have been an accounting distinction made between local funds from aid sources and those from domestic taxation or central bank loans, there were no genuine differences as far as the budget was concerned.

The giving of aid results in a certain fixed availability of goods in the economy, a combination of domestic production plus aid. The central problem with an aid economy is how to allocate the goods available among the factors of production (which may or may not be producing) in such a way as to achieve all the goals of a country at war: an effective military force, a relatively equitable distribution of real income, a maximum amount of domestic production and a stable price level. In an aid economy, such as the Khmer Republic, the government policies and objectives become the dominant factor in the economic life of the country simply because the government controls a large fraction of available goods. (In fact, in the Phnom Penh area it almost certainly controlled the majority.)

As aid replaces domestic production, the tax system becomes a less and less important source of government revenue and, by default or design, tends to become a neglected area of government policy except for that portion tied to the aid system. Typically, and certainly in the incipient stages of aid, the domestic tax system is linked to aid through the tariff-collection process. This kind of economy can be modelled with a very simple algebraic system. Let $X^*$ be total availability of goods and services measured in dollars, $A^*$ be aid measured in dollars, $Y$ be domestic output measured in riels, $R$ be government revenue in riels, $C$ be counterpart funds generated to the account of the United States government through the sale of aid, $\alpha$ be the ratio of domestic taxes to domestic income, $\beta$ be the *ad valorem* import tax rate, $V$ be the equilibrium 'exchange value', and $\delta$ be a policy variable that relates the official exchange rate $E$ and the import tax rate to the exchange value. Using these symbols we can express the important relationships for the economy in a series of equations. Total availability measured in dollars is

$$X^* = A^* + \frac{Y}{V} = A^* + Y^* \tag{1}$$

If availability is measured in riels, it is

$$X = VA^* + Y = A + Y \tag{2}$$

(dollar values are always starred and riel values unstarred). The ratio of the price at which exchange is sold to the exchange value is

$$\delta = \frac{(1 + \beta)E}{V} \tag{3}$$

Thus we can refer henceforth to $\delta V$ as the 'exchange price', to differentiate it from the 'exchange value'. In simplest terms, exchange value is what foreign exchange is worth and exchange price is what an importer must pay for it. Direct local government revenue is

$$R = \alpha Y + \beta EA^* \tag{4}$$

The remainder of the revenue from the sale of aid foreign exchange accrues in counterpart accounts that are normally controlled by the United States Government:

$$C = EA^* \tag{5}$$

Total revenues available to *some* governmental entity are thus

$$\hat{R} = \alpha Y + (1 + \beta)EA^* = \alpha Y + \delta VA^* \tag{6}$$

If $\delta < 1$ there is some fraction of the aid that is being diverted to people involved in the import process, either officials or importers. We shall call this importers' rent and let the symbol for it be $Q$:

$$Q = (1 - \delta)VA^* \tag{7}$$

It is evident from eq. (6) that if aid, as valued at the exchange value, replaces domestic output on a 1:1 basis, the revenue received by government entities increases as a fraction of total availability provided $\delta > \alpha$. The fraction of total availability that accrues *directly* to the aid-receiving country will be a function of $\beta$, however. The counterpart that is acquired by the United States government is an extra-budgetary accumulation of local currency which is controlled by the local representatives of the United States with certain restrictions imposed by Congress.

Although the model is an extremely simple one, it illuminates several aspects of an aid economy. First, the total amount of real goods $Z^*$ is fixed in the short run by the amount of domestic production and the budgeted quantity of aid. Policies that do not affect these two things will not affect total availability. Second, as aid becomes a larger and larger part of total availability, the exchange rate becomes increasingly important in determining the nominal revenue acquired by government entities; for a given amount of aid dollars, the greater the ratio of exchange rate plus tariffs to the exchange value, the greater the amount of riels collected by the governments. Third, the larger the fraction of aid relative to domestic income, the less important import tax policy becomes as a means of raising revenue and the more important it becomes as a means of allocating between two government entities the revenue collected. If the expenditure objectives of the two entities are identical, as they tended to be in Cambodia during the early part of the four-year period, tax policy with respect to aid and imports becomes irrelevant; $\beta$ can be anything between 1 and 0 without affecting anything other than administrative procedures. If the objectives are different, as they became after June 1974, or if different administrative procedures result in different degrees of corruption, $\beta$ becomes important. Finally, the greater the fraction of total availability supplied by aid, the more closely the economy approximates the typical exchange economy of economic theory where everyone starts with an 'endowment' and trade takes place to move people to preferred positions.

Before expanding these themes, we should look at the other side of government budgetary process — expenditures — and see how the total budget determined the money supply. The Khmer government had three *direct* sources of funds: the revenue from domestic taxes, the revenue from import duties on sale of foreign exchange, and the money it printed. If we define $G_k$ as government expenditures in local currency and $\Delta M_k$ as the increase in money supply due to Khmer government expenditures, we have

$$\Delta M_k = G_k - \alpha Y - \beta E A^* \tag{8}$$

The Khmer government was not the only government spending local currency in Phnom Penh, however. The United States government became the main source of funds for two separate (and to some extent competing) operations: refugee relief, handled by international voluntary agencies, and refugee rehabilitation, under the auspices of the Rural Development Foundation (R.D.F.). Both these activities were almost completely outside the control of the Khmer government. By the beginning of 1975 the projected budgets for these two operations exceeded the official government budget. If we define $G_{us}$ as United States government expenditure in local currency and $\Delta M_{us}$ as the change in money supply due to the United States expenditures, we have

$$\Delta M_{us} = G_{us} - C = G_{us} - E A^* \tag{9}$$

Since the United States government could not print Khmer money or borrow from the central bank, United States expenditures could not exceed counterpart revenue. If the United States spent less than United States counterpart receipts, the difference offset money growth by the Khmers so that the total change in money supply was

$$\Delta M = \Delta M_k + \Delta M_{us} = G_k + G_{us} - \alpha Y - \delta V A^* \tag{10}$$

In a situation such as Cambodia's it was evident that the major determinant of inflation was the increase in the money supply augmented by any decline in the availability of goods and increase in velocity. Anything that affected the money supply could be expected to affect inflation.

Eq. (10) indicates succinctly the important policy variables that influenced the growth rate of money supply: Khmer government spending, United

States government spending, and the exchange price, $\delta V$. In addition to emphasising the importance of the exchange price in the inflationary process, it illustrates well another aspect of the aid-dominated Khmer economy. There were two independent governmental entities making expenditure decisions. To the extent that the United States released its counterpart funds to be spent on non-government activities, the Khmer government was forced either to print money or reduce its own budget expenditures.

But these observations are peripheral to the main problem we wish to address, that of the role of the exchange price in generating government revenue and affecting the price level. For any level of aid and government expenditures, the rate of growth of money supply and the rate of inflation will be minimised by keeping the exchange price at the highest possible level at all times. The relationship between the exchange price and the rate of growth of money supply means that the exchange price becomes a fiscal instrument whose importance increases in direct proportion to the volume of aid being given.

We have distinguished between two important concepts, the 'exchange value' and the 'exchange price'. The exchange price is a policy variable that is simply the combination of exchange rate plus taxes and can be affected by changing the value of either one. The exchange value, on the other hand, is a phenomenon of market clearing that one somehow ought to be able to observe. Both are important because any difference between them represents revenue the government could be collecting. To the extent that the revenue is not collected it is income that skews the income distribution towards importers and government officials involved in importing and away from people on fixed salaries.

As important as it is, however, we have not suggested how to estimate the exchange value. It is the position of this paper that the best approximation of the exchange value is the black-market rate for foreign exchange. Although there is no space for a complete mathematical model of the official and black markets, it may be useful to indicate diagramatically how the two are related and why the black-market rate should be approximately an equilibrium value for exchange. Fig. 1 shows the official and the black markets back to back under the assumption that there are no links between the two so that exchange is unable to flow from one to the other. $R_0$ is the official exchange price, including tariffs, and $R_2$ is the value of official exchange to importers. $R_1$ would be the value of the exchange in the black market. In this particular example, the value of exchange for imports happens to be above that for financial transactions, as long as the two markets are isolated.

In fact, however, in Cambodia, as in most countries, the two markets were not isolated, they were linked through the process of over- and under-invoicing of imports so that flows could occur from one market to the other. In the diagram shown, it would be profitable to purchase dollars in the black market to be used for imports in the official market. There would be an incentive for this to continue (essentially through net under-invoicing)

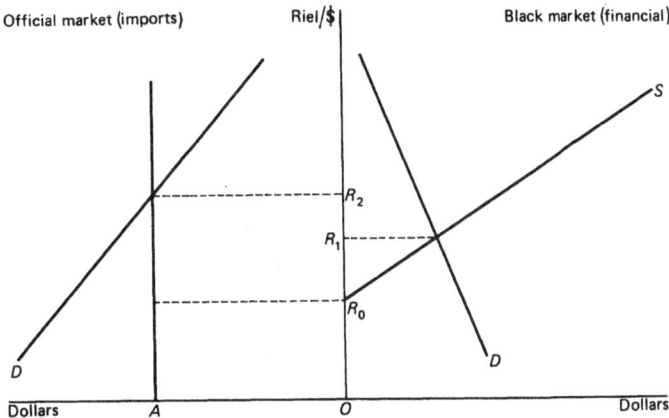

Fig. 1. Isolated official and black markets.

until the value of exchange in the two markets was the same. The result is shown in Fig. 2. When the value in the two markets is equal, the excess demand for dollars in the black market (*CF*) is just equal to the excess supply in the official import market, and the actual value of imports will exceed the official exchange availability by the amount *AB* (in Fig. 2).

The equilibrium exchange value is thus approximately equal to the black-market rate. As a result, as long as the official exchange price is below the black-market rate, the government will not be maximising its revenue from the sale of aid dollars. Part of the exchange value will still be available for absorption by the import community. The model implies that only by setting the official rate at least equal to the black-market rate can the government expect to maximise its revenue.

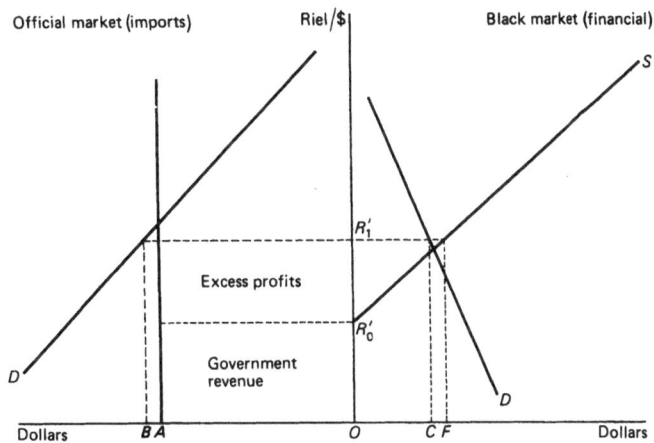

Fig. 2. Linked official and black markets.

It is easy to see from Fig. 2 that the black-market rate will be affected by a shift in either the official or the black-market demand curves. An outward movement in the demand for imports will result in an *increase* in under-invoicing and a rise in the black-market rate, while a shift in the black-market demand curve will also raise the black-market rate but will *reduce* under-invoicing — and eventually lead to net over-invoicing at the expense of total imports. These results should not be unexpected. The markets are linked through the false invoicing process and, as a result, behave very much like one market. With one market or two, an increase in demand for dollars to pay for airline services or some other invisible transfer (such as government missions) should lead to a decrease in exchange available for imports.

Although the model has aspects of apparent great simplicity, its implications were not well recognised nor by any means universally accepted as a basis for policy decisions in Cambodia until near the end of the four-year period over which aid was so important. A large faction in the Khmer government, and several advisers from international organisations, maintained throughout the period that raising exchange rates could only contribute to inflation through effects on import prices and on the psychology of the people. As a result, increases in the official exchange rate tended to come about sporadically following confrontations between the United States aid mission and the Khmer government, with representatives from the I.M.F. sometimes on one side and sometimes on the other. The confrontations tended to follow a pattern. After the official exchange rate had been pegged for a period of time, the price level would have risen substantially and the black-market rate would be well above the official rate and rising continuously. At a point when a new agreement releasing aid funds was to be signed between the United States and the Khmer government, the mission would insist on a readjustment of the exchange rate and use the threat of not signing the agreement to force a revaluation. The new rate would inevitably be a compromise arrived at through negotiation but would not be the maximum rate the market would bear, nor would it be based on any hard analysis of what an appropriate price (albeit extremely temporary) ought to be. In other words, the concept of the exchange price as an anti-inflationary fiscal tool and the black-market rate as an estimate of exchange value was not universally understood. Only in the summer and autumn of 1974 were the policy implications fully accepted by both the United States mission and (again reluctantly in some quarters) by the Khmer government. But before discussing these events and their outcome it is necessary to provide some background on the actual exchange markets and their operation in the Khmer Republic prior to September 1974.

We have spoken about 'a' rate and 'a' market as though there existed only one of each. The exchange system in Cambodia was always a complicated one, even before the war, with several markets governed by different rates. As exports declined with the war, however, and aid became the dominant factor in the supply of exchange, the old markets were phased out or modified so that by the summer of 1974 there were basically three exchange markets of any importance. There were the Nouveau Marché de Change (N.M.C.), the Exchange Stabilisation Fund (E.S.F.) and the Commercial Import Programme (C.I.P.).

The N.M.C. corresponded most closely to the usual concept of any ex·change market, although it effectively operated only to permit the government to purchase exchange from exporters at a fixed rate and then use the exchange as it wished, either to put into the E.S.F. or to pay its own foreign exchange bills. The government had complete control of the exchange.

The Exchange Stabilisation Fund was a hybrid sort of fund, organised in 1972 at the suggestion of the I.M.F. as a means of accomplishing two things: establishing an institutional arrangement to channel multilateral aid to the Khmers and providing a means whereby American aid could be given that was not tied to procurement of American goods. Since the Khmer also contributed to E.S.F., the fund was both aid and domestic exchange. The Commercial Import Programme was the main body of the United States aid programme. Imports could be obtained only from the United States or a limited number of underdeveloped countries, and purchases of exchange required enormous paperwork to satisfy the bureaucratic controls enacted by Congress.

In September 1974 the Khmer government promulgated a reform package that completely revised the way in which foreign exchange was priced and sold. It recognised that, for political reasons, three foreign exchange markets had to continue to exist in Phnom Penh: the C.I.P. market for aid tied to American procurement, the E.S.F. for untied aid, and what came to be called the *marché libre*, theoretically a free market in which the government could purchase exchange and also sell it to satisfy all the legitimate financial demands that, because of various restrictions, could not be accommodated by the other two markets. Many of the transactions that had formerly been handled by the black market were now to be accepted on the *marché libre*.

The reforms also adopted the principle that the exchange price was a full-fledged fiscal instrument when applied to aid-derived exchange. All exchange prices had to be treated differently, however. The *marché libre*, which had to be open continuously for buying and selling, was to have a single quoted rate with a small spread between buying and selling. The rate was to be set twice a week by a committee chaired by the governor of the National Bank and was to be based on the black-market rate. Thus an official market could compete with the black market.

Exchange from the E.S.F. was to be sold through the N.M.C. twice weekly in fixed quantities under a Dutch auction system with a floor price set and bids accepted above that floor price. The lowest acceptable bid was to be the bid that just absorbed all the exchange available, but each successful bidder would have to pay the rate he bid. The government was thus presumably able to act as a discriminating monopolist and collect all the area under the demand curve.

The C.I.P. rate was still set up by the United States government but would be a fixed percentage below the floor rate of the E.S.F. It would be licensed, as it had always been, by going through massive amounts of red tape.

As a final innovation, all taxes on imports not matched by taxes on domestic production were to be eliminated so that the exchange rate became the true price of exchange and the device through which government revenues were collected. This rendered impossible differential taxation of imports, but presumably at least a portion of the lost revenue would be collected through the bid system on the E.S.F.

Complete data on revenue collections are not available, but information is available on E.S.F. sales and exchange rates between September 1974 and January 1975. In interpreting these figures, it should be kept in mind that almost no exchange had been sold from the E.S.F. for two months prior to September. The exchange rate before September had been 420 riels per dollar and the exchange price around 685 riles per dollar.

Between the time of the reforms in mid-September 1974 and mid-January 1975, the Nouveau Marché witnessed a spectacular rise and partial decline in the level of exchange-rate bids for E.S.F. funds. It also recorded an equally spectacular fall in the amount of foreign exchange demanded. During the period from mid-September until the beginning of November the bid volume per session ranged between $1 million and $2 million, with the average demand being around $1·75 million. After mid-November demand declined sharply and during early January averaged slightly above $125,000 per session. This was approximately one-twentieth of the demand during the first few markets. Exchange-rate movements over the period were equally dramatic. From an initial September level of around 1,200, the average bid rate moved up to 1,880 in mid-November and declined to a level in early January just slightly above 1,650.

It is interesting to compare the average bid rate and the black-market rate. With the exception of a short period in early November and another in early December, the black-market rate maintained a fairly regular relationship to the average bid rate. It should not be surprising that the two tended to move tandem since they had to be determined by the same forces and were linked through the invoicing of imports.

In terms of the primary objective of raising revenue, it should be clear, even without detailed figures, that the reforms represented an enormous improvement over the previous system. The actual sales were made at prices very close to and occasionally above the black-market rate. In additon, the elimination of tariffs meant that there was little opportunity to divert government income from imports into private pockets. In terms of stabilisation, the policy also seemed to be effective. The Phnom Penh working-class price index rose 24 per cent from August to September 1974 and only 13 per cent from September 1974 to January 1975. The USAID price index rose 32 per cent between August and September and another 32 per cent between September and January. By either measure there was a vast improvement.

The reforms were not without problems of their own, however. The major one was the allocation of income from the sale of aid-derived foreign exchange. When the import duties were eliminated, all revenue went into the counterpart fund controlled by the United States mission. The Khmer consented to this only because they believed that the counterpart would be allocated to them for budget support. In the event, political pressure and a large increase in refugee inflow forced the United states mission to promise most of the counterpart revenue to the voluntary agencies, leaving the Khmer high and dry. The Khmer were attempting to correct this situation by applying an exchange tax directly to the sale of exchange when time ran out.

The economic reforms based on the model presented in this paper were by no means meant to be final steps. For example, to the extent they were successful in forcing the exchange rate to the black-market rate and eliminating most of the trading in the black market, they would have also eliminated a target variable for the exchange value. A new decision rule would have been required. One possibility would have been to accept the purchasing power parity theory and move the exchange rate up with the domestic price level. This would have meant also accepting the idea that the equilibrium exchange value was the price that maximised revenue. An alternative policy would have been to force the floor price up on the E.S.F. more rapidly than the price level rose. If the bidding process involved a large degree of conjectural interdependence so that the cut-off rate affected the bids received, then it could be argued that pushing the rate up beyond what we have called the equilibrium exchange value might push the entire demand curve outward and increase revenue, perhaps substantially (see Chapter 7). It seems equally plausible, however, to theorise that rather than pushing out the entire demand curve, only those people bidding close to the cut-off rate would be affected. They might raise their bids rather than lose the opportunity to buy exchange, causing a blip to appear on the demand curve as the cut-off rate moved up, but there is no reason to believe that everyone throughout the curve would raise his bid as the cut-off rate moved up. If bids were not affected by the expected cut-off rate, the policy would have simply eliminated low bidders.

Conceptually a forced loan would have been another innovative way to absorb cash from the private sector, appearing less onerous than a tax increase to the middle class on whom it would be imposed, and yet yielding perhaps the same revenue (see Chapter 7). But from a practical point of view a forced loan poses the same dilemma as a tax. It requires that some visible, measurable sign of wealth be taxed and it requires a bureaucracy backed by a degree of government will in order to collect it. It is debatable whether these things were present in Phnom Penh at the end of the war. It is also debatable whether the political benefit of a marginally reduced rate of inflation would sufficiently offset the political cost of a forced loan to make the process of collecting the loan worthwhile.

Military and political events made superfluous any further economic experiments and, to some extent, render difficult interpretation of what happened after the reforms. It appears, however, that the policies were successful in contributing to an increase in government revenue and a reduction in the rate of inflation.

Without belittling the value or quality of the economic analysis done in Cambodia, it was nevertheless apparent that all the economic policies were to a certain extent somewhat analogous to picking fleas off a dog that has cancer in hopes of restoring him to health. It will make him more comfortable, more faithful, and save energy by keeping him from scratching and thus prolong his life. But the ultimate result will be the same unless the cancer is cured. Regardless of the appropriateness of the policy and correctness of the thoery underlying it, economic reform was necessary but not sufficient. The fundamental problems in Cambodia were political. Had the policies adopted in September 1974 been followed throughout the period of aid, however, they could have helped stabilise the economic situation and led to a more equitable distribution of income and war burden. As a result, they may have permitted more emphasis to have been placed on the political problems that ultimately led to what must be recorded as one of the saddest events of current history.

## APPENDIX: A MODEL OF EXCHANGE MARKETS

The equilibrium state for a simple exchange marketing system that includes a black market can be expressed as a series of equations. The symbols used are:

$A$    = aid
$S$    = total supply of non-aid foreign exchange
$D_1$ = demand for exchange in the black market
$D_2$ = demand for exchange to be used for imports
$S_1$ = supply of dollars in the black market
$S_2$ = supply of non-aid dollars in the official market
$B$    = black-market exchange rate
$R$    = official market exchange price.

Eq. (A.1) says that aid plus all exchange from other sources is equal to the demand for imports plus demand for dollars in the financial market. Written this way, it assumes easy transfer of funds from one market to another.

$$A + S = D_1 + D_2 \qquad (A.1)$$

The total supply of non-aid dollars is a function of the highest rate of exchange available, i.e. the black-market rate. If certain exports are forced to go through official channels at official rates rather than be smuggled or under-invoiced or if a large proportion of the diplomatic community buys riels officially rather than on the black market, this will not be true.

$$S = a_4 + b_4 B \qquad (A.2)$$

The supply of dollars in the black market is a function of the percentage differential between the black market and the official market rates. If the supply dries up completely when the official and black-market rates are equal, the intercept term of eq. (A.3) would be equal to zero. Otherwise, the intercept is whatever amount would trade at a zero differential.

$$S_1 = a_1 + b_1 \frac{B - R}{R} \qquad (A.3)$$

The supply of dollars going into the official market is equal to the total less the black-market supply:

$$S_2 = S - S_1 \qquad (A.4).$$

Demand for financial dollars is a function of the black-market rate:

$$D_1 = a_2 - b_2 B$$

Demand for imports will also be a function of the black-market rate (or value of exchange) under the assumption that importers (or someone) collect any rent that is available above the official rate and that through false invoicing they can convert dollars from official markets to black markets and vice versa.

The solution values for the six endogenous variables are as follows:

$$S = -A + a_2 + a_3 - \frac{(b_2 + b_3)(a_2 + a_3 - a_4 - A)}{(b_2 + b_3 + b_4)}$$

$$S_1 = a_1 - b_1 + \frac{b_1}{R} \frac{(a_2 + a_3 - a_4 - A)}{b_2 + b_3 + b_4}$$

$$S_2 = b_1 - a_1 + a_4 - (b_1/R - b_4) \frac{(a_2 + a_3 - a_4 - A)}{b_2 + b_3 + b_4}$$

$$D_1 = a_2 - b_2 \frac{(a_2 + a_3 - a_4 - A)}{b_2 + b_3 + b_4}$$

$$D_2 = a_3 - b_3 \frac{(a_2 + a_3 - a_4 - A)}{b_2 + b_3 + b_4}$$

$$B = \frac{a_2 + a_3 - a_4 - A}{b_2 + b_3 + b_4}$$

The solution to the system, using these assumptions, indicates that the black-market rate, the amount of imports, the amount of financial demand satisfied and the total non-aid dollars supplied are independent of the official exchange rate. The official exchange rate influences only the decision on where to exchange dollars, but has no effect on their quantity or use. This cannot be true if there are some kinds of enforceable limits on false invoicing. Then, the system will come up against a constraint before it reaches equilibrium. It will also not be true if some exports can only be sent out officially at official rates. Then a portion of dollar earnings will be a function of the official rate rather than the black-market rate.

The solution also indicates that legitimising some activities that normally take place on the black market (such as payments for airline operations in Cambodia) will not increase total demand, merely shift it over and reduce net over-invoicing or else encourage sales in the official market. Changing rules about capital flight, to the extent that it shifts the financial demand curve outwards, will offset the rates and the amounts exchanged.

All these conclusions depend also upon the linearity of some of the behavioural equations. It may be that they are independent of the linearity assumption, but this will require further investigation.

# Part II
# Economic Policy

SECTION 1: PETROLEUM ECONOMICS

# Introduction

Since October 1973 the international oil industry has been shaken up in ways heavily affecting the global economy. The most obvious effects have been those of higher oil prices (cf. Jefferson, Chapter 12). But the effects of higher oil prices on the 1973–4 inflationary episode are quite difficult to gauge (cf. Burstein, Chapter 7, on higher versus rising prices). Sargent (Chapter 11) is concerned with just this point. He argues that the continuing effects of the higher oil price will be deflationary – and will depress rates of profit and rates of real growth.

Jefferson centres on the ramifications of the emergence of OPEC as a significant force. Some ramifications are internal: witness the inherently 'surplus' Saudi Arabian financial position and the inherently 'deficit' financial position of Algeria (Iran?). External ramifications include aspects of placement of net surplus funds (recycle) and likely elasticities of response of supplies of oil from other sources and of oil substitutes (e.g. nuclear power).

Canes (Chapter 10) and Kennedy (Chapter 9) contribute papers in the tradition of neo-classical economic theory. Abstract constructions, well within established controlling theorems, are set out and interestingly analysed and then interpreted in terms of the oil industry – directly by Canes (vertical integration), indirectly by Kennedy. Kennedy need not offer much direct interpretation: all agree that current investment in oil-search and oil-production activity is risky. Will freely operating capital markets discount these risks in ways conforming to social risk preferences?

Canes and Kennedy participate in what might be called the *laissez-faire* counter-revolution. Not many years ago Pigovian welfare economics were rampant. Economists searched each market for its controlling externalities, indivisibilities, frictions, etc. Well-oiled economic theory always seemed to call for some kind of corrective intervention. There were few dissenters. Now a powerful reverse thrust is pervasively operating. Seeming externalities repeatedly are shown either to be in fact internalised by markets more intricate than had been realised or existent only because of official interventions.

The counter-revolution may be politically rooted to some extent. But duality's conquest of price theory is, we think, more important. It is impossible for many to believe that bureaucracy could develop the extremely complex algorithms required to solve resource allocation problems. But the interaction of numerous agents solving comparatively simple problems can indeed solve complex global problems under reasonably realistic stipulations. Not that the counter-revolution is ideological: optimisation problems, including embedded dual price systems, are defined over consumption and production sets, action spaces, etc., all invariant against ownership forms (cf. Bod, Chapter 5).

# 9 Public Investment in Energy Production under Price Uncertainty

MICHAEL KENNEDY

## 1. Introduction

Recent sharp increases in the price of imported oil, and consequent uncertainty about its price in future, have provoked much discussion about the desirability of government investment in energy production. Can firms be expected to undertake investments in high-cost energy despite the chance that energy prices may plummet in the future? This paper examines the conditions, in a stylised model of an economy facing import-price uncertainty, under which standard optimality criteria would call for government investment in energy. We assume that there exists a social welfare function of the Paretian class which policy-makers wish to maximise.[1]

Previous work on the economics of public investment under uncertainty, e.g. Arrow and Lind (1970) or Saandmo (1972), began from assumptions differing from ours, although the basic approaches are quite similar. Arrow and Lind assume that the returns from government investment are independent of the other stochastic elements an in individual income. Both papers assume that government investment opportunities are independent of the intensities of private activity. These assumptions are inappropriate for our case; we assume that government investments occur on margins at which private investors have stopped. And the earlier papers assume identical subjective probability distributions for all consumers; we allow for differing degrees of risk-aversion and differing beliefs about the future in studying the ability of various market structures and policy measures to promote optimal allocation of risk-bearing.[2]

This paper has two goals. First, we hope to gain some insight into real-world problems of government resource allocation; emergent policy implications will be discussed in the conclusion. Second, the root problem comprises a natural application of the familiar two-sector models of econonomic equilibrium (cf. Johnson, 1975, for an excellent survey of this model's properties).

## 2. Economic Framework and Optimality Conditions

The idealised economic model comprising the framework for this paper assumes that there are two consumers ($i = 1, 2$) and two goods ($E$, energy; $Q$, other goods). $Q$ serves as numeraire. There are two possible states of nature, characterised by the price of energy, assumed to be set by a foreign source exogenously to the agents of 'our' economy. These states are $s = o$, in which the price of energy is unity, and $s = m$, in which $p > 1$. Only one period is considered. There is a fixed stock of capital available in this period, allocated either for the production of energy or the other good. After the allocation, completely determining each sector's output level, the state of nature becomes known.[3] Consumers can then trade the goods produced, which become their endowments, at the fixed prices established by the foreign energy source, adjusting their consumption patterns to these prices.

Each consumer has an ordinal utility function defined over consumption of energy and other goods and denoted $U_i(Q_i, E_i)$. His endowment, generally depending upon the state of nature that occurs, is represented as $(Q_i^o, Q_i^m, E_i^o, E_i^m)$. $E_i^s$ = the amount of energy consumer $i$ receives if state $s$ occurs. Given the state of nature, consumers can trade feeely at the international price ratio. Thus in state $o$ the consumer faces unitary prices and has income $Q_i^o + E_i^o$; in state $m$ income is $Q_i^m + pE_i^m$. Given the indirect utility function $Y_i^*(r, I)$, we can represent the consumer's utility in state $o$ as $Y_i^*(1, Q_i^o + E_i^o)$ and in state $m$ as $Y_i^*(Q_i^m + pE_i^m)$.

It is convenient to work with a single variable representing real income. So we renumber the indifference curves in the following way. Each curve is numbered by the level of income which, at $r = 1$, would just allow the consumer to reach the utility level represented by it; for each indifference curve we find a point of tangency with a straight line of slope $-1$ and number the curve by the $Q$ intercept of the straight line so determined. The new utility index is defined by $Y(1, Y^*(r, Q + rE))$, using $Q$ as numeraire, $r$ being the price of energy.[4] The function $Y^*$ satisfies by definition $Y^*(r, Q + rE) = Q + E + CV(p, 1; Q + rE)$ where CV is the compensating variation[5] of income restoring the consumer to the original utility level, at a fixed income of $Q + pE$, after the energy price has fallen from $p$ to 1. Now we assume unitary income elasticity of demand for energy at all prices.[6] This implies that the indifference curves are homothetic so that, for a given price change from 1 to $p$, the compensating variation is a constant proportion of income expressed in terms of the numeraire. Thus here we can express utility (or real income) in state $o$ as $Y^o = Q^o + E^o$ (CV being zero in state $o$) and in state $m$ as $Y^m = c(Q^m + pE^m)$, $c$ depending only on $p$.[7]

We have found an index of ordinal utility in each state, namely $Y^o = Q^o + E^o$ and $Y^m = c(Q^m + pE^m)$. Following Hirschleifer,[8] we can construct a von Neumann—Morgenstern utility function $V(Y)$ measuring expected utility. That is, given the belief that the probability of state $m$ occurring is $\pi$, the well-being of the consumer is measured by $(1 - \pi)V(Y^o) + \pi V(Y^m)$.

Concerning the economy's production possibilities, there is a fixed stock of capital, $K$, available for the production of $E$ or $Q$. It is convenient to assume that there are two firms able to produce energy according to the production functions $E_1 = h_1(k_1)$ and $E_2 = h_2(k_2)$. If $k_i$ units of capital are allocated to firm $i$, $h_i(ki)$ units of energy will be produced by that firm. The functions $h_i$ satisfy $h_i' \geq 0$ and $h'' \leq 0$, i.e. diminishing returns to scale. Production of other goods is assumed to occur under constant returns to scale; the total production of other goods is $K - k_1 - k_2$.

Now we derive real-income production possibilities of the economy from the commodity production possibilities. (Recall that the definition of real income in each state conditional on a given homothetic ordinal utility function.) Productive efficiency requires that $h_1'(k_1) = h_2'(k_2) = h'$. Real income then is

$$Y^o = Q^o + E^o = K - k + h(k) \tag{1}$$

$$Y^m = c(Q^m + pE^m) = c[K - k + ph(k)] \tag{2}$$

where $k = k_1 + k_2$ and $h(k) = h_1(k_1) + h_2(k_2)$ subject to $h_1' = h_2'$. Trade-off between real-income levels in the two states is defined as

$$\frac{dY^o}{dY^m} = \frac{dY^o/dk}{dY^m/dk} = \frac{h' - 1}{c(ph' - 1)} \tag{3}$$

The marginal rate of transformation, the opportunity cost of incremental consumption in state $o$, is usually defined as

$$\mathrm{MRS} = \frac{h' - 1}{c(1 - ph')} \tag{4}$$

For this to be positive,

$$1 \leq 1/h' \leq p \tag{5}$$

The marginal cost of energy will be set between the two possible prices; in the model, increasing energy production is equivalent to increasing real income in state $m$ at the expense of real income in state $o$. Stipulated properties of $h$ assure that the economy-wide $(Y^o - Y^m)$ production-possibility frontier will be concave.

The conditions for a Pareto-optimum resource allocation can now be derived. Let consumer $i$'s utility function be $(1 - \pi_i)V^i(Y_i^o) + \pi_i V^i(Y_i^m)$. Subjective beliefs about and attitudes towards risk can vary, but ordinal preferences concerning energy consumption and other goods are identical. The social objective is to maximise consumer 1's utility subject to a given consumer 2 utility level:

$$\max (1 - \pi_1) V_1(Y_1^o) + \pi_1 V_1(Y_1^m) \tag{6}$$

subject to

Associated Lagrange<br>multiplier

$$(1 - \pi_2)V_2(Y_2^o) + \pi_2 V_2(Y_2^m) = \bar{V} \qquad\qquad \beta \qquad\qquad (7)$$

$$Y_1^o = Q_1^o + E_1^o \qquad\qquad \mu_1 \qquad\qquad (8)$$

$$Y_1^m = c(Q_1^m + pE_1^m) \qquad\qquad v_1 \qquad\qquad (9)$$

$$Y_2^o = Q_2^o + E_2^o \qquad\qquad \mu_2 \qquad\qquad (10)$$

$$Y_2^m = c(Q_2^m + pE_2^m) \qquad\qquad v_2 \qquad\qquad (11)$$

$$Q_1^o + Q_2^o = Q \qquad\qquad \tau_0 \qquad\qquad (12)$$

$$Q_1^m + Q_2^m = Q \qquad\qquad \tau_m \qquad\qquad (13)$$

$$E_1^o + E_2^o = E \qquad\qquad G_0 \qquad\qquad (14)$$

$$E_1^m + E_2^m = E \qquad\qquad G_m \qquad\qquad (15)$$

$$E = b_1(k_1) + b_2(k_2) \qquad\qquad \rho \qquad\qquad (16)$$

$$Q = K - k_1 - k_2 \qquad\qquad \phi \qquad\qquad (17)$$

The variables are defined as:

$Y_i^s$ = consumer $i$'s real income in state $s$.

$Q_i^s$ = consumer $i$'s endowment of other goods in state $s$.

$E_i^s$ = consumer $i$'s endowment of energy in state $s$.

$E$ = total production of energy.

$Q$ = total production of other goods.

$k_i$ = allocation of capital to energy firm $i$.

Manipulation of the first-order conditions of the problem's Lagrangean leads to

$$b_1{}'(k_1) = b_2{}'(k_2) = \phi/\rho \qquad\qquad (18)$$

The marginal product of capital should be equalised between the two firms. Let $\rho/\phi = \theta$, the certainty-equivalent price of energy: if energy's price were known with certainty to be $\theta$, firms would produce according to eq. (18), equating marginal cost and price. Define $\lambda_1$ and $\lambda_2$:

$$\lambda_1 = \pi_1 V_1{}'(Y_1^m)/(1 - \pi_1)V_1{}'(Y_1^o) \qquad\qquad (19a)$$

$$\lambda_2 = \pi_2 V_2{}'(Y_2^m)/(1 - \pi_2)V_2{}'(Y_2^o) \qquad\qquad (19b)$$

The $\lambda_i$ are then marginal rates of substitution of real income in state $o$ for real income in state $m$. The rest of the first-order conditions yield

$$\lambda_1 = \lambda_2 = \theta - 1/c(p - \theta) = \lambda \qquad (20)$$

Marginal rates of substitution must be equalised and jointly set equal to the marginal rate of transformation between real income in state $o$ and real income in state $m$. Since the common $\lambda$ must be positive, the certainty-equivalent price of energy will fall between the two possible future values.

So the analysis − for purposes of determining Pareto-optimal outcomes − can be reduced to that of a two-good economy (cf. $Y^o$ and $Y^m$). Any market arrangement equalising $\lambda_1$ and $\lambda_2$ to the opportunity cost of producing $Y^o$, i.e.

$$\frac{\theta - 1}{c(p - \theta)} = \frac{1 - b'}{c(pb' - 1)} \qquad (21)$$

will achieve Pareto-optimality.

### 3. Attainment of Optimum under Different Market Structures

*Contingent Commodities*

It is well known that, if a market existed for delivery of energy and other goods contingent upon occurrence of a given world price for oil, trade in these commodities under conditions of perfect competition would lead to a Pareto-optimum (see Arrow, 1971; Debreu, 1959). Furthermore, since production of goods in this model promotes utility only through purchasing power thus conferred on consumers, equilibrium trade in the composite contingent commodities, 'income in state $s$', would lead to a Pareto-optimum.

*Future Markets*

Will existence of a market for future oil also serve to allocate risk optimally? In a future market, agents agree now to make transactions in energy after the state of the world is known, but at a fixed price determined before this state is known. The problem for a consumer owning capital $K$ with energy production possibilities $b(k)$ becomes

$$\max (1 - \pi)V(Y^o) + \pi V(Y^m) \qquad (22)$$

so that

Associated Lagrange<br>multiplier

$$Y^o = E + Q \qquad\qquad \mu_0 \qquad (23)$$

$$Y^m = c(Q + pE) \qquad\qquad \mu_m \qquad\qquad (24)$$

$$P = h(k) \qquad\qquad \rho \qquad\qquad (25)$$

$$M = K - k \qquad\qquad \beta_a \qquad\qquad (26)$$

$$E = P - S \qquad\qquad \beta_E \qquad\qquad (27)$$

$$Q = M + rS \qquad\qquad \beta_Q \qquad\qquad (28)$$

$P$ is production of energy; $M$ is production of other goods; $S$ is sale of future energy (and can be negative if future energy is purchased); $r$ is the price at which future transactions will be carried out. Manipulation of the first-order conditions of the associated Lagrangean leads to $h'(k) = 1/r$: production will be carried to the point where the marginal cost of a unit of energy is its marginal value in exchange after uncertainty has been resolved. And

$$\lambda = (r - 1)/c(p - r) \qquad\qquad (29)$$

Eqs (18) and (20) show that this is the correct common MRS for attainment of Pareto-optimality. Thus, for each agent in the economy, rates of technical substitution and marginal rates of consumption preference are brought into equality through the future market; again there is an optimal allocation of risk-bearing. Consumption and production decisions again can be separated: firms maximise the well-being of their shareholders by maximising profits at the certainty price $1/r$. Again no government action is needed for Pareto-optimality.

### Stock Market

Suppose, following Diamond (1967), that neither contingent commodity nor future trading can take place, but that consumers can buy stocks (shares of unsure profits) from and sell bonds (loans with certain returns) to various firms in the economy. For simplicity, assume that there is but one energy-producing firm, with a production function $E = h(k)$. Consumers take as exogenous the state-determined profit level of the energy firm $- h(k) - k$ in state $o$ and $p \cdot h(k) - k$ in state $m$. The total value of energy-firm shares is $D$; that of consumer assets, $A$. Since the profitability of investing in the other-goods sector is zero in both states, such investment, equivalent to selling bonds, will be suppressed here. The endogenous variables for the consumer are $s$, the share of energy-firm stock purchased, and $B$, bonds purchased. State-distributed income, and thus consumption, is totally determined by this.

Formally, each consumer's problem is

$$\max (1 - \pi) V(Y^o) + \pi V(Y^m) \qquad\qquad (30)$$

subject to

Associated Lagrange
multiplier

$$Y^o = B + s(b(k) - k) \qquad \mu_0 \qquad (31)$$

$$Y^m = c(B + s(p \cdot b(k) - k)) \qquad \mu_m \qquad (32)$$

$$sD + B = A \qquad \beta \qquad (33)$$

We now define two net variables, $F_0$ and $F_m$, representing the profits of the energy firm in each state of nature:

$$F_0 = b(k) - k \qquad (34)$$

$$F_m = p \cdot b(k) - k \qquad (35)$$

Combining first-order conditions,

$$\lambda = (D - F_0)/c(F_m - D) \qquad (36)$$

The marginal rate of substitution for each consumer is determined by objective data: these rates will therefore be brought into equality throughout the economy by the stock market. Will firms act so as to bring the rates of technical substitution into line as well?

Again following Diamond (1967), we assume that the goal of the firm is to maximise its value to its owners: the total value of stock outstanding, i.e. $D$. Inverting eq. (36),

$$D = (1/1 + c\lambda)F_0 + c\lambda/(1 + c\lambda)F_m \qquad (37)$$

The value of the firm is a convex combination of profit in the two states, the weights depending on the consumers' marginal rate of substitution. Assume that the firm takes this value of $\lambda$ as given (the analogue of price-taking). The firm will try to maximise $D$ by setting $dD/dk = 0$:

$$dD/dk = (1/1 + c\lambda)dF_0/dk + (c\lambda/1 + c\lambda)dF_m/dk = 0 \qquad (38)$$

$$= \frac{b'(k) - 1 + c\lambda[p \cdot b'(k) - 1]}{(1 + c\lambda)} = 0 \qquad (39)$$

leading to

$$b'(k) = (c\lambda + 1)/(1 + c\lambda p) \qquad (40)$$

exactly equivalent to condition (21): with a stock market, Pareto-optimality again is guaranteed.

This section has shown that, under assumptions of profit maximisation and two not implausible institutional arrangements, a future market and a stock-market, competition will indeed efficiently allocate production and risk-bearing. We now turn to market imperfections which may lead a private economy to an interior allocation, thus making government intervention desirable on Pareto-optimality grounds.

## 4. Market Imperfections

*Absence of Profit Motivation*

In discussing the stock-market economy we assumed that the firm had a specific preference structure over its state-distributed profit pattern; the most desired profit structure would maximise the total value of its shares. But perhaps managers of the firm might have preferences over profit levels independent of the well-being of the stockholder.[9] So we should generalise the model to include existence of a managerial utility-of-profits function, $Z(F_0, F_m)$, which is independent of the stock-market value of the firm.[10] Assume managerial risk-aversion leading to under-investment in energy; firms will choose an $F_0$ which is too high and an $F_m$ which is too low, insensitively to consumer preferences; the stock market no longer affects selected levels of $F_0$ and $F_m$. But since we assume that consumers can still trade on the stock market to reach exchange equilibrium, state-distributed endowments will be determined by von Neumann–Morgenstern utility functions according to eq. (37). *Given* the pattern of production, risk is optimally allocated among consumers, but a Pareto-optimum for the whole economy is not attained.

The possibility of a Pareto-improvement as a result of government investment in energy is now obvious. Each consumer's MRS between $Y^o$ and $Y^m$, $\lambda$, is equal to $(D - F_0)/c(F_m - D)$, but the government can transform $Y^o$ into $Y^m$ at a rate equal to the generally higher slope of the production-possibility curve. Thus, small equal amounts of $Q$, taxed away from consumers in a lump-sum fashion and returned to them in the form of $E$ at the technically possible rate, will make them better off. A presumptive case for government action has now been made on 'Pareto-optimum" grounds.

Given our assumptions, we can easily determine whether the preferences of consumers really are such that corporate action is suboptimal for them so that government investment is appropriate. So long as $b'(k)$ is observable, we need merely ask consumers: 'Would you be willing to give up $1 - b'(k)$ dollars of income if the price of energy should be unity in return for an increase of $[p \cdot b'(k) - 1]$ dollars of income if the price should be $p$?' Given the stock market's role in allocating risk among consumers, all answers should be the same. If they are 'yes', it becomes established that corporations are under-investing in energy relative to Pareto-optimality criteria.

But such a government policy will not *necessarily* aid both consumers. Any such investment will move each consumer's endowment to a new point in the $Y^o - Y^m$ trade-off curve. If stock-market trading is still allowed, the terms of trade between $Y^o$ and $Y^m$ will in general change. Ordinarily $p$ could be expected to fall. This will aid some consumers, but price and income effects will move in different directions for others. In terms of compensation possibilities, the move is desirable for obvious reasons.[11] In general, some interpersonal welfare judgements would be required before a government investment policy could be endorsed.

*Price controls*

The stock market's role in risk-allocation pivots on the stipulation that consumers can expect high profits from energy shares if state $m$ occurs. This stipulation would be vitiated by a government policy of domestic price control in the face of high foreign prices. We proceed to explore implications of such regulation for the working of the stylised economy.

Assume that the price at which domestic energy production can be sold is legally fixed at unity: (1) profits in the energy sector are independent of the state and equal to $b(k) - k$; the profit-maximising firm produces where $b'(k) = 1$; (2) the income of consumers, in terms of the numeraire, is independent of the state of nature and invariant against stock-market trading as well. Consumers' ordinal utilities will be determined by their income; the consumer price of energy will be a datum.

Extending the analysis, assume once more that consumers have equal endowments, i.e. initial capital $K_i$ and production function $b_i(k_i)$. In the price-control case, each consumer's income is equal in both states to

$$I_i = K_i + H_i(k^*) - k^* \tag{41}$$

where $b_i'(k^*) = 1$. Line $DD'$ in Fig. 1 is the Marshallian demand function for energy when each consumer's income is unity and prices vary. Let $E^*$ be the amount of energy domestically produced (invariant against price in the true state of nature to be revealed). If state $o$ occurs, there is no problem: consumers consume $C_0$ and an amount $E^* C_0$ is purchased from abroad at $p = 1$. What if state $m$ occurs? Assume that the government operates the price-control system so that total revenues equal total costs. It must then find a price to consumers, $n$, that satisfies

$$nC = E^* + p(C - E^*) \tag{42}$$

where $C$ is consumption, itself a function of $n$. Fig. 1 shows that at such a price the ratio of the line segment $(pn)$ to the segment $(p1)$ equals that of $OE^*$ to $OC$: the price consumers will face if state $m$ occurs depends upon $E^*$ and is a decreasing function of $E^*$.

Relative to state $o$, each consumer's level of ordinal utility is $I$ (cf. the utility definition at p. 90). Relative to state $m$, it is $C^* I$, $C^*$ being a reduction factor to be applied to the value of income in terms of the numeraire when the price of energy increases from 1 to $n$. Since $n < p$, $C^* > C$: each consumer's level of von Neumann–Morgenstern utility before the state is known is

$$(1 - \pi_i) V_i(I) + \pi_i V_i(C^* I) \tag{43}$$

The amount of nominal income pertaining to state $o$ which consumers would be willing to give up for one unit pertaining to state $m$ is

$$\lambda_i = \frac{\pi_i}{1 - \pi_i} \cdot \frac{V_i'(C^*I)}{V_i'(I)} \tag{44}$$

assuming that the price of energy will remain at $n$ in state $m$. If $\pi_i \geq \frac{1}{2}$, $\lambda_i \geq 1$ and $\lambda_i = 0$ only when $\pi_i = 0$. In this economy the $\lambda_i$'s are *not* equalised across consumers by the stock market.

How can government investment change each consumer's state-distributed utility? A small investment in energy will decrease nominal income in state $o$ by $1 - b'(k^*)$. Assuming that prices remain at $n$, it will increase income in state $m$ by $B = nb'(k^*) - 1$. Since an increase in energy supplies, given our assumptions of unitary income elasticities, will lower the relative price of energy, $B$ will underestimate the welfare gain so long as each

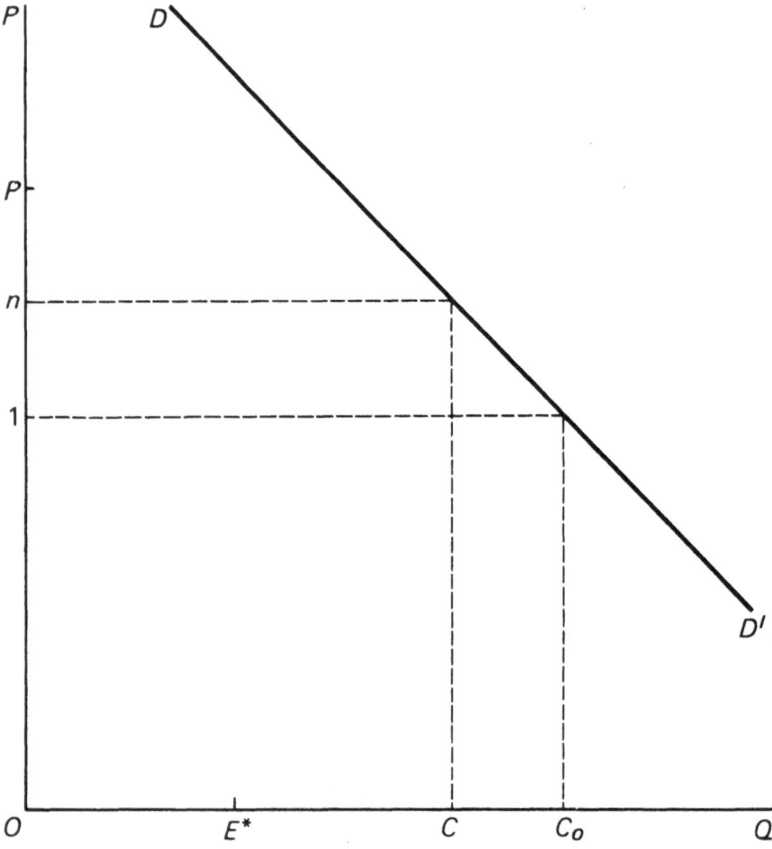

Fig. 1. Price controls on energy

person's share of government energy production is less than his energy consumption, an assumption we adopt. So

$$(1 - b'(k^*))/(nb'(k^*) - 1)$$

is the most attractive rate at which state $o$ income can be transformed into state $m$ income in the private economy. But $1 - b'(k^*) = 0$! Pareto-optimality demands some government investment in order to offset the discouragement of energy production due to price controls.

Costs and benefits will have to be recalculated after each dose: $n$ will fall as more energy is produced. As soon as the lowest of the $\lambda_i$ is below the social opportunity cost, interpersonal welfare judgements become necessary: no longer does investment make for unambiguous welfare gain.

As long as price controls exist there is no way for the $\lambda_i$'s to come into equality; a Pareto-optimum cannot be achieved, in contrast to the first case of market failure when government intervention could produce a competitive-equilibrium outcome.

### Lack of Access to the Stock Market

Analogous to the case in which consumer's MRSs are equalised to each other, but not to the rate of technical substitution, is a case in which only one consumer's MRS is equal to the technical rate: only one consumer owns shares of firms capable of producing energy; the other consumer cannot operate in the stock market to acquire an interest in energy production, owing to institutional barriers. (High transactions costs for small-lot trading or simple information gaps are examples.) We assume that excluded groups are lightly endowed: this case is meant to shed light on income-distribution issues.

In Fig. 2, consumer 1's production-possibility frontier is $PP'$; in autarky he maximises welfare by producing and consuming at $P^*$ along indifference curve $U_1$. Consumer 2's endowment is restricted to $Q$. In $(Y^o - Y^m)$ space it corresponds to point $E$ whose $Y^m$ co-ordinate is exactly $c$ times its $Y^o$ co-ordinate. Point $E$ lies along indifference curve $U_2$.

If stock-market trading were to develop, a new set of implied prices for $Y^o$ and $Y^m$ would be formed, say according to line segments $BB'$. Then a Pareto-optimum would be obtained; both consumers would improve upon the *status quo ante*.

Without a stock market no government investment policy and energy-production can improve the positions of both consumers. In fact, since consumer 1's energy production possibilities correspond to those of the society, and since he is in equilibrium at $P^*$, *any* government energy investment which gives him an equal share of costs and proceeds will make him worse off. A public production programme will improve consumer 2 if $\lambda_2 > \lambda_1$ or if consumer 2 values consumption in state $m$ relatively more than does consumer 1. This premiss, satisfied in Fig. 2, is by no means

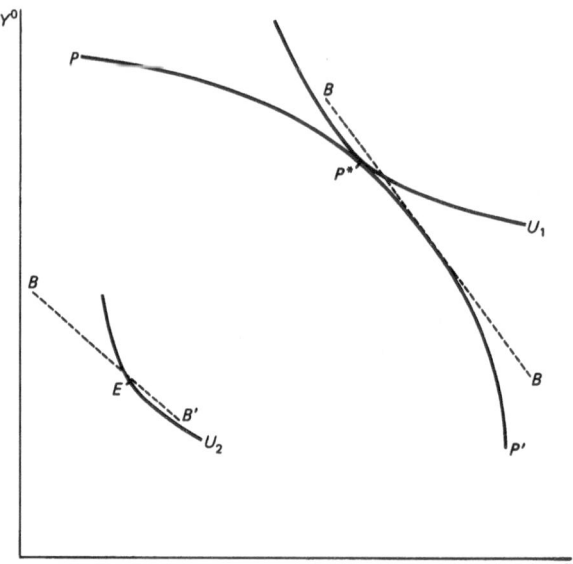

Fig. 2. Equilibrium with and without access to stock market

necessarily true. True, consumer 2's $Y^o/Y^m$ consumption ratio can be expected to be higher than that for consumer 1: the latter can enjoy energy profits if state $m$ occurs. But if 1 is substantially more risk-averse than 2, or if $\pi_1$ is substantially higher than $\lambda_2$, the condition $\lambda_1 > \lambda$ could easily occur. Then government investment would disadvantage both groups.

Certainly, investigation into preferences of consumers thought to be excluded from stock-market trading ought to precede any government investment policy. And even if investigation led to the conclusion that $\lambda_2$ were greater than the social opportunity cost of producing $Y^m$ ($= \lambda_1$), the undoubted loss which would accrue to group 1 consumers must be inserted into the social welfare calculus.

## 5. Conclusion

This paper has investigated, for a simplified economic model, the implications of various kinds of institutional arrangements for government investment in energy in a Pareto-optimum theory context. We found that under conditions of consumer risk-diversification through a stock market, and maximisation of present value by firms, full Pareto-optimality could be achieved without government intervention. Only if these conditions broke down owing to independent managerial preferences, price controls or exclusion from the stock market would government investments shift the economy from a non-Pareto-optimum state to a Pareto-optimum state.[12]

Surely, those who call for government investment should specify exactly which market failure has occurred. Which Pareto condition has been violated? In particular, empirical determination of $b'(k)$ and of values of $\lambda$ (perhaps through surveys) are needed for proper assessment of government policy.

## Notes

1. See Bergson (1938).
2. For a general discussion of the economics of risk-bearing, see Arrow (1971, chaps. 2–4).
3. We abstract from another important source of uncertainty, that concerning the cost of domestic energy resources. Hopefully the paper could incorporate this generalisation without damage to its conclusions, but the matter is still to be fully investigated and is subject to ongoing research.
4. See Uzawa (1964) for a discussion of the expenditure function $Y(p, U)$ underlying the analysis.
5. See Hicks (1944) and Mishan (1971, chaps. 48–51) for discussions of the compensating variation.
6. This assumption is supported by many econometric studies. See, for example, Darmstadter (1971) and Kennedy (1974).
7. We have computed $c$ for $p = 4$. In the Leontief case, with $E = 0.07(E + Q)$, $c = 0.83$. In the Cobb–Douglas case, with $E = 0.07E + Q)$ when $r = 1$, $c = 0.90$. At relative prices prevailing in 1972, energy was about 7 per cent of total U.S. consumption.
8. See Hirschleifer (1970, pp. 235–9).
9. Implications of such managerial preferences have been explored by Saandmo (1971) and Leland (1972). Arrow and Lind (1970, pp. 375–6) briefly discussed in the implications of such a situation for the optimal allocation of risk-bearing in the global economy.
10. This implies a certain imperfection in the stock market: otherwise speculators could buy all the shares of the firm's stock at depressed prices, adjust production levels to a pattern more preferred by consumers and sell their stock at a profit.
11. See von Graaff (1957) for a discussion of compensation tests.
12. Conference participants commented on the model. Beazer noted that the existence of differential (and possibly not well known) marginal tax rates in the economy, besides undermining the Pareto-optimality of the competitive outcome, made the calculus of costs and benefits of government interference much more complicated in principle. Burstein pointed out that in the real world firms may hold closely information which, if published, would change consumers' subjective probability density functions, thus attenuating the linkage between consumers and producers via the stock market. Motivation for thus holding information includes confidentiality vis-à-vis prying rivals or a host of other 'zero-sum-like' considerations. Concerning the lack-of-access-to-the-stock-market model, Canes showed that there were other possible forms of investment, such as education, which would be differentially rewarded according to the state of nature, thus permitting a closer approach to Pareto-optimality. Tardos objected to the use of consumer utility functions as indicators here of public welfare; he perceived no inherent correlation between *ex-ante* and *ex-post* welfare, especially if probability distributions should in some sense be wrong. Tardos considered Pareto-optimality irrelevant to the Pareto-optimum conceptions of this paper. The present writer disagrees with him but admits that the linkages between uncertainty and welfare economics are so insecure, so unexplored, that new research into social preferences under uncertainty is urgently required.

102 *Resource Allocation and Economic Policy*

## References

Arrow, K. J. (1971). *Essays in the Theory of Risk Bearing* (Amsterdam: North-Holland).
Arrow, K. J. and Lind, R. C. (1970). 'Uncertainty and the Evaluation of Public Investment Decisions', *American Economic Review* (June).
Bergson, A. (1938). 'A Reformulation of Certain Aspects of Welfare Economics', *Quarterly Journal of Economics,*
Darmstadter, J. (1971). *Energy in the World Economy* (Baltimore: Johns Hopkins Press).
Debreu, G. (1959). *Theory of Value* (New York: Wiley.)
Diamond, P. A. (1967). 'The Role of a Stock Market in a General Equilibrium Model with Technological Uncertainty', *American Economic Review*, (Sept.).
Hicks, J. R. (1944). 'The Four Consumers' Surpluses', *Review of Economic Studies.*
Hirschleifer, J. (1970). *Investment, Interest and Capital* (Englewood Cliffs, N.J.: Prentice-Hall).
Johnson, H. G. (1975). 'The Problem of Inflation', in *On Economics and Society: Selected Essays* (Chicago and London: Univ. of Chicago Press).
Kennedy, M. (1974). 'An Economic Model of the World Oil Market', *Bell Journal* (Autumn).
Leland, H. E. (1972). 'Theory of the Firm Facing Uncertain Demand', *American Economic Review*, (June).
Mishan, E. J. (1971). *Cost–Benefit Analysis* (New York: Praeger).
Saandmo, A., (1971). 'On the Theory of the Competitive Firm under Price Uncertainty', *American Economic Review* (Mar.).
Saandmo, A. (1972). 'Discount Rates for Public Investment under Uncertainty', *International Economic Review* (June).
Uzawa, H. (1964). 'Duality Principles in the Theory of Cost and Production', *International Economic Review*, (May).
von Graaff, J. de (1957). *Theoretical Welfare Economics* (Cambridge: Cambridge Univ. Press).

# 10 The Vertical Integration of Oil Firms

MICHAEL E. CANES

*This paper is for study and discussion and does not necessarily represent the views of the American Petroleum Institute or any of its members.*

## 1. Introduction

Recent events in world petroleum markets have focused attention on the vertical integration of oil firms. In the United States, Congressional hearings have inquired into the consequences of oil industry vertical integration.[1] Bills are presently before the Congress to force integrated oil firms to divest themselves of parts of their holdings.[2] And a complaint has been brought by the Federal Trade Commission against eight large vertically integrated United States oil firms.[3] In addition, recently enacted United States tax legislation and recently proposed price-control legislation seem intended to discourage oil industry integration.[4]

Policy-maker suspicion of vertical integration has found little support in the economics literature. Though some writers have argued that vertical integration has non-competitive consequences,[5] most have asserted that if firms in some market have monopoly power, their vertical integration into other markets is likely to reduce the misallocative effects.[6]

On the other hand, economists have yet to provide a strong theoretical basis for the claim that vertical integration under conditions of open competition results in real resource savings.[7] A common assertion in the literature is that backwards vertical integration offers 'security' of supply, forward integration 'security' of markets.[8] But this ignores the fact that the acquisition of 'security' is costly, and it is unclear under what conditions this cost is worth bearing. Further, a consequence of this sort of language is that policy-makers worry that non-integrated firms (unfairly) confront 'insecure' supply sources, and some have been sympathetic to proposals to increase such firms' security by legislative fiat.[9]

To be sure, efforts to explain vertical integration in terms of costs and returns exist. Coase (1937) explained the 'firm' as an institution to economise the use of markets. According to him, there are costs of market transactions that can be economised by directing resources within the firm, but there are also costs to this direction, and these increase relative to those of using markets with firm size. By this view, vertical integration is a means to economise costs of transacting across stages of production but is limited by diseconomies of size.

Although this is a powerful insight, it is not a theory of vertical integration. Without further specification of the determinants of costs and gains from integration, it is impossible to predict in which markets vertical integration will occur and which not. For example, why do oil refiners often integrate into crude production but rarely into refinery construction? Further, if diseconomies of size were the only constraint on vertical integration, it would be difficult to explain why some large firms are vertically integrated whereas some smaller ones are not. Are costs of transacting between manufacturer and retailer markedly different, say, in oil and cigarette markets? Or does some other phenomenon explain why (large) oil companies often are integrated into retailing whereas (smaller) cigarette manufacturers generally are not?

A somewhat different theory of vertical integration has been offered by Stigler (1951). From Adam Smith's famous theorem that the division of labour is limited by the extent of the market, Stigler reasoned that vertical integration is non-specialisation of production occurring when the volume of a good employed in some production process is insufficient to support specialised firms. By implication, firms in industries that grow larger over time will vertically disintegrate, whereas firms in industries that decline will integrate. Although Stigler's thesis yields refutable implications, he himself noted that it does not explain several instances of vertical integration and he proposed both monopoly and public regulation of prices as additional forces leading to integration.[10]

Recently, Williamson (1971) compared the strategy of vertical integration to those of engaging in short- or long-term contractual relationships. He described a number of transactions costs associated with the latter two alternatives and how these might be economised through integration. The identification of specific transactions costs associated with alternatives to vertical integration is an important step to formulating an operational theory of vertical integration.

More recently, Green (1974) examined markets in which openly competing firms intermittently are subject to costly non-price rationing. Under reasonably general assumptions, he derived conditions under which vertical integration reduces costs to such firms. Green's identification of another specific cost of non-integration is also an important step towards a theory of integration. Further, the cost that Green identifies has often been mentioned in previous discussions of integration in the oil industry.

Finally, Arrow (1975) has explained vertical integration as a means of acquiring valuable market information about an input to a production process. The explanation is limited, however, because it leaves unclear under what conditions this method of acquiring information is cheaper than more direct means.

In this paper we proceed to formulate the vertical integration problem in a general way. This is done so as to provide a theoretical framework within which we can analyse oil industry integration. More specifically, after briefly defining and describing vertical integration, we examine some costs and returns from integration and some determinants of these costs and returns. These considerations are then brought to bear on the petroleum industry, and we argue that vertical integration in that industry is plausibly explained by an economic theory of integration under conditions of open competition. We conclude the paper with a brief discussion of recent changes in the world petroleum market and the implications for vertical integration.

## 2. Definition and Description of Vertical Integration

We define vertical integration as a combining of the owned resources of market transactors (i.e. buyer and seller) in common ownership. Such a combining does not necessarily involve physical changes, but rather a revised property right structure governing the resources. The rights involved include the right to transfer or sell those resources, the right to direct their use (including the structuring of physical relationships among them) and the right to the net return from their economic activity. The essence of a positive theory of vertical integration under open competition is that under certain conditions this revision in property right structure yields real economies.

A firm would be totally vertically integrated if it transacted only with final consumers, producing all its inputs, as well as the inputs to those inputs, on back to the ownership and production of raw materials. In reality, few if any firms are so integrated and one of our tasks is to explain why firms integrate vertically into some markets but not into others.

The oil industry is often divided into five stages: (1) exploration and crude oil production; (2) crude oil transportation; (3) refining of oil products; (4) product transportation; and (5) product marketing. A firm that engages in two or more of these stages is vertically integrated and there are some thirty American firms which have extensive operations in all five of these stages. By our above description, however, it is clear that a firm which operated *only* in these lines of business would hardly be completely vertically integrated. For example, crude oil transportation modes include pipelines, tankers, railroad cars and barges, and by definition such a firm would not produce any of these equipments or the inputs necessary to construct them. In fact, oil companies generally do not produce transportation equipment, or refineries, oil drilling equipment, retail service station equipment, oil storage equipment, etc. Further, they do not buy many of these devices, choosing usually to rent such things as offshore exploration services, drilling rigs, etc.[11]

Because there is no precise measure of vertical integration, it is difficult to assess its relative extent in the oil industry. However, Adelman's study of

United States vertical integration (1955) indicated the oil industry to be less integrated than most other manufacturing industries.[12]

## 3. Gains from Vertical Integration

In this section we ignore the effects of monopoly on vertical integration. Wealth-maximising firms in all industries are assumed openly competitive, so that integration is not explained either as a method of circumventing monopoly pricing or of strengthening existing monopoly power. These explanations have dominated discussion of public policy towards vertical integration, but their consideration here would divert us from our primary task.[13]

A firm can purchase inputs on spot markets, make long-term contracts for their delivery, or itself engage in their production. The use of spot market transactions allows the firm to sample market prices continually in assessing how much of each input to purchase and to adjust its input purchases sequentially to changing market prices. Similarly, the use of such transactions allows an input supplier to sample market prices in assessing how much to produce and to adjust his production sequentially to these changing prices. A firm will gain from the information provided by continued sampling of market prices and from the opportunity to engage in sequential decision-making, but it will acquire the information and opportunity at a cost. This cost has three main components: the cost of searching for terms at which goods can be exchanged, the cost of concluding a short-term contract for each transaction, and the cost of adjusting production to stochastic variation in prices or quantities of the good transacted for. Costs of searching for market terms will increase the less predictable are these terms over time and among transactors. More variability of terms over time and less product uniformity will result in less predictability. Costs of negotiating and concluding contracts will increase the more contracts are used to transact a given volume of product and the greater the cost per contract negotiated. This latter will be greater the less standardised the product involved and the fewer the transactors with whom to negotiate.

Costs of adjusting to stochastic price variation will increase the more variable are prices and the more costly are means to make such adjustment. For example, a sudden unanticipated increase in the price of an input will impose costs on a producer because he will require additional finances to cover the purchase of any quantity of the good. He might economise these costs by holding fungible assets, including cash, or by prearranging lines or credit, etc. The more costly (the cheapest of) these alternatives, the more costly the adjustment.

Alternatively, transactors may find it profitable to hold prices constant in the face of short-term changes in demand or supply conditions.[14] More predictable stable prices reduce costs of search and other adjustment to price variation, but result in non-price forms of rationing when quantities supplied and demanded are temporarily unequal owing to unanticipated demand or supply changes. The costs of non-price rationing are the costs of competing along non-price criteria, and these costs can fall differentially among different market transactors. For example, under 'shortage' conditions if first-come/first-served rationing is used, then buyers will bear costs of queueing and those with higher time value will bear higher costs. Similarly, if an input to a production process is suddenly and unexpectedly rationed by suppliers, those customers with relatively more investment in specific complementary capital and those whose supplies are absolutely the more reduced will bear the greater reduction in wealth. Transactors can reduce the consequences of being rationed by holding buffer stocks, and the cheaper the holding of such stocks, the less costly non-price rationing will be.

Higher costs per contract imply longer-term contractual relationships. Long-term contracts reduce costs associated with numbers of contracts reached, but in turn involve other costs. First, unless such contracts exhaustively specify all terms (e.g. product characteristics, terms of payment, etc.), the contracting parties may later differ on what terms have been agreed to and engage in costly negotiation or litigation. Since the exhaustive specification of terms itself is costly, some latitude is likely to remain. Second, even if initial contractual terms are well specified, unanticipated changes in demand or supply conditions are likely to make original contractual conditions costly to adhere to. This problem can be partially mitigated through contingency, renegotiation or escape clauses, but it is difficult to comprehend all possible contingencies and the exercise of renegotiation or escape clauses also has costs (e.g. of determining whether such clauses can be legally exercised and of renegotiating the contract or finding a new trading partner). Third, long-term arrangements pose contractual enforcement problems. A firm continually utilising market transactions to secure inputs or sell outputs can punish a derelict trading partner by taking its business elsewhere, but under long-term arrangements this alternative will be more costly to implement. Since the threat to turn to a competitor is one means to enforce a trading arrangement, the more costly this is the more costly such enforcement will be. The above suggests that costs of long-term contracts will be higher the more terms must be initially specified, the more subject to change are demand or technology, and the more costly the use of the courts or other sources of arbitration when contractual disagreement occurs.

The vertical integration of a buyer and seller accomplishes at least three things. First, the rearranged structure of property rights provides an opportunity to bring the costs and rewards facing the buyer and seller more into accord with one another. In particular, if the integrated firm can restructure incentives facing what otherwise would be independent parties so that their wealth is more positively (or less negatively) related, then their inducement to strive for bargaining advantage will be less and costs of negotiation, enforcement, etc., will be reduced. Second, where disagreements between buying and selling organisations arise, these can be settled by fiat within the firm, without costly resort to outside arbitrators such as the courts. And third, vertical integration allows a firm to reduce costs of adjusting to unanticipated changes in transaction prices or quantities. Essentially, vertical integration allows specialisation within the firm of the monitoring of buyer–seller relationships and the development of techniques to reduce costs associated with changes in open-market relationships. Thus, the gains from integration will be greater the more costly are alternative means to negotiate, conclude and enforce buyer–seller transactions, and the more costly is adjustment to changed market terms.

## 4. Costs of Vertical Integration

In this section we ignore possible legal barriers to vertical integration which exist in the United States. Obviously, such legal barriers impose real costs on firms wishing to integrate.

Two sources of market-imposed costs are apparent. First, a firm that vertically integrates is likely to be larger because it takes on a new business that it otherwise does not.[15] This larger size imposes costs because it is costly to organise factors of production within a firm and this cost will rise the more factors there are. The director of a firm will find that the more assets under his control, the greater the rate at which he must make decisions or the more decision-making he must delegate to others. The results will be more mistaken decisions, more layers of review (implying a longer time to implementation), etc. These imply that the costs of vertical integration will be greater the larger the increase in firm size and the greater the rate of increase of decision-making costs with firm size.

A second diseconomy arises from non-specialisation of production. This is distinguished from the first in that a firm can increase in size by producing more of its traditional product or by producing a new product in addition to the old. But the production of any product involves specialised knowledge, and vertical integration involves more acquisition of new specialised knowledge than expansion of existing product lines. Such knowledge acquisition is costly and these costs will increase the more new knowledge to be acquired; that is, the less related is the new knowledge to the firm's existing stock of knowledge and the more of it there is.

Generally speaking, the extent of knowledge associated with a production process will be positively related to the number of markets in which its inputs are acquired and its outputs sold. More efficient use of any market can be made by acquiring more knowledge of its supply and demand characteristics, and the more different inputs or outputs there are, the more such market knowledge must be acquired. Further, a production process involves interaction among inputs to produce outputs, and the more different inputs and outputs there are, the more complex these interactions are likely to be and hence the more knowledge required to direct the process. By implication, the greater the number of different inputs or outputs in two production processes, the more knowledge required to operate both efficiently, and hence the more costly their vertical integration.

## 5. A Proposition

We now offer a proposition concerning vertical integration. More vertical integration of production will occur the more costly is the use of markets relative to costs of non-specialisation and of firm size. Changes in the cost of using markets and changes in costs of managing additional assets or of acquiring more specialised information will change the gains relative to costs of vertical integration and hence the amount of integration that will occur. We proceed to draw implications of this proposition and to describe observable phenomena that would refute it.

If transactions in a particular market became more costly to carry out, more such transactions would be carried out within vertically integrated firms, and more transacting firms would vertically integrate. For example, if a government imposed price controls on a particular good, the cost of transacting for that good would rise. This is so because if the controls were effectively enforced, the good would be rationed according to non-price criteria and buyers would expend resources to develop such criteria. Further, it is probable that buyers and sellers would seek costly means to avoid the controls (e.g. tie-in sales), and would also expend resources to avoid detection by governmental authorities. If these arguments are correct, our proposition would be refuted if effective price controls over a good resulted in no increase in vertical integration in the market for that good.

A direct tax on transactions for a good would make those transactions more costly and hence would increase vertical integration among buyers and sellers of the good. Conversely, a tax on *not* transacting for the good in an open market (i.e. a tax on vertical integration) would lead to less vertical integration. The United States Congress has recently enacted a tax bill that repeals the oil and gas percentage depletion allowance for producers of oil who own over 50,000 barrels per day refining capacity or who control retail service stations, but exempts 2,000 barrels per day production from repeal for producers without such 'downstream' assets. Our proposition implies that such legislation will decrease vertical integration between producers and refiners or marketers of oil in the United States, and would be refuted if no such decrease occurs.

We have stated earlier that costs of using markets will rise the less predictable are market terms. One measure of predictability is the variance of a distribution of prices taken over time; the smaller this variance, the more predictable are prices. Our proposition implies that an increase in the variance of such a distribution will increase vertical integration; observation to the contrary would refute it.

Similarly, we argued that fixed market prices coupled with non-price rationing of positive excess demand or supply would impose costs on market transactors and that these costs would be greater the more specific complementary capital used with the good and the greater the costs of holding buffer stocks. This implies that the more often non-price rationing occurs in a market for a good, the greater the extent of this rationing; the more capital complementary to the good, the more specific this capital; and the greater the costs of holding inventories of the good, the more buyer–seller vertical integration. Evidence, say, that, all else equal, companies with more complementary capital integrated less into raw material supply than companies with less would refute the proposition. Similarly, evidence that, all else equal, companies bearing higher per unit raw material inventory costs integrated less than companies with lower per unit costs would refute it.

If costs of organising activity within a firm increase with firm size, then the cost of integration will rise with the scale of activities integrated. But if costs of using markets also rise with firm size, then size has an indeterminate effect on integration. Evidence below (p. 113) suggests that integration between crude oil production and refining increases with firm size, but we have no other data with which to estimate the relative magnitude of these costs.

Costs of non-specialisation will increase the more costly is the acquisition of knowledge required to operate efficiently in each of two successive production stages. We argued earlier that the cost of acquiring knowledge in a given stage is positively related to the number of distinct inputs or outputs in the production process. If this is so, our proposition would be refuted if more vertical integration occured among production processes using greater numbers of different inputs or producing more distinct outputs than among processes using or producing less. For example, the proposition would be refuted if manufacturing and retailing were integrated more where the manufacturers' product were a smaller portion of the retailer's total product line than where it is a larger portion. Similarly, we would expect less integration between input supply and manufacture where the particular input is but one of several input supplier outputs than where it is the sole output, and evidence to the contrary would refute the propostion.

## 6. Vertical Integration in the Oil Industry

We now turn to whether vertical integration in the oil industry can be plausibly explained by the industry's technical, cost and demand conditions. As noted earlier, we are ignoring monopoly pricing as a cause of vertical integration, and therefore assume openly competitive conditions.[16]

It will be useful to describe briefly the characteristics of oil industry investment.

Both the refining and pipeline transportation of oil involve large initial investments in specialised forms of capital that are long-lived and immobile. The initial cost of a refinery will vary with its size and location, but at present in the United States runs as much as $1,500 per barrel per day (b/d) of rated capacity. Thus, a refinery of 200,000 b/d capacity will cost roughly $300 million to construct, plus additional sums to operate.

Generally, the cheapest means of transporting crude oil from fields to refineries and oil products from refineries to market areas is by pipeline.[17] The cost of pipeline services will vary with the size of pipe and the length of line laid, so that no one cost figure is meaningful. However, it is not unusual for feeder lines to cost several millions of dollars, trunk lines in the hundreds of millions. Oil pipeline service is subject to large economies of scale, and by nature is specific both to oil and to the particular refineries, fields or market areas served.

Marketing facilities for oil products involve smaller capital investments than transportation or refining, but generally are specialised to oil. Some larger facilities such as pipeline terminals involve fairly large capital investments, and the development of a brand name for oil products such as gasoline and motor oil involves large-scale capital commitments.

The discovery and production of oil requires investment in leaseholdings and in drilling and production equipment. Lease costs vary with local conditions, such investment in the United States running anywhere up to $40,000 per acre. This investment, of course, is specific to a particular location. Drilling and production costs also vary with local conditions, several thousands of dollars sufficing to drill a shallow onshore well but many millions of dollars being necessary to conduct deep drilling under conditions such as the North Sea. In general, drilling and production equipment is specific to oil, but much of it is mobile and can be reused.

Both the supply of crude oil and the demand for oil products in an area are subject to variation over time. To some extent this variation is predictable, as with declining production rates from mature oil fields or seasonal demands for gasoline and heating oil, but each also contains stochastic elements. New discoveries of oil follow in somewhat unpredictable fashion from exploration activity, and it is also difficult to forecast supply changes caused by changes in recovery technology, natural disasters and changes in government policy. In addition, estimates of changes in demand through time and by region are subject to error because it is difficult to predict precisely such causal factors as future weather conditions or local economic conditions.

Stochastic supply-and-demand of crude oil inputs and product outputs is of particular consequence because of the industry's large, long-lived and immobile capital investments and because of the costs of oil inventories. Because much refinery and pipeline investment involves long-term capital commitments, unanticipated 'shortages' of crude oil and 'surpluses' of products significantly increase the long-run average cost per barrel refined or transported by pipeline. One means of economising costs of such unanticipated variation is to hold large oil inventories. But at present crude prices, the investment necessary to hold three months' stock of crude for a refinery of 100,000 b/d capacity would be about $100 million for the crude plus another $50 million or so for storage tanks, and the cost of storing products is higher. The magnitude of these investments makes it likely that oil companies will seek other means to economise costs of random variation in supply or demand.[18]

At least two other means are apparent: long-term contracts between refiners and crude oil suppliers and between refiners and marketers of oil products, and vertical integration of these industry stages. Long-term contracts will be the more costly to use the more negotiation, renegotiation and enforcement procedures these arrangements involve. Stochastic variation of crude and product supply and demand imply costly means to adjust within long-term contracts or adjustment of these contracts, and the greater the wealth consequences of this stochastic variation for the contracting parties, the more costly these adjustments will be. Since much investment in crude oil production, refining and product marketing involves capital which is specific to particular location and use, its commitment under contract implies negotiation costs to specify and respecify contractual conditions, and policing and enforcement costs to assure contractual compliance. The greater the capital invested the greater these various costs, and hence the greater the relative return to vertical integration.

Similar arguments apply to relationships between refiners and pipeline transportation suppliers. One means for refiners and pipeline suppliers to transact is for the former to advertise prices to be paid for transportation of given quality characteristics over specified routes and the latter to respond by offering such transportation. Because both refining and pipeline transportation involve investment of large sums in specific and immobile capital, contracts for such services would likely be long-term. But because of the sums of money at stake, each party would devote considerable resources to anticipating contingencies and negotiating contingency clauses, and to negotiating mechanisms to ensure enforcement of contractual agreement. The greater the magnitude of investment and the longer the time-period involved, the more costly such preparation and negotiation are likely to be. Vertical integration is a means to reduce the costs of negotiating and policing such contracts and of service delays while contract terms are being arranged or rearranged, and the greater the magnitude of investment and the longer the period and the contract is to cover, the greater the cost reduction such integration is likely to achieve.

In sum, we hypothesise that oil industry vertical integration is a means to economise costs of transacting arising from stochastic variation of input and output supply and demand and from large-scale investment in long-lived specific assets. But we asserted earlier that vertical integration in any industry is more costly the greater the degree of non-specialisation, defined in terms of the number of input and output markets involved. We proceed to draw implications of these hypotheses for the behaviour of firms in the oil industry.

Integration between oil transportation and other parts of the oil business is more likely the more specialised is transportation equipment to oil, because the more specialised this equipment the less the diseconomies from non-specialisation of knowledge. For example, though oil has been transported both by railroad and by pipeline, oil companies have integrated less into ownership of railroads than pipelines, and less into ownership of entire railroads than into rail tank cars (which are specialised to oil). The railroad business involves the transportation of many more goods than oil, and integration into railroading would require knowledge of many more transportation markets than are required to operate oil transportation pipelines or tank cars.

Earlier we asked why oil companies integrate more into retailing than do cigarette manufacturers. Oil and gas products comprise a greater percentage of all products sold by the retail establishments where they are offered than cigarettes where they are retailed, and hence vertical integration into cigarette retailing involves more additional knowledge and is the more costly of the two.

We also asked why oil refiners integrate more into oil pipeline ownership and operation than into refinery construction. We conjecture this is so because firms which build refineries also build other types of industrial complexes whereas pipeline operation is specific to oil. Because of this, integration into refinery construction would require more market knowledge for company survival than integration into pipeline operation.

If integration is a means to avoid costly non-price rationing, then companies which expect greater costs from such rationing and those which expect it to occur more frequently will more vertically integrate. Earlier we reported that the Exxon Corporation recently decided to integrate into the ownership of offshore mobile drilling rigs. According to a trade publication, the company is doing so 'to carry out a thorough, long-range exploration and development program without having to stand in line to lease drilling equipment'. The company's offshore exploration division manager is then quoted as stating that 'the availability of suitable mobile drilling rigs is potentially a major constraint facing operators' (*The Oil Daily*, 26 Feb. 1975, p. 1).

Finally, if the cost of transacting for crude oil rises relative to the cost of integration with the amount transacted per period, then firms with more refinery capacity will tend to integrate more, and firms that increase their refinery capacity will more than proportionately increase their owned crude oil production. The cost of transacting for oil will rise relative to the cost of integrating if, for example, there are constant marginal costs of transacting while marginal costs of integration decrease over some range because of 'set-up' or initial costs of acquiring the information necessary to take on a new line of business. Data produced by McLean and Haigh (1954, p. 43), and data gathered by the author but not reported here, tend to support the contention that production—refining integration is subject to decreasing cost relative to open-market transacting.[19]

## 7. The Simultaneous Existence of Integrated and Non-Integrated Oil Firms

An explanation of oil industry vertical integration should be able to explain why both integrated and non-integrated firms persist. If our propositions are not to be refuted, then some companies must face different costs and benefits of integration from others.

A simple explanation is that different directors of oil firms have different comparative advantages. In other words, some have better abilities to direct some particular phase of industry operations relative to their abilities to direct multiple phases than others. If this is so, then changes in the directorship of oil companies over time should result in their choosing different integration strategies, and companies should not change their strategy much during the tenure of any particular director.

An alternative possibility is that costs and gains to integration vary with local demand and supply conditions. Where oil suppliers or demanders are subject to common random forces, peak demands or supplies will coincide and 'shortages' or 'surpluses' and other inducements to integrate will occur. But where these peaks differ as among customers or suppliers there will be a higher return to trading with multiple partners and therefore the relative return to integration will fall.[20]

Still another alternative is that non-specialisation costs vary locally. For example, the specialised market information involved in retailing gasoline within a city (i.e. where to locate, what hours to operate, whom to employ) may be greater than that in retailing on an interstate throughway. If this is so, then more integration will occur among throughway gasoline retailers and refiners than among city retailers and refiners.

We cannot here pursue these explanations. Rather, we conclude that our explanation of oil industry vertical integration does not preclude the simultaneous existence of integrated and non-integrated firms.

## 8. Alternative Explanations of Oil Industry Vertical Integration

A number of previous studies have sought to explain vertical integration in the oil industry. We briefly describe these to determine whether they provide an alternative explanation to our own.

De Chazeau and Kahn (1959, p. 115) explain oil industry vertical integration in terms of 'assurance' of crude supplies and of market outlets. They write:

> the essence of integration . . . is the protection it offers or seems to offer against the uncertainties and instabilities of reliance on often highly imperfect intermediate markets. It is a means by which oil companies have attempted, in an industry that is potentially highly unstable, to stake out and insulate market positions by securing dependable sources of supply (of raw materials and products) and dependable market outlets (for crude oil and products) . . . The thrust, in short, has been market control.

Similarly, Frankel (1953) notes a tendency towards large-scale capital investment in refineries, and explains firm integration of production and refining as a means to increase the 'security' of continuous refinery operation via a balancing of crude supply and demand. One way of interpreting references to 'dependability', 'control' and 'security' is in terms of avoiding costly non-price rationing and contractual negotiation. If this is a correct interpretation, then the assertions are close to our own. But since neither study develops a calculus of the costs and benefits of dependability, control or security, they are more descriptions than explanations of oil industry integration.

By far the most comprehensive work on oil industry integration is that of McLean and Haigh (1954).[21] These authors trace the history of such integration, and develop three central theses why oil firms integrate. We discuss each in turn.

First, they argue that vertical integration is a source of risk reduction because profits in various phases of the industry are imperfectly correlated. Thus, vertical integration is argued to be a means to diversify a portfolio of oil industry assets.

Taken alone, this argument is unconvincing. It is unclear why investors would be better off allowing firm managers to diversify among phases of the oil industry than to do so themselves. There are transaction costs to investor diversification, but so too are there costs of company diversification. Further, it is unclear that investor diversification within the petroleum industry will reduce risk more efficiently than diversification between petroleum and other industries. Nevertheless, if there are other economies to vertical integration, risk reduction may provide positive value to oil industry investors.

Second, they argue that vertical integration in the oil industry reduces risk associated with investment in large-scale capital facilities such as refineries. The essence of the argument is given in the following quotation (McLean and Haigh, 1954, p. 665):

> Vertical integration represents a means of reducing the risks associated with refinery investments. . . . Integration forward into marketing activities constitutes one of the best means by which a refiner may guard against a forced reduction of throughput in times when the refined products markets are oversupplied and backward integration into crude oil production constitutes one of the best means by which a refiner may be assured of adequate oil supplies at reasonable prices in times of crude oil shortages. Similarly, integration into transportation operations constitutes one of the best means by which a refiner may be assured of having the transportation facilities necessary to his situation. For example, once a refinery location has developed economic characteristics which permit or require the use of pipelines to move crude oil inward, or refined products outward, a refiner often cannot afford to wait for the pipeline in-

vestments to be made by outside interests but must build the lines himself to keep his operations on a competitive basis.

Restated, the authors appear to be saying that the refining business is subject to costs associated with variation of supply or demand in crude and product markets, and that a refiner can economise such costs by integrating into crude production and marketing. Further, there are costs of delayed refinery pipeline investment, and these can be economised by the refiner owning and operating such pipelines rather than transacting for them. So restated, this explanation of the benefits of oil industry vertical integration is similar to our own. However, since McLean and Haigh do not discuss benefits of oil industry integration *relative to costs*, their statement provides little insight into conditions under which the industry would *not* be integrated.

The third reason given for integration is that 'planning' economies can be achieved These include-es crdination of investment mnong different levels of the business and the handling of logistics of oil processing in the face of changing market demand conditions. Reinterpreted, market transactions could    used to co-ordinate investments and to alter product mix in the face of changing demand conditions, but in the oil industry the costs of so transacting can be reduced by co-ordinating such information within the firm. Our comment above pertains: there may be benefits to investment co-ordination within a firm, but without conditions under which these benefits exceed costs, we do not have an explanation of integration.

Finally, Cross (1953) ascribes many of the same advantages to vertical integration as McLean and Haigh. He attributes to integration better control over logistics to meet seasonal and cyclical demand shifts, diversification of risk, planning and co-ordination economies, and savings in transactions costs of distributing products. Disadvantages of integration are described in terms of gains from specialisation. For example, independent distributors are in a better position to gain information concerning local market conditions, including customer preferences and relative credit riskiness, and there is less need for the filing of operating data with a central organisation (an economy of smaller size). This description of advantages and disadvantages of integration provides insight into several aspects of the industry, but it is not a general explanation of the extent and type of vertical integration that occurs.

## 9. Concluding Remarks

Finally, a few words pertinent to the current international petroleum situation. We shall try to use the material developed above to say something about the future of vertical integration in world oil markets.

There have been two major developments in world oil markets in the past few years. First, the Organisation of Petroleum Exporting Countries has managed a substantial increase in the world price of crude oil. And second, in several countries oil-producing properties once owned by integrated private oil firms have been taken over by local governments. These developments have caused a disequilibrium concerning industry vertical integration. For a number of reasons, such integration can be expected to increase.

Consider first the rise in price. Because this rise is caused by monopoly restrictions on the supply of crude oil, there is inducement for refiners and users of oil products both to acquire producing oil properties and to search for new sources. This acquisition and search will result in greater integration of oil use and production. A further effect results from the higher cost of holding oil inventories. Since the holding of inventories is an alternative to vertical integration, the higher this cost the relatively more attractive is vertical integration and the more integration will occur.

The takeover of producing oil properties by host governments has several consequences for integration. First, in so far as producing country governments export oil according to political rather than market criteria, refiners and distributors face additional uncertainty concerning future oil prices and availability. This additional uncertainty will induce backward integration into crude oil production. Second, the takeovers have increased transactions among independent organisations based in different countries. There are few legal means to enforce international contracts, and the weaker are contractual alternatives the greater the gains to integration. Third, if integration achieves real economies, then national as well as private companies will be induced to undertake it. Since our analysis suggests there are real economies to integration, we predict that the national oil companies of the OPEC and other oil-producing countries will integrate from production into exploration, refining, transportation and distribution.[22] Further, since a principal cost of integration is the cost of acquiring market knowledge, we expect more integration and integration more quickly by countries whose civil servants are more experienced in dealing in oil. This explains, for example, why the British National Oil Corporation is to be set up initially as a holding company of producing properties, but will have powers to extend its activities ultimately to become a fully integrated company.[23]

In sum, the future of worldwide oil industry vertical integration is bright. Since such integration will probably conserve real resources, there is reason to applaud. But since the sources of the integration imply economic inefficiencies, the applause should be muted. And if present United States policy towards integration is continued, our hands should remain still.

## Notes

1. U.S. Congress (1974).
2. For example, H.R. 309 and H.R. 310, both introduced as of 14 January 1975, would divorce the marketing of petroleum products from their production, refining and transportation, and would divorce the pipeline transportation of oil from pipeline

ownership. In addition, H.R. 5213 of 1975 would prohibit oil and natural-gas companies from engaging in more than one phase of their industries.

3. F. T. C. Docket No. 8934, in the matter of Exxon *et al.* According to newspaper sources, the F.T.C. staff contemplates divesdture of refining and certain transportation operations by the companies as a method of relief.

4. The tax legislation is the Tax Reduction Act of 1975. This Act completely repealed the oil depletion allowance for integrated firms but only partially repealed it for non-integrated. The proposed price-control legislation would slightly weaken controls over natural gas discovered after 1 January 1975 if produced by a non-integrated firm, but would maintain a strict ceiling price of 75¢ per thousand cubic feet if produced by an integrated oil or gas firm. As at the time of writing this paper, the legislation had passed a Committee of the U.S. Senate and will come to that body for a vote (*Wall Street Journal*, 7 May 1975, p. 2).

5. See especially Edwards (1953) and Mueller (1969).

6. See, for example, Spengler (1950), Liebeler (1968), Bork (1969), Peltzman (1969), Vernon and Graham (1971) and, with some qualification, Schmalensee (1973 and Warren-Boulton (1974).

7. M. L. Burstein attempted to provide such a basis in 1968. Cf. M. L. Burstein, *Economic Theory* (London: Wiley, 1968) pp. 171–2. Consider an industry subject to continual perturbation so that it normally is off its equilibrium course. Quoted prices then normally would pertain to what Hicks has called 'false trading'. One might observe non-integrated firms employing 'a non-optimal programme except in full equilibrium when, ideally, the competitive-market processes solve the dual and, hence, the primal problem or problems'. Ibid., p. 172. (Editor's note.)

8. See Frankel (1953) and De Chazeau and Kahn (1959, esp. pp. 102–4) for arguments to this effect concerning vertical integration in the oil industry.

9. The U.S. Congress has investigated whether over the past few years non-integrated marketers of petroleum products were deprived of their 'rightful' market share. The General Accounting Office, an investigative arm of the Congress, was requested to determine changes in the market position of these non-integrated retailers with an eye to possible legislative remedy. Putting the matter in terms of conditions under which vertical integration is more or less viable might reveal that temporal changes in relative market shares of integrated and non-integrated firms can be the result of competitive market forces rather than of monopolistic control over resources.

10. Stigler (1951, p. 190).

11. However, Exxon recently announced a decision to integrate into the ownership of offshore mobile drilling rigs. The reason for this will be explored below.

12. Adelman measured vertical integration via the ratio of value added to sales. A company that produced all its own inputs would show a ratio of 1; companies buying some of these inputs, lower ratios. But the measure is marred because it is affected by whether integration occurs backwards towards raw resource production or forwards towards marketing, and by other factors (see Barnes, 1955).

13. The most complete discussion of these issues to date is contained in Weston and Peltzman (1969, section IV, pp. 139–76).

14. This point is developed by Alchian and Allen (1969, pp. 156–7). Its application to labour markets is examined by Gordon (1974).

15. In the United States oil industry, firms that are integrated from crude oil production through product marketing are larger than non-integrated firms by virtually any measure.

16. Vertical integration in the industry predates the emergence of OPEC as an effective cartel body. A number of studies have empirically tested whether the United States oil industry is competitive (see McKie, 1967; Erickson and Spann, 1974a, 1974b; Mitchell, 1974). The evidence of these studies is consistent with the assertion that the industry is competitive. Also, Duchesneau (1975) summarised the findings of a Ford Foundation study of United States energy markets by concluding that government policies

have had anti-competitive effects in the oil market, but that the conduct and perfor-mance of firms in that market is consistent with competitive behaviour.
17. Of course, for transocean transportation tankers are cheaper.
18. At historically lower prices for crude, inventory costs were lower. But the storage of large oil quantities in steel tanks has always been an expensive proposition. This is probably the chief reason why oil futures markets have not prospered.
19. The data referred to are company United States refinery capacity and United States crude oil production in 1950 and 1973. Ratios of crude production to refining capacity by size category of refining showed generally increasing numbers with capacity. McLean and Haigh's data were gathered by survey, the author's from publicly available sources.
20. Frankel (1953, p. 120) reasons along these lines to explain independent suppliers of oil tankers. It may also explain why there are independent oil drilling services, seismic survey services, etc.
21. McLean apparently understood something of what he studied. Professor of Business Administration at Harvard University when the study was undertaken, he later became the Chief Executive Officer and Chairman of the Board of the Continental Oil Co., presently the sixteenth largest United States firm (by 1974 sales).
22. The prediction is safe. There already exist fully integrated national oil companies (e.g. PEMEX, ENI, ELF ERAP), and the Norwegian government intends that Statoil, its newly set-up state oil corporation, should become fully integrated (see Dam, 1974, p. 235).
23. Reported in Dam (1974, p. 247).

## References

Adelman, M. A. (1955). 'Concept and Statistical Measurement of Vertical Integration', in *Business Concentration and Price Policy* (Princeton: Princeton Univ. Press, for National Bureau of Economic Research).

Alchian, A. A. and Allen, W. R. (1969). *Exchange and Production: Theory in Use* (Belmont, Calif.: Wadsworth Publishing Co)

Arrow, K. J. (1975). 'Vertical Integration and Communication'. *Bell Journal of Economics*, VI (1), 173–83.

Barnes, I. R. (1955). 'Comment' on 'Concept and Statistical Measurement of Vertical Integration' by M. A. Adelman, in *Business Concentration and Price Policy* (Princeton: Princeton Univ. Press, for National Bureau of Economic Research pp. 322–30.

Bork, R. H. (1969). 'Vertical Integration and Competitive Processes', in J. F. Weston and S. Pelzman (eds.), *Public Policy Towards Mergers* (Pacific Palisades, Calif.: Goodyear Publishing Co.) p. 139.

Coase, R. H. (1937). 'The Nature of the Firm'. *Economica*, IV, 386; reprinted in G. J. Stigler and K. E. Boulding (eds.), *Readings in Price Theory* (Homewood, Ill.: 1952) p. 331.

Cross, J. S. (1953). 'Vertical Integration in the Oil Industry'. *Harvard Business Review*, XXXI (4), 69–81.

Dam, K. W. (1974). 'The Evolution of North Sea Licensing Policy in Britain and Norway', *Journal of Law and Economics*, XVII (2), 213–63.

De Chazeau, M. and Kahn, A. E. (1973). *Integration and Competition in the Petroleum Industry* (Port Washington, N.Y.: Kennekat Press).

Duchesneau, T. D. (1975). *Competition in the U.S. Energy Industry*, a Report to the Energy Policy Project of the Ford Foundation (Cambridge, Mass.: Ballinger Publishing Co.).

Edwards, C. D. (1953). 'Vertical Integration and the Monopoly Problem', *Journal of*

*Marketing*, XVII, 404–10; reprinted in Werner Sichel (ed.), *Industrial Organization and Public Policy* (Boston: Houghton Mifflin, 1967).

Erickson, E. W. and Spann, R. W. (1974*a*). 'The U.S. Petroleum Industry', in E. W. Erickson and L. Waverman (eds.), *The Energy Question: An International Failure of Policy* (Toronto: Univ. of Toronto Press).

Erickson, E. W. and Spann, R. W. (1974*b*). 'An Analysis of the Competitive Implications of the Profitability of the Petroleum Industry with Special Reference to the Comparison Between the Cost of Equity Capital and the Rate of Return Earned on Stockholders' Equity', in *Market Performance and Competition in the Petroleum Industry*. Hearings before the Special Subcommittee on Integrated Oil Operations of the U.S. Senate Committee on Interior and Insular Affairs, 93rd Congress, 2nd Session (Washington, D.C.: Government Printing Office) pp. 1756–95.

Frankel, P. H. (1953). 'Integration in the Oil Industry'. *Journal of Industrial Economics*, II, 202–11.

Gordon, D. F. (1974). 'A Neo-Classical Theory of Keynesian Unemployment', *Economic Inquiry*, XII (4), 431–59.

Green, J. R. (1974). 'Vertical Integration and Assurance of Markets'. Discussion Paper No. 383 (Cambridge, Mass.: Harvard Institute of Economic Research).

Liebeler, W. J. (1968). 'Toward a Consumer's Antitrust Law: The Federal Trade Commission and Vertical Mergers in the Cement Industry', *U.C.L.A. Law Review*, XV (4).

McKie, J. W. (1967). 'Incentives for Sound Growth: Gas Price Regulation', in S. H. Hanke and S. L. Gardner (eds.), *Essays in Petroleum Economics* (Golden, Colo.) p. 144.

McLean, J. and Haigh, R. (1954). *The Growth of the Integrated Oil Companies* (Cambridge, Mass.: Harvard Univ. Press).

Mitchell, E. J. (1974). *U.S. Energy Policy: A Primer* (Washington, D.C.: American Enterprise Institute).

Mueller, W. F. (1969). 'Public Policy Towards Vertical Mergers', in J. F. Weston and S. Peltzman (eds.), *Public Policy Towards Mergers* (Pacific Palisades, Calif.: Goodyear Publishing Co.) pp. 150–66.

Peltzman, S. (1969). 'Issues in Vertical Integration Policy', in J. F. Weston and S. Peltzman (eds.), *Public Policy Towards Mergers* (Pacific Palisades, Calif.: Goodyear Publishing Co.) p. 167.

Schmalensee, R. (1973). 'A Note on the Theory of Vertical Integration', *Journal of Political Economy*, LXXXI, 442.

Spengler, J. J. (1950). 'Vertical Integration and Antitrust Policy', *Journal of Political Economy*, LVIII, 347–58.

Stigler, G. J. (1951). 'The Division of Labor is Limited by the Extent of the Market', *Journal of Political Economy*, LIX, 185–93.

U.S. Congress (1974). Senate Committee on Interior and Insular Affairs, Special Subcommittee on Integrated Oil Operations, *Market Performance and Competition in the Petroleum Industry*. Hearings, 93rd Congress, 2nd Session (Washington, D.C.: Government Printing Office).

Vernon, J. M. and Graham, D. A. (1971). 'Profitability of Monopolization by Vertical Integration', *Journal of Political Economy*, LXXIX, 924–5.

Warren-Boulton, F. R. (1974). 'Vertical Control and Variable Proportions', *Journal of Political Economy*, LXXXII (4), 783–802.

Weston, J. F. and Peltzman, S. (eds.) (1969). *Public Policy Towards Mergers* (Pacific Palisades, Calif.: Goodyear Publishing Co.).

Williamson, O. E. (1971). 'The Vertical Integration of Production: Market Failure Considerations', *American Economic Review*, LXI (2), 112.

# 11 The Macroeconomic Effects of the Higher Oil Price

## J. R. SARGENT

What happens when a powerful group contributing to the output of an economy seeks to appropriate to itself a larger proportion of that output than it has previously been receiving? The question seems to many to have direct relevance both to the domestic situation in the United Kingdom in recent years and to the international economy since the rise in the price of oil induced by OPEC at the end of 1973. For this reason, it may be useful to approach the macroeconomic analysis of the effects of the rise in the price of oil via the rather better-explored territory of 'wage-push' in the domestic setting. The analogy lends itself readily because we are concerned with the effects of the rise in the price of oil on the world economy at large; we can therefore assume the kind of closed economy which features in most analyses of 'wage-push', avoiding the complications which the latter encounter when foreign trade has to be brought into the picture. It is not intended to suggest that the autonomous increases in money wages which adherents of 'wage-push' believe to be the prime mover in the United Kingdom's inflation in recent years can be ascribed to concerted action of the sort taken by the oil producers' cartel. Nor do we mean to deny that either autonomous 'wage-push' by trade unions in the domestic setting, or the oil producers' concerted action, may be explicable in terms of the desire to recoup earlier losses of relative real income experienced for reasons outside their control. We intend simply to trace the consequences of a decision taken at a point in time by an important productive agent to bid for a higher share of a given level of output of the economy (of the United Kingdom, of the world) as its reward for what it contributes to that output. We begin, then, with trade unions pushing for higher money wages in a closed economy, intending later to interpret the model as one of the world economy in which the part of trade unions is played by OPEC.

So we imagine an economy with the following characteristics:

1.  Money wages are autonomously determined by trade unions. The existence and extent of excess supply or demand in the labour market have no direct or systematic influence on the size of the money

wage, although these factors will no doubt enter with others into
what the trade unions autonomously decide this is to be.

2. The actual level of employment is determined by the employers'
   demand for labour. The latter varies inversely with the real wage;
   higher money wages, at a given price level, cause employment to be
   contracted because at the margin it becomes unprofitable to maintain it. The state of demand for goods and services makes its impact on the demand for labour via the prices at which goods and
   services can be sold. A higher price level, with given money wages,
   increases the demand for labour (also, it may be added, might reduce the supply); and this raises the question whether the actual
   level of employment may sometimes fail to conform to what employers
   want. This possibility we are able to ignore because, as it turns out,
   the operation of the model in response to 'wage-push' takes it only
   to lower, and never into higher, levels of the demand for labour
   than the original equilibrium, in which we take the demand to be
   satisfied.

3. The possibility that the demand for labour at a given real wage
   might increase as a result of increasing productivity of labour,
   owing to capital accumulation or technical progress, is excluded.
   The model is static and short-term; output is determined by employment.

4. The demand for goods and services, in real terms, reacts to the
   traditionally Keynesian variables such as the level of real income
   (or output) and interest rates, but also in monetaristic style to the
   real value of the stock of money. The interest rates which affect
   demand in a model of ongoing inflation should in principle be real
   rather than nominal; but this raises complications which it is convenient to treat as flavouring rather than as ingredients of the
   model. We do, however, include real wages as a specific influence
   on demand; a higher real wage, at a given level of output, means
   a distribution of income more favourable to labour, and this may
   affect the demand for goods and services. The redistribution
   effect is worth isolating in the domestic 'wage-push' situation particularly because it is the basis of the argument that money wage
   increases may be needed at certain times in order to reflate the
   economy. But it is especially relevant to the oil case, when the
   consequences of a redistribution of income brought about by a rise
   in the price of oil may be significantly different.

5. Interest rates are conflated into a single, nominal rate, which is
   determined by the supply of and demand for money balances. The
   former is autonomously determined; the latter by the level of
   money income and the interest rate itself, but without any special
   Keynesian assumptions about the interest-elasticity of the demand
   for money.

The model embodying these characteristics is formally set out and operated in the Appendix.

Now consider the repercussions of a decision by trade unions to seek a higher real wage, at the going level of employment, through the agency of an autonomous increase in money wages; and bear in mind that we shall later be wishing to transform this into a decision by OPEC to seek a higher real price of oil, at the going level of output, via an increase in its money price. We trace the repercussions through three stages. In the first stage we consider the balance of supply and demand in the market for goods and services before any adjustment of their prices has taken place. We must not imagine that this adjustment happens automatically. Our model neither requires nor invokes any kind of 'cost-plus' method of pricing by the suppliers of goods and services. The question we ask of it is rather: 'does the autonomous increase in money wages introduce a disequilibrium into the balance of supply and demand for goods and services, at their original prices, such as to bring about a market situation in which those prices must be forced upwards?' We find that it does. On the supply side, the increase in money wages at the going price level reduces the amount of employment offered and therefore the level of output. Provided the marginal propensity to spend is less than unity — an assumption which we make for the time being, but will later qualify— the reduction in output is greater than the consequential reduction of demand, so that the net effect so far is the emergence of excess demand. But this excess demand is enhanced by two factors operating on the demand side. First, wage-earners get a bigger share of real income, and since they are commonly supposed to enjoy a higher marginal propensity to consume than non-wage-earners, the demand for consumer goods rises. (The effect on the demand for investment goods we take to be neutral; it is equally encouraged by the higher cost of labour and discouraged by the reduced flow of profits.) Secondly, the lower transactions demand for cash balances reduces interest rates and stimulates both consumption and investment demand. From all these effects, it follows that the introduction of a higher money wage generates excess demand for goods and services, and creates the conditions under which an upward adjustment of prices can take place.

The second stage of the process sees the adjustment take place, while money wages remain at the higher level to which they were autonomously lifted in the first stage. As prices rise, the excess demand is bled out of the system. This happens partly because the upward movement of prices begins to cancel some of the increase in the real wages, and to reverse the downward movement of interest rates, which occurred in the first stage. But another factor which comes into operation to reduce the excess of demand over output is the fall in the real value of cash balances—since we hold their nominal value constant. The upward movement of prices continues until no excess demand is left to drive them further up. The process is illustrated in Figs. 1(a), 1(b) and 1(c) of the Appendix.

At the end of the second stage, the net result will be to leave the real wage higher than it was before the beginning of the first stage. This can be demonstrated by imagining what would be the case if somehow or other the price level were to have increased in the second stage in full proportion to the original increase in money wages. Compared with the situation before this increase autonomously occurred, real wages would be unchanged; hence employment and output would be unchanged. But demand would be lower, because the higher price level would have raised interest rates, through the transactions demand for cash balances, and lowered the real value of the latter. There would therefore be excess supply in the event that prices rose in proportion to money wages, just as there would be excess demand if prices rose not at all. It follows that equilibrium will be restored in the market for goods and services if and only if prices rise to some positive extent which is less than the autonomous increase in money wages. Since this involves an increase in real wages, it also means a fall in employment and output. The absolute size of the fall will always be greater, the smaller is the demand effect of the redistribution of income in favour of wage-earners brought about by the wage increase, and the greater is the marginal propensity to spend; for these factors reduce the scale of the excess demand which the wage increase generates and therefore the scale of the subsequent price rise required to eliminate it.

A third stage may now ensue in which the government, being inclined or committed to the maintenance of full — interpreted to mean the former level of — employment, and observing that a lapse from it has occurred, will step in to expand demand and the money supply. This allows prices to rise further than they have done by the end of the second stage; and when they have risen to the full extent of the autonomous wage increase, the former level of employment is regained. But paradise regained is also paradise lost; for the return to the original level of employment is the result of a return to the original real wage; and the unions' original aim to raise the real wage has been frustrated. Out of this frustration springs the renewal of 'wage-push', and the persistence of the inflationary process.

In my view some such mechanism as this has been at work in the economy of the United Kingdom in recent years. Compared with the monetarist hypothesis that money wages have been dragged up in the wake of price increases engendered by an excessive creation of credit, it seems more consistent with the observed trend of a rising share of wages in the national income. But this is not the place to argue this interpretation of the United Kingdom's recent economic history. The intention is merely to present a plausible and analytically familiar mechanism which may help us to consider the actions of OPEC and their consequences. We now therefore paint OPEC into the place hitherto filled by trade unions in the picture presented.

If we were simply to repeat the old story in the new context, it would

run as follows. The immediate effect of the rise in the price of oil is to make some marginal uses of oil unprofitable, so that the world's output of goods and services is cut back. But world demand is cut by less than output; and at the same time it is stimulated by the redistribution of real income away from the rich oil-consuming countries, and by the fall in interest rates which accompanies the fall in income. Hence there is excess demand for goods and services which causes non-oil prices to follow the price of oil upwards. Thus the objective of OPEC to achieve a higher real price of oil is at least partially frustrated. It may even by wholly frustrated, if the world's governments allow the world stock of money to expand in such a way as to create sufficient additional demand — a process assisted by the redepositing of currency surpluses of oil-producing countries in the financial centres of the oil consumers, so that they are added to the former's reserves without being deducted from the latter's. In these ways the increase in the price of oil could be shown to give another twist to world inflation to a smaller or larger degree.

But of course the old story cannot be reiterated word for word with the simple substitution of 'OPEC' for 'trade unions'. For at least in the first half of 1974, following the big rise in the price of oil, there were certain distinguishing features attending the 'OPEC price-push' which might have led to a result very different from that of 'union wage-push'. The first of these was that the redistribution of income in the world effected by the rise in the price of oil was towards economies with a relatively low marginal propensity to spend. This was partly because the sheer size of the redistribution to oil producers, and the fact that it was skewed towards those like Saudi Arabia and the Gulf States with relatively small populations, made it impossible for them to respond in the short run with more than a limited addition to their demands for goods and services either internally or from abroad. In the not so short run their income elasticities of demand are proving unexpectedly resilient; but in 1974 the redistribution of income tended to reduce demand rather than, as in the 'union wage-push' case, to increase it. In the second place, the fall in interest rates, which in the basic model was supposed to occur in response to the decline in economic activity, was muted in 1974 by the monetary restraints being applied in most of the economies of the oil consumers for anti-inflationary purposes. The effect was aggravated because the weight of OPEC financial surpluses seeking relatively liquid investment bore down on short-term interest rates rather than on the long-term rates which would have been most relevant to stimulating fixed investment. Thus the creation of extra demand via financial markets was relatively weak in the particular circumstances of the OPEC case. A third peculiarity of this case can also be discerned. The uncertainties brought into the world economy by the unprecedented rise in the price of oil were superimposed upon those already present and associated with the incipient end of an unusually inflationary boom. Given the lack of confidence and the fear of a deep and prolonged recession, it was likely that an initial fall in economic activity in the world of 1974 would lead to an unusually large consequential fall in both consumption and investment demand, and a preference for the accumulation of liquid assets despite the inflationary situation. In other words, the marginal propensity to spend was probably rather high, and could have exceeded unity.

In these peculiar circumstances of 1974, following the rise in the price of oil, the model might have worked in a different way from the one we sketched in the 'union wage-push' case, and show in Figs. 1(*a*), 1(*b*) and 1(*c*) of the Appendix. These circumstances would certainly operate to reduce the size of the excess demand created in the first stage of the adjustment. But they could have done more; they might actually have turned it into excess supply. Such a result might have flowed from the combined effect of the oil price rise redistributing income, at a given level of activity, to those less inclined to spend it; of a tendency, as economic activity fell, for demand to fall even more rapidly; and of the failure of monetary influences to generate enough countervailing demand. Thus the prices of other goods and services might not merely have responded very little to the rise in the price of oil, but might actually have fallen—as actually occurred for some commodities. In the latter case the initial or primary increase in the real price of oil as its money price was autonomously raised would lead on to a secondary increase in its real price as the general world price level fell. (This is illustrated in Figs. 2(*a*) and 2(*b*) of the Appendix). The larger the total increase in the real price of oil, the less profitable its marginal uses become and, at least in the short run, the larger the contraction in world output and correspondingly in the demand for oil itself.

There is a more frightening possibility. In the circumstances which bring it about that the rise in the price of oil actually reduces the demand for goods and services in the world economy by more than it reduces the output – that is, circumstances combining a low marginal propensity to spend, a negative effect on demand of the redistribution of income, and weak monetary stimulants – it is possible that the consequential fall in the world price level could even aggravate the excess supply situation, so that the fall in the price level becomes self-reinforcing. (This is illustrated in Fig. 3 of the Appendix.) In this case of an unstable equilibrium, the rise in the price of oil could plunge the world economy into a severe recession, which would end only when the real value of the world stock of money had been sufficiently increased by the falling price level to mop up the deficient demand, or alternatively when the fall in the demand for oil itself built up pressures within the oil cartel to reverse the price rise which had brought matters to such a pass.

It is possible that the model working in the ways described in the last two paragraphs may illuminate and help to explain the relative severity of the 1974–5 recession, the damping of the world rate of inflation despite the large increase in the money price of oil, and the success of OPEC in achieving a substantial increase in the real price of oil, rather than finding itself largely thwarted in this aim, as it would be normal to expect, by market forces inducing an adjustment of the world price level.

But this *modus operandi* of the model may be only for a short term which is already passing. In the longer term, it seems likely that the redistribution of income to the oil producers from the oil price rises of 1973–5 will actually turn out to be a redistribution in favour of countries which do have a relatively high, rather than a relatively low, marginal propensity to spend. This is less obvious when we consider the shift of income to the oil producers, not from the developed countries, but from the non-oil-producing developing countries, which presumably have a very high marginal propensity to spend. But the adjustment forced upon the non-oil developing countries will be reduced by the unexpectedly large scale of the aid commitments entered into by OPEC countries. The current build-up of OPEC imports suggests that the readjustment of the parameters of the model from their magnitude immediately following the rise in the price of oil may well be complete in the medium term, say two or three years from now rather than longer. As that readjustment completes itself, the model will begin to operate in a way directly analogous to the 'union wage-push' case, in which an autonomous increase in money wages generates the excess demand which causes the subsequent increase to prices – and by doing so thwarts, and provokes a repetition of, the initial push for higher real income.

But the period during which the OPEC countries will be reverting towards a relatively high propensity to spend – the next few years – will also be the period which sees the coming to fruition of the government measures of monetary and fiscal expansion now almost universally adopted to counter the recession. These autonomous stimuli to world demand – corresponding to the third stage of the inflationary process which we described for the domestic economy under 'wage-push' – will add to the stimulus from the build-up of the demand for goods and services in the OPEC countries. The coincidence of these stimuli will perhaps be reinforced by yet another, which has not hitherto entered our model: the heavy investment in alternative sources of energy induced by the increase in the real price of oil from OPEC. Thus we shall have experienced a sequence of events in which the initial slackness of the demand for goods and services in OPEC aggravated the recession; the recession made it necessary for the industrial countries to stimulate domestic demand; and the stimuli made their impact at the very time when OPEC's demand for goods and services was changing from sluggish to torrential. Under this double dynamic, the 1977–8 boom may be difficult to contain. The rise in the price of oil which OPEC brought about at the end of 1973 will turn out not merely to have made the 1974–5 recession deeper than it would otherwise have been, but also to have made the subsequent expansion sharper and even more inflationary. Will the awareness of the possibility enable the world to avert it?

## APPENDIX

The model of 'wage-push' which lies behind the argument is as follows. The economy consists of three markets: for goods and services, for labour, and for interest-bearing bonds. Settlements are in non-interest-bearing cash, and the sum of the excess demands in the three markets must equal the excess supply of cash. It is convenient (and more familiar) to refer explicitly to the properties of the supply and demand functions for cash in place of those for interest-bearing bonds. We therefore set out briefly what we consider these properties to be for goods and services, labour and cash.

A. *Goods and Services*

$$\text{Demand} = D = D\left(Y, \frac{\overline{W}}{p}, r, \frac{\overline{M}}{p}\right) \tag{1}$$

$$\text{Output} = Y = Y(N) \tag{2}$$

where   $D$ = aggregate demand (for consumption and investment) in real terms;
   $Y$ = aggregate actual (observed) real output;
   $N$ = aggregate actual (observed) employment;
   $W$ = money wage rate;
   $p$ = price level of goods and services;
   $r$ = nominal rate of interest on bonds;
   $M$ = supply of cash.

The bars on $W$ and $M$ indicate that we take them to be autonomously determined. The real wage is included as an argument in the demand function as well as real output in order to allow for the influence on the demand for goods and services of changes in the distribution of income between wages and other incomes. Aggregate demand is allowed to be influenced not only by the 'Keynesian'-type variables $Y$ and $\overline{W}/p$, but also by the 'monetarist' real value of cash balances $\overline{M}/p$. Output obeys a short-run production function which ignores the influence of technical progress and changes in the capital stock.

The presumed signs of the partial derivatives are:

$$D_Y > 0, D_{\overline{w}/p} > 0, D_r < 0, D_{\overline{M}/p} > 0; \ Y_N > 0, \ Y_{NN} < 0.$$

B. *Labour*

We assume that the actual level of employment is determined by employers, who choose it in such a way as to equate the value of the marginal product of labour with the autonomously determined money wage:

$$Y_N = \frac{\overline{W}}{p} \tag{3}$$

There is in principle a supply of labour, presumably influenced by the real wage, which could thwart the employers' choice. We assume, however, that within the range of values of the real wage which the working of the model encompasses, there is always a positive margin of the supply of labour over the level of employment which the employers choose, so that the latter can always determine the actual level of employment. Since the money wage is autonomously determined, it is not influenced by the excess of the supply of labour over actual employment. Clearly there are levels of the excess at which this assumption will fail, but the purpose of the model is to trace what happens to the economy as long as it holds — in particular, to the level of employment and unemployment in conditions of autonomous 'wage-push' — and how the monetary authorities may react to what happens.

## C. *Cash balances*

$$\text{Demand:} \quad L = L(pY, r) \tag{4a}$$

$$\text{Supply:} \quad M = \bar{M} \tag{4b}$$

$M$ and $L$ are expressed in money terms, and the signs of the partial derivatives are: $L_{pY} > 0$, $L_r < 0$. It is convenient to suppose that equilibrium always prevails in this market, namely:

$$L = M \tag{4c}$$

We can then treat cash balances in terms of a single equation:

$$\bar{M} = L(pY, r) \tag{4}$$

The model as specified in the four equations (1) to (4) has five variables: $D$, $Y$, $N$, $p$ and $r$. It can, of course, be closed by imposing on the market for goods and services the equilibrium condition:

$$Y = D$$

and evaluating the total derivatives which emerge. But one of the possibilities in which we are interested is that of unstable equilibrium, which makes this procedure inappropriate. Instead we shall use eqs (1) to (4) as specified to discover the way in which the balance of output and demand for goods and services is changed by changes in the autonomous elements $\bar{W}$ and $\bar{M}$, and by the changes in the endogenous variable $p$ which we presume to react to this balance. Differentiating (1) to (4) we have:

$$dD = D_Y dY + D_{\bar{W}/p} \, d(W/p) + D_r dr + D_{\bar{M}/p} \, d(\bar{M}/p) \tag{1a}$$

$$dY = Y_N dN \tag{2a}$$

$$Y_{NN} dN = d(\bar{W}/p) \tag{3a}$$

$$d\bar{M} = L_{pY}d(pY) + L_r dr \tag{4a}$$

Eliminating $r$ and $N$, we find:

$$dD = \left[\frac{D_Y\bar{W}}{Y_{NN}p} + D_{\bar{W}/p} - \frac{D_r L_{pY}}{L_r Y_{NN}}\bar{W}\right]\frac{1}{p}d\bar{W}$$

$$- \left[\frac{D_Y\bar{W}}{Y_{NN}p} + D_{\bar{W}/p} - \frac{D_r L_{pY}}{L_r Y_{NN}}\bar{W} + D_{\bar{M}/p}\frac{\bar{M}}{W} + D_r L_{pY}Y_p{}^2\right]\frac{W}{p^2}dp$$

$$+ \left[\frac{D_r}{L_r} + D_{\bar{M}/p}\frac{1}{p}\right]dM \tag{5}$$

$$dY = \left[\frac{\bar{W}}{Y_{NN}p}\right]\frac{1}{p}\,d\bar{W}$$

$$- \left[\frac{\bar{W}}{Y_{NN}p}\right]\frac{\bar{W}}{p^2}\,dp \tag{6}$$

Hence for the change in excess demand:

$$dD - dY = \left[\frac{(D_Y - 1)}{Y_{NN}p}\bar{W} + D_{\bar{W}/p} - \frac{D_r L_{pY}}{L_r Y_{NN}}\bar{W}\right]\frac{1}{p}\,d\bar{W}$$

$$- \left[\frac{(D_Y - 1)}{Y_{NN}p}\bar{W} + D_{\bar{W}/p} - \frac{D_r L_{pY}}{L_r Y_{NN}}\bar{W} + D_{\bar{M}/p}\frac{\bar{M}}{W} + \frac{D_r L_{pY}Y_p{}^2}{L_r}\frac{\bar{W}}{W}\right]\frac{\bar{W}}{p^2}\,dp$$

$$+ \left[\frac{D_r}{L_r} + D_{\bar{M}/p}\frac{1}{p}\right]d\bar{M} \tag{7}$$

To isolate the primary effects of 'wage-push', we shall set $d\bar{M} = 0$; that is, we consider what would be the effect of an autonomous increase in money wages if the supply of cash were held constant. Let us then write (5) to (7) as:

$$dD = A\,d\bar{W} - (A + B)\frac{W}{p}\,dp \tag{5a}$$

$$dY = C\,d\bar{W} - C\frac{W}{p}\,dp \tag{6a}$$

$$dD - dY = (A - C)\,d\bar{W} - (A + B - C)\frac{\bar{W}}{p}\,dp \tag{7a}$$

where

$$A = \left[\frac{D_Y\bar{W}}{Y_{NN}p} + D_{\bar{W}/p} - \frac{D_r L_{pY}}{L_r Y_{NN}}\right]\frac{1}{p}$$

$$B = \left[ D_{\bar{M}/p} \frac{\bar{M}}{W} + \frac{D_r L_p Y}{L_r} \frac{Y_p{}^2}{W} \right] \frac{1}{p}$$

$$C = \left[ \frac{\bar{W}}{Y_{NN} p} \right] \frac{1}{p}$$

If the partial derivatives have the signs given to them above, it follows that $B > 0$ and $C < 0$. But the sign of $A$ is uncertain. If $D_Y$, though always positive, is small absolutely, the positive sum of the last two terms in $A$ will prevail and make $A$ itself positive; but as $D_Y$ increases, $A$ may become negative. However, if we introduce an additional restriction, namely $D_Y < 1$ (the marginal propensity to spend is less than unity), we can unequivocally assert that

$$A - C > 0$$

and hence

$$A + B - C > 0 \text{ (since } B > 0 \text{ always)}$$

In this case — which we will call the 'normal' case — it follows that, starting from equilibrium in the market for goods and services, and with an unchanged supply of cash:

(a)　at the going price level ($dp$ assumed zero), an autonomous increase in the money wage creates excess demand;

(b)　at the going money wage ($d\bar{W}$ assumed zero), an increase in the price level generates excess supply.

The 'normal' case can now be represented in diagrams referring to the market for goods and services. In Figs. 1(a) to 1(c) the schedule $Y_{W_0}$ shows the relation between output and the price level when the money wage is held at an original level $\bar{W}_0$. From (6) it is clear that it always has a positive shape. $Y_{\bar{W}_1}$ shows the corresponding schedule for a higher money wage; it is clear from (6) that output at any given price level will be lower. Both the slope and the shift of the $Y$ schedule are the same in all three diagrams. The difference concerns the demand schedules, $D_{\bar{W}_0}$ and $D_{\bar{W}_1}$. In Fig. 1(a), $D_Y$ is assumed small enough to allow $A$ to remain positive. Hence the $D$ schedule has a negative slope and shifts to the right when money wages rise. At the original equilibrium price level, $\bar{p}_0$, excess demand $AB$ results and propels the price level upwards towards a new equilibrium at $\bar{p}_1$. In Fig. 1(b), $D_Y$ is bigger and $A$ has become negative. Hence the increase in $\bar{W}$ reduces aggregate demand at $p_0$ — but by less than output itself (since $A - C$ remains positive). Again there is excess demand $AB$ and the impetus for $p$ to rise. In this case the positive effect on demand which a higher money wage has via its redistributive effects is outweighed by the negative

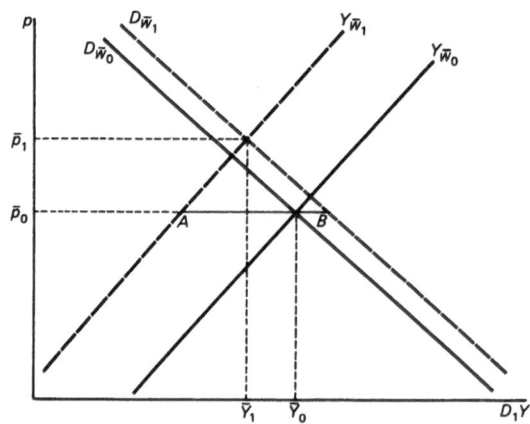

Fig. 1(a)

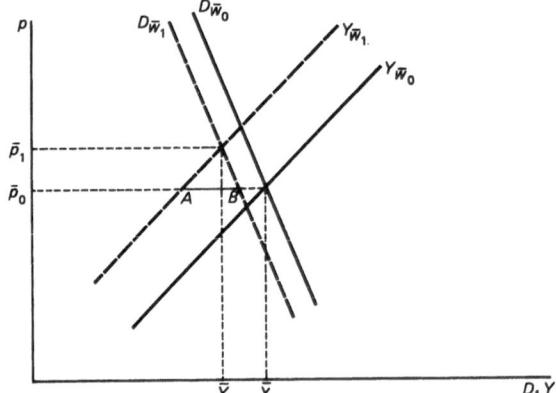

Fig. 1(b)

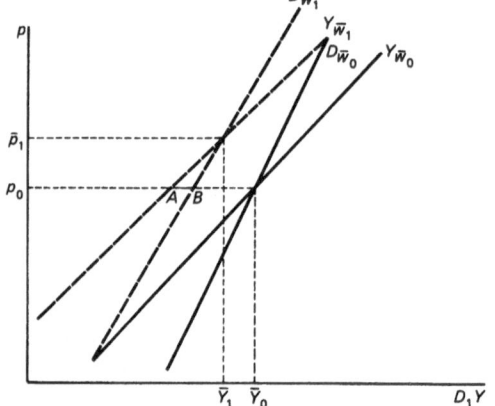

Fig. 1(c)

effect which results via $D_Y$ from the fall in output which it causes. In Fig. 1(c), $D_Y$ has become large enough (though still less than unity) to make the slope of the $D$ schedule actually positive. But the schedules still shift in response to higher $\bar{W}$ in such a way as to create excess demand and upward pressure on prices.

In all these three cases the price level rises, but (with an unchanged supply of cash) by proportionately less than money wages. This is easily shown from (7a), setting $dD = dY$, and evaluating

$$\frac{d(\bar{W}/p)}{d\bar{W}} = \frac{1}{p} \frac{B}{A + B - C} > 0$$

It follows from (6a) that output and employment must fall.

Now let us move from these comparatively well-known general-equilibrium properties of the 'normal' case and allow for the special features which we have suggested might characterise the situation when the role of organised labour autonomously raising the money wage is played by organised oil producers raising the price of oil. Of this 'special' case there were two possible features on which we based our argument:

(i)   the partial derivative $D_{\bar{W}/p}$ might be negative instead of positive, because the redistribution of income in the oil case would be in favour of a group with a relatively low marginal propensity to spend;

(ii)  the partial derivative $D_Y$ might exceed unity given the peculiar uncertainties of the world situation of inflation-cum-recession on which the rise in the price of oil was superimposed.

These features are not by themselves sufficient to overturn the conditions of the 'normal' case; the mainly monetary term in $A$:

$$\frac{D_r L_{pY}}{L_r Y_{NN}} \bar{W}$$

could be large enough absolutely to keep $A$ positive. We assume that this is not so, and that the effect of $D_{W/p} < 0$, $D_Y > 1$, is such as to give us

$$A - C < 0$$

but at the same time, as in the 'normal' case,

$$A + B - C > 0$$

We call this 'special case A', and its two variants are set out in Figs. 2(a) and 2(b). The $Y$ schedules are exactly the same as before.

In Fig. 2(a), although $A$ is negative, $(A + B)$ remains positive, and the $D$ schedules have negative slopes. But the increase in $\bar{W}$ shifts the $D$ schedule leftwards from its original position by more than the $Y$ schedule (since

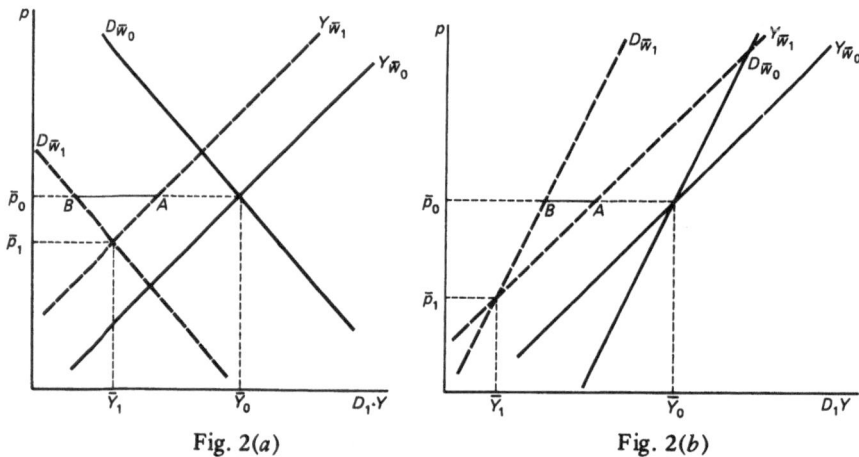

Fig. 2(*a*)                     Fig. 2(*b*)

$A - C < 0$) and at the original price level there is excess supply $BA$, causing the price level actually to fall. In Fig. 2($b$), $A$ is negative enough to make $(A + B)$ negative, and the demand schedules have positive slopes; but again the shift of the schedules creates excess supply, and the price level falls but more sharply than in Fig. 2($a$).

In the 'normal' case, the price level rose in response to increased $\bar{W}$ but less than proportionately, causing some reduction of output and employment. In 'special case A', which we have just considered, the price level falls while money wages rise; hence the rise in the real wage, and the consequent fall in output and employment, are more marked than in the 'normal' case. But there is a stable equilibrium at which the economy can come to rest. This is no longer so in 'special case B', to which we now turn. Here the absolute size of $D_{\bar{W}/p} < 0$ and $D_Y > 1$ are such as to bring it about that not merely do we have

$$A - C < 0$$

as in 'special case A', but also

$$A + B - C < 0$$

The result is shown in Fig. 3. Here the positive slope of the $D$ schedules is greater, with respect to $p$, than that of the $Y$ schedules; we are in conditions of unstable equilibrium. The shift of the schedules when $\bar{W}$ increases creates excess supply $BA$. Although a new equilibrium theoretically exists at $C$, the system cannot get to it; instead, it is driven away from it by the excess supply, which worsens as the price level falls. Real wages rise, and output and employment fall, with nothing to stop them, until at some point or other the power of labour to maintain $\bar{W}$, or the power of the oil cartel to maintain the oil price, is undermined.

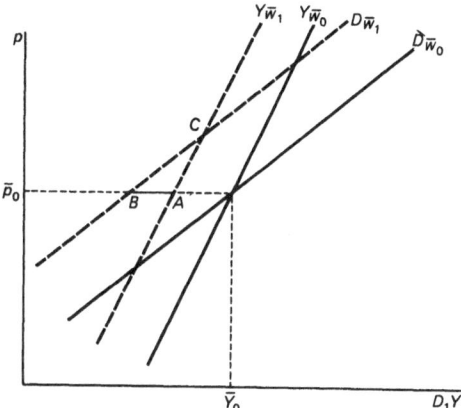

Fig. 3

EDITORS' NOTE

Diagram A suggests an alternative exposition of Professor Sargent's special (unstable) case. The gamma curve concerns pairs of interest-rates and price-levels sustaining aggregate demand at a given level ($Y^f$ being a special case), the wage-unit being given. The beta curve determines the (non-oil) com-modity-price level appropriate for that level of aggregate demand (output); the beta curve concerns the supply-of-all-goods. Here the commodity market is unstable in isolation: excess demand increases with $p$. Prof. Sargent shows that here, in the event of an increased price of oil, the com-modity-price level in general ($p$) will fall; cf. the arrow above. But excess supply will be consequent to $p < p^*$, assuming for the moment that output adjusts more slowly than demand to the commodity-price.

Our diagram cannot carry more weight than that of a demonstration in the special case an increased price of oil sets off a cumulative depressive process. But elementary Keynesian reasoning would, relative to a given wage-unit and a presumably upward-shifted oil price, yield diagram B, also descriptive of Prof. Sargent's special case.

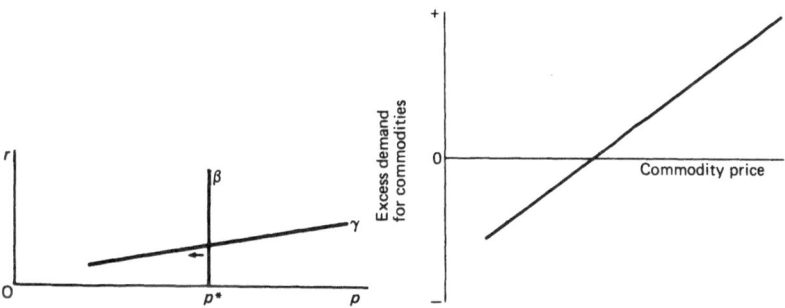

A. Stability of the Commodity-Market in Isolation (relative to a given wage-unit)

B. Instability of the Commodity-Market in Isolation

# 12 Conflict and Co-operation in an Era of High Oil Prices

MICHAEL JEFFERSON

## 1. Introduction

Academic economists have long been criticised for idle speculations made from an armchair and easy circumstances, but here I wish to indulge in the sort of speculations which form an integral part of the planning activities of a large international oil company.

Such operational speculation should not be lightly dismissed. As a relative newcomer to the oil industry, joining close to the beginning of the major crisis in the autumn of 1973, I was deeply impressed by the foresight of my colleagues and predecessors in earlier years. The crisis had been foreseen at least three years before it broke. The consequences and characteristics, from uncannily correct forecasts of oil import costs per barrel to problems of absorptive capacity and surplus oil revenues for individual OPEC member-nations, were worked out shortly thereafter. For two years prior to the events of October 1973, warnings went out from top oil executives to national governments and international institutions as to what was likely to happen, and the need for emergency measures to be put in a state of pre-paredness using the oil companies as the only practicable vehicle for the allocation of unusually scarce supplies.

Little action followed those warnings, although they did not go entirely unheeded. It should also be made clear that the oil companies thought the crisis would break from the second half of 1974 as a probable prelude to the renegotiation of the Teheran Agreement which would have expired in December 1975, although the oil supply/demand situation was such that there was an awareness in the oil companies of the significance of surprise political or military incidents. That the crisis was to be an accompaniment to the October 1973 Arab–Israeli war was no more precisely foreseen by the oil companies than by the Israelis. Nevertheless, the experience confirmed the suspicion that, contrary to popular mythology, industrial companies can take a longer view of things than most politicians and civil servants, buffeted by day-to-day events and motivated by considerations of electoral gain and national advantage. It encourages the thought that such speculation

136

within business enterprises may often be better founded than speculation within the academic halls, and for as long as the gift of perfect prophecy eludes us all is unlikely to be much worse.

## 2. Economic Prospects and Oil Prices

We are all aware that the higher oil prices since October 1973, combined with the effects of economic recession, some energy conservation, and mild weather conditions, have resulted in downward pressure on OPEC oil export demand, and there has been downward adjustment in the prices of the more expensive crude oil supplies. On top of this there have been the ravages of inflation, both domestic inflation within the OPEC member-nations and in the prices of their imports. By the end of 1975 average OPEC government revenue per barrel of oil would have to increase by about $3·50 in order to bring it back to the real revenue per barrel ruling in January 1974.

We are therefore in a position where downward pressures on real oil prices have been considerable over the past eighteen months. They may have been insufficient, as those who have predicted the imminent collapse of oil prices to $6–7 per barrel, or even $2–3 per barrel (at 1974 prices?), presumably believe. One looks, on the basis of past history, to the early collapse of cartels — although it may be argued that OPEC does not have many of the characteristics of a cartel. One may hope that oil prices are constrained by the cost of alternative oil and other energy supplies, although this application of the theory of monopolistic competition seems a will-o'-the-wisp for as long as these alternative energy sources remain unavailable or only in limited supply at rapidly escalating costs.

The question is whether any of these considerations will have a powerful influence in the short term — and perhaps even up to 1980. Most of the advanced industrial nations are not far from the point of recovery from the present recession. The timing and speed of the recovery cannot be foreseen with precision, but it could provoke an unsustainable boom. Or, and perhaps more likely, it could proceed in an orderly way in most major countries. Either way the demand for oil imports will expand considerably, enhancing the capacity of OPEC member-nations to raise oil prices — to recoup at least some of the toll taken by recent inflation. Only in the event of a severe recession following a coming boom would it be reasonable to expect oil prices to fall very significantly over the next five years. Poor weather conditions in the industrial nations could exacerbate the situation in the opposite direction, and result in greatly increased pressure on supplies.

Over this period, too, the willingness of oil exporters to allow prices to fall dramatically will be constrained in some cases by the depletion of their oil reserves, and to an increasing extent in all cases by their rising demand for imports. The jargon of reserve/production ratios and OPEC absorptive capacities has become commonplace, but it remains true that the OPEC member-nations with the largest populations tend to have the lowest reserve/

production ratios and the greatest demand for imports. The two or three countries with the smallest populations have high reserve/production ratios and a low demand for imports.

### 3. Oil Reserves and Oil Prices

There has been a tendency to assume that the first requirement for the supply of oil is the successful recycling of oil revenues. While it is true that success on this score demands a lengthening time-profile of petrodollar investments, because the market in liquid and near-liquid assets is finite, it has always seemed that, provided no artificial constraints were placed on capital markets — including international direct and equity investment — the primary recycling process would proceed and that capital markets could handle even the higher OPEC cumulative surplus revenues foreseen for the late 1970s.

By primary recycling we mean the process whereby oil revenues surplus to domestic requirements are invested externally in more or less liquid assets. This is now to be distinguished, in a world in which jargon flourishes more than weeds in the late spring, from secondary recycling between oil-importing nations in external account surplus and those in deficit, and from tertiary recycling whereby oil-importing governments take steps to restore some of the purchasing power lost by consumers of oil and oil-using products owing to higher oil prices.

Of course, if the primary recycling process broke down this would encourage oil exporters to keep their oil in the ground. But as we have seen in recent months, several OPEC member-nations are not unhappy to eke out their oil reserves over a longer period on various grounds, some of them unrelated to low prices. This desire to constrain production on conservation grounds has helped, and will help, to place a higher floor on oil prices than would otherwise be the case.

### 4. OPEC Surplus Revenues and Oil Prices

It is curious that those who have recently argued that the aggregate OPEC surplus (to, say, 1980) would rapidly disappear have not also recognised that the appearance of deficits would create pressures for a major increase in oil prices. But if it is argued that OPEC in aggregate will, say, be in annual deficit by 1978, then some OPEC member-countries will be heavily in deficit well before then, even after consideration of previously accumulated surpluses. If OPEC imports of goods and services by 1980 were to reach $227 billion, and OPEC oil revenues were only $143 billion, then what would be the deficit of most OPEC member-countries? Which other OPEC member-countries would be either willing or in sufficient surplus to lend vast sums with little chance of repayment? Is there, in short, room for mechanical extrapolations of this sort?

The answer is, of course, that such exercises are extremely hazardous and open to serious misinterpretation. They suggest that earlier estimates of OPEC surplus revenues were grossly exaggerated, that OPEC will soon be in aggregate annual deficit, and that the whole episode has been a storm in a teacup. It is true that a number of earlier estimates now look far too high, but those estimates were mainly of the 'If . . . then . . .' kind. If, for example, OPEC's oil exports were to continue their rise at the rates achieved during much of 1973, and at 1974 revenues per barrel, then they could have cumulatively exceeded $650 billion by 1980. But surely nobody seriously thought that the world would just continue, *ceteris paribus*, as oil exports and revenues escalated — because we do not live and never have lived in a *ceteris paribus* world.

The higher estimates might have had the effect, and sometimes had the purpose, of encouraging action among policy-makers and others where there had previously been inaction. Lower estimates, intentionally or otherwise, are liable to have the contrary effect: to encourage complacency where a sense of urgency is more appropriate; to undermine measures aimed at energy conservation and the development of alternative energy sources, where these should instead be encouraged. If the evidence is overwhelmingly in favour of the lower estimates then all is well, but in one or two recent instances the estimates have been so low as to be well beneath the range of likely outcomes. I do not say that an OPEC aggregate cumulative surplus revenue of under $200 billion by 1980 is beyond the realms of possibility, for who knows what the future may bring, but such singleline projections at the present time may have seriously adverse consequences for us all in circumstances where the cumulative surplus could equally well exceed $450 billion by 1980.

### 5. OPEC Imports and Oil Prices

One area of misunderstanding was the belief that those who advanced higher estimates of OPEC surplus revenues by 1980 had failed to recognise the rapid increase in OPEC member-countries' merchandise imports which would occur after the oil price rise. Those who advanced low estimates of OPEC surplus revenues congratulated themselves on foreseeing the rapid upward trend in imports. In fact at least some of those who advanced, and still advance, higher figures have not needed to change their estimates of these imports in any significant way. Table 1 shows our estimates of the position on OPEC imports in aggregate; disaggregated figures are also available (see Appendix).

It should be noted that our estimates are in current dollars, applying declining rates of real increase in merchandise imports and high but declining rates of inflation. They represent something close to the mid-point in a multiple scenario approach which we adopt on both real and price changes, and which produces forty possible outcomes in order to understand and

TABLE 1

*Estimated OPEC Imports and Aid*
*($ billion)*

|      | Merchandise imports (f.o.b.) | Net services | Grants/Aid |
|------|------------------------------|--------------|------------|
| 1974 | 35·1 | −7·7 | 6·8 |
| 1975 | 60·1 | −7·9 | 6·6 |
| 1976 | 77·2 | −5·3 | 7·0 |
| 1977 | 96·6 | −1·1 | 7·6 |

illustrate the uncertainties. Although OPEC countries will pay for their merchandise imports c.i.f., delays in delivery due to shipment and port congestion, combined with a rising trend, make it more sensible on a cash transactions basis to ignore the rule-of-thumb 10 per cent differential between f.o.b. and c.i.f. import costs. And it should be recognised that OPEC grants/aid is defined very broadly to include such attractive investments as World Bank bonds, and is not evenly distributed among the most seriously affected developing nations.

The first requirement of the oil-exporting nations is to earn sufficient revenue from oil sales to cover their domestic economic requirements, particularly imports of goods and services. However, not all the oil-exporting nations are of equal strength on this score. Thus in 1974 Saudi Arabia imported about $ 3¾ billion worth of merchandise goods but received from oil-sales about $ 29 billion, and received about $ 22 billion in cash from these sales. She was left, therefore, with a nominal surplus over merchandise imports of around $ 25 billion and an actual surplus of about $ 18 billion.[1] Indonesia and Algeria, on the other hand, already have only a small margin over their import costs at current oil revenues. Other oil exporters with large populations, ambitious to develop their economies and power rapidly but with much more modest oil reserves than Saudi Arabia, will rapidly join the ranks of those in difficulty over their balance of payments if present import trends were to continue.

In fact, real rates of increase of the magnitude we have seen in recent months are unlikely to be maintained for very long. Look around the OPEC members today. We read in the press that ships are laid up outside Lagos harbour for 90 days before being able to enter, and for over 80 days outside the port of Basra. Increased penalties have been applied on the Yembo and Jeddah shipping routes into Saudi Arabia. Consignments of chemicals and other goods urgently required are being flown in. Civil servants and government ministers are desperately overworked as the pace of economic development quickens and the number of vital decisions that need to be taken multiplies. Transport and communications facilities are found to be inadequate in relation to the extra demands suddenly placed upon them, and must be expanded. The labour required, sometimes relatively unskilled labour, is often not readily available. There is some resentment in neighbouring countries already at the outflow of their more adventurous workers, skilled and un-skilled, into the oil-rich countries.

Even with declining real rates of increase in imports, however, there is upward pressure on oil prices by countries with insufficient foreign exchange earnings from oil and other exports to meet their requirements. Those re-quirements will of course be scaled down in time and where necessary, but with an upturn in economic growth in the main industrial nations the capa-city of OPEC members to raise oil prices is enhanced in the short term.

## 6. OPEC Output Constraints and Oil Prices

But suppose OPEC member-nations are more interested in raising total ex-port earnings by higher production than in raising oil prices through impos-ing higher revenue claims per barrel. What freedom of action do they have?

The mid-1975 range for OPEC oil exports in aggregate is widely consid-ered to be about 22 million barrels per day (b/d) at the bottom end and about 35 million b/d at the top end. This latter figure assumes that countries like Venezuela and Libya do not follow previously announced conservation policies, and that OPEC's productive capacity has increased a little in recent months. It assumes that Iran is prepared to produce for export in large vol-umes, thus reducing the prospects for developing domestic oil-using indus-tries. And it assumes that Saudi Arabia is prepared to produce at full capa-city and earn huge surplus revenues.

Two comments should be made here. First, it is quite conceivable that economic recovery from late 1975 in the major industrial nations, combined with stockbuilding in anticipation of higher prices and a poor winter, could quite quickly result in OPEC producing at close to full capacity. This could lead to upward pressure on prices. Second, if OPEC member-countries — especially Saudi Arabia — were unwilling to produce at full capacity, then the upward pressure on oil prices would intensify.

## 7. The Scope for Conflict

The seeds of future conflict in the period to 1980 therefore seem to lie much more in the reactions to higher oil prices among oil-importing nations than in the reactions of oil exporters to a major fall in oil prices.

The problems are now familiar. Oil import costs rise, not merely because volumes go up closely in line with economic growth, but because producer revenue per barrel rises. This has consequences for the balances of trade and payments, and means a transfer of financial — and subsequently real — re-sources from the oil-importing nations to the oil-exporting nations. There are deflationary consequences in so far as the oil price rise has an effect similar to a rise in indirect taxation.[2] Costs also rise, and hopefully we all now recognise that the inflationary consequences of oil price rises have second-round effects on domestic energy sources and energy-using activities which were not encompassed by O.E.C.D. and some other commentators when they produced rather low estimates of oil-induced price increases last year.

Perhaps more significant for the economic outlook, the faster an incipient boom began and the more substantial it seemed likely to be, the greater the likelihood that higher oil import costs — whether through increased volumes or, more especially, higher prices — would undermine it. In some senses, of course, this sort of self-correcting mechanism would have its attractions. But undeniably it would provoke the reaction in the oil-importing countries that they were being held to ransom to a quite unacceptable degree.

## 8. The Need for Co-operation

It is not my purpose here to advocate or even suggest what steps might constructively be taken by the oil-importing nations or the oil-exporting nations in order to overcome the problems that appear likely to arise between now and 1980.

What should be stressed is that the oil crisis has not miraculously gone away, that the oil supply problem has not been solved, and that oil prices are not about to collapse. Perhaps when alternative energy sources are readily available things will be very different, but for the next decade at least this seems little more than a pious hope.

We appear to be on the threshold of a period of renewed activity on the oil price front after some months of deceptive calm. In this new phase there will be even greater need than before of caution in decision-making by oil exporters and importers alike, greater recognition of mutual interdependence between oil importers themselves and between oil importers and exporters, and a greater desirability of co-operation among the richer and the poorer nations of the world.

## 9. The Place of the United Kingdom

In many respects the United Kingdom is placed in an unenviable position with regard to all these matters in the period to 1980. But despite all the grounds for pessimism, not least the failure of successive British governments to recognise that the errors of past interventions argue for less intervention in the future, there is North Sea oil. The United Kingdom is, after all, the only major industrial nation with energy self-sufficiency now in sight.

There is still a serious danger that the existence of North Sea oil will be regarded as a panacea for Britain's economic problems. Nothing would be more foolish than to subscribe to such a view. Before self-sufficiency in oil supplies can be achieved, by 1980 or shortly thereafter, the United Kingdom's balance of trade will continue under its traditional strain and the nation's indebtedness and outgoings on servicing such debt will have risen. Appropriate action to improve the balance of payments is likely to have been postponed in the light of expectations about North Sea oil. The undoubted eventual benefits to the United Kingdom balance of payments should be seen in this context.

British industry has been slow to recognise the importance of what was happening on its doorstep, and even where the response has improved, the performance of companies has often been marred by poor productivity and endless labour disputes (many over demarcation practices inherited from shipbuilding). Fortunately there is a growing number of satisfactory performances, but still not enough. Perhaps most important of all, the contribution of North Sea oil to the United Kingdom's annual gross national product in the early 1980s will not be all that great. If North Sea oil were available now in the quantities expected in the early 1980s the contribution would be less than 5 per cent of G.N.P.; thus by then it could well be significantly less — less per capita than the sort of annual per capita G.N.P. growth that, say, Japan can be expected to enjoy in the early 1980s. And the danger is that efforts to put other parts of the British economic and political house in order will have been undermined by a mistaken belief in a coming bonanza.

How much oil is there in the North Sea, and how quickly can it be produced? Oil reserves from existing fields in the United Kingdom sector currently exceed 12 billion barrels, but the ultimate figure is a matter of public controversy on which it would be foolish to take a hard-and-fast line. A theoretical estimate for the development of these reserves, which assumes very favourable economic and political conditions and minimal technical problems, would suggest a production level in 1980 of between $2\frac{1}{2}$ and 3 million b/d. However, this can be regarded as the maximum technically feasible, and is higher than the $2-2\frac{1}{2}$ million b/d in the United Kingdom Department of Energy's 'Brown Book' published in May 1975 — which in turn represents a scaling down of the forecast made a year earlier. The adjustment took in to account delays that are occurring in start-up dates and the downward revision in reserves of one or two fields.

Such forecasts are critically dependent upon economic conditions, the United Kingdom Government's policy on participation, and the technical problems to be resolved.

The recent economic situation and the high level of inflation have caused financing and cash-flow problems for a large number of companies. Highly capital-intensive projects characterised by long lead times and heavy so-called 'front-end loading', such as the development of North Sea oil fields, are being more closely scrutinised. The deferment of some development plans, the declaration of sub-economic finds and the curtailment of exploration activity has occurred and could proliferate.

The policy of successive United Kingdom governments towards participation has been unfortunate in several respects, and none more so than its timing. Most of the major traditional oil-exporting countries have an established industry and a substantial nucleus of well-trained nationals, and are able to generate future capital requirements from oil income. In the United Kingdom, on the other hand, the finance, expertise and materials necessary to ensure the continued development of the North Sea are heavily dependent upon foreign resources and are being applied in unusually difficult conditions. Government participation, largely for ideological reasons, is liable to hinder investment and the planned development of projects yet to be capitalised. There is a real danger that operators might decide to opt out, although psychological mood here is so critical that changes in ministerial responsibilities or welcome decisions on quite unrelated matters could have a powerful influence for good as well as bad. But if operators were to opt out, then the ability of the United Kingdom government or other companies to take over such operations in the short term would be severely hampered by lack of funds and expertise.

Looking to the longer term, it may be that a future United Kingdom government will feel the need to exercise production controls in the interests of conserving reserves after 1980. There is a strong awareness in the oil industry that present oil reserves generate a potential production level which could coincide with government policies to place limits on maximum permissible production. If such limits were to be placed on fields where development funds had already been committed, the effects would be particularly serious. These uncertainties also provide a disincentive towards further exploration, if companies believe that the development of future fields might be held back and return on investment deferred.

Then there are the technical issues. Although the Department of Energy's recent 'Brown Book' acknowledges the technical problems involved in North Sea operations and revisions have been made for known delays, no allowance appears to be incorporated for future delays. In the circumstances this seems a little unrealistic. During the rest of the 1970s continuing delays in the delivery of equipment, shortage of equipment and of skilled labour are likely to feature prominently in most development programmes. Furthermore, engineering problems associated with starting up production and achieving optimum production rates tend to be understated. In the absence of production experience, future reservoir performance is predicated upon limited appraisal well-testing and theoretical concepts which on balance are more likely to be over-optimistic than pessimistic. Teething problems are also likely to be longer drawn out than expected.

At the present time, therefore, it seems realistic to assume that U.K. North Sea oil production may reach only 2 million b/d by 1980, and even then is dependent upon the removal of some of the present political uncertainties. The lower the availability of alternative oil supplies, the stronger the price of OPEC oil.

10. Conclusion

The drift of these speculations has been towards the likelihood of even higher oil prices over the next five years and away from the view that oil prices 'must', somehow, fall dramatically over this period. The view that OPEC oil prices are past their peak, economic prospects are rosy, and North Sea oil a bonanza for all, is not realistic.

Notes

[1] Net service payments made inroads into these figures, to the tune of $0·6 billion, but did not upset the overall picture of vast surpluses.
[2] Studies of United Kingdom inflation and trade union behaviour show that rises in taxation may also have inflationary implications for wage demands.

APPENDIX: OPEC COUNTRIES' ABSORPTIVE CAPACITY, 1974–7

The following figures should be read in the light of these comments:
1. Absorptive capacity is here defined as merchandise imports plus net service outflows plus grants/aid in current dollars. This is a generally accepted definition, but for both theoretical and practical reasons it is not the sole definition.
2. Merchandise imports (f.o.b.) data are in some cases actuals for 1974, and in most other cases are estimated from figures available for a substantial part of 1974.
3. Estimates of future merchandise imports (f.o.b.) are in current dollars, applying declining rates of real increase and declining rates of inflation. Although we have alternative scenarios for both real and price increases, we believe the single-line estimates provided are a reasonable guide.
4. Although OPEC countries will pay for their imports c.i.f., delays in delivery due to shipment and port congestion have been and are likely to continue to be substantial over the period. As a rough rule-of-thumb, c.i.f. costs are 10 per cent over f.o.b. costs, but many vessels are experiencing delays of 80 days and beyond at OPEC ports of entry. Given widespread concern with OPEC cash flows, and the rising trend of imports, f.o.b. data can safely be used.
5. No remotely reliable data are available on Soviet-bloc exports to most of OPEC. It has been guessed that the Soviet bloc exported $1 billion of merchandise to Iran in 1974, $0·5 billion to Iraq and $0·6 billion to Algeria. It can be reliably estimated that the Soviet bloc exported $0·3 billion of merchandise to Indonesia in 1974, and $0·07 billion to Kuwait.
6. Whereas statisticians in some international institutions would claim that all military items are included in their balance-of-payments data, mystery surrounds the handling of military transactions between the

United States and Iran. Some observers believe that $4·5 billion of United States military equipment was delivered to Iran during 1974; other well-placed observers do not believe it.

7. Net services can be only very roughly estimated, and our estimates show OPEC's net service outflows declining through 1977. Expenditure on professional and advisory services, and on private invisible outgoings such as tourism, can be expected to rise. However, interest earned on the investment of surplus revenues will be a decisive factor and is properly included under service inflows.

8. Aid disbursements are widely defined, to include participation in the I.M.F. oil facilities and investment in World Bank bonds. The figure for 1974 may therefore seem surprisingly high. On the other hand, we are inclined to disbelieve the significantly higher figures for aid in future years now being bandied about.

9. Since this paper was prepared Gabon has become a full member of OPEC, but is excluded here.

*OPEC Absorptive Capacity, 1974–7*
*($ billion)*

|                      | 1974 | 1975 | 1976 | 1977 |
|----------------------|------|------|------|------|
| Algeria              | 4·2  | 5·9  | 7·3  | 7·8  |
| Ecuador              | 0·9  | 1·1  | 1·3  | 1·6  |
| Indonesia            | 6·0  | 7·2  | 9·0  | 10·9 |
| Iran                 | 10·1 | 16·8 | 20·3 | 24·5 |
| Iraq                 | 4·0  | 7·2  | 8·4  | 11·2 |
| Kuwait               | 2·1  | 3·2  | 3·3  | 3·5  |
| Libya                | 3·6  | 6·2  | 7·2  | 7·2  |
| Nigeria              | 4·0  | 7·3  | 9·3  | 11·7 |
| Qatar                | 0·5  | 0·9  | 1·7  | 1·5  |
| Saudi Arabia         | 6·9  | 9·0  | 10·2 | 12·5 |
| United Arab Emirates | 1·9  | 2·8  | 3·5  | 3·7  |
| Venezuela            | 5·4  | 7·0  | 8·0  | 9·2  |
|                      | 49·6 | 74·6 | 89·5 | 105·3 |

*Estimated OPEC Imports and Aid, 1974*
*($ billion)*

|  | Merchandise imports (f.o.b.) | Net Services | Grants/Aid |
|---|---|---|---|
| Algeria | 3·7 | −0·5 | 0·0 |
| Ecuador | 0·8 | −0·1 | 0·0 |
| Indonesia | 4·5 | −1·5 | 0·0 |
| Iran | 7·2 | −1·8 | 1·1 |
| Iraq | 3·2 | −0·4 | 0·4 |
| Kuwait | 1·4 | +0·5 | 1·2 |
| Libya | 2·7 | −0·7 | 0·2 |
| Nigeria | 2·4 | −1·4 | 0·2 |
| Qatar | 0·2 | −0·1 | 0·2 |
| Saudi Arabia | 3·8 | −0·9 | 2·2 |
| United Arab Emirates | 1·2 | −0·1 | 0·6 |
| Venezuela | 4·0 | −0·7 | 0·7 |
|  | 35·1 | −7·7 | 6·8 |

*Estimated OPEC Imports and Aid, 1975*
*($ billion)*

|  | Merchandise imports (f.o.b.) | Net services | Grants/Aid |
|---|---|---|---|
| Algeria | 5·6 | −0·3 | 0·0 |
| Ecuador | 1·0 | −0·1 | 0·0 |
| Indonesia | 5·5 | −1·7 | 0·0 |
| Iran | 13·8 | −2·4 | 0·6 |
| Iraq | 6·6 | −0·5 | 0·1 |
| Kuwait | 2·2 | +0·8 | 1·8 |
| Libya | 5·0 | −0·8 | 0·4 |
| Nigeria | 5·2 | −1·6 | 0·5 |
| Qatar | 0·6 | −0·1 | 0·2 |
| Saudi Arabia | 6·5 | −0·6 | 1·9 |
| United Arab Emirates | 2·3 | −0·1 | 0·4 |
| Venezuela | 5·8 | −0·5 | 0·7 |
|  | 60·1 | −7·9 | 6·6 |

*Estimated OPEC Imports and Aid, 1976*
*($ billion)*

|  | Merchandise imports (f.o.b.) | Net services | Grants/Aid |
|---|---|---|---|
| Algeria | 6·5 | −0·8 | 0·0 |
| Ecuador | 1·2 | −0·1 | 0·0 |
| Indonesia | 7·0 | −2·0 | 0·0 |
| Iran | 18·0 | −1·5 | 0·8 |
| Iraq | 7·5 | −0·7 | 0·2 |
| Kuwait | 3·0 | +1·5 | 1·8 |
| Libya | 6·2 | −0·5 | 0·5 |
| Nigeria | 7·5 | −1·2 | 0·6 |
| Qatar | 1·0 | −0·5 | 0·2 |
| Saudi Arabia | 9·0 | +1·0 | 2·2 |
| United Arab Emirates | 3·0 | 0·0 | 0·5 |
| Venezuela | 7·3 | −0·5 | 0·2 |
|  | 77·2 | −5·3 | 7·0 |

*Estimated OPEC Imports and Aid, 1977*
*($ billion)*

|  | Merchandise imports (f.o.b.) | Net services | Grants/Aid |
|---|---|---|---|
| Algeria | 7·0 | −0·7 | 0·1 |
| Ecuador | 1·5 | −0·1 | 0·0 |
| Indonesia | 8·5 | −2·4 | 0·0 |
| Iran | 22·0 | −1·5 | 1·0 |
| Iraq | 10·0 | −1·0 | 0·2 |
| Kuwait | 4·0 | +2·0 | 1·5 |
| Libya | 7·5 | +0·6 | 0·3 |
| Nigeria | 10·0 | −1·0 | 0·7 |
| Qatar | 1·5 | +0·1 | 0·1 |
| Saudi Arabia | 12·5 | +3·0 | 3·0 |
| United Arab Emirates | 3·6 | +0·5 | 0·6 |
| Venezuela | 8·5 | −0·6 | 0·1 |
|  | 96·6 | −1·1 | 7·6 |

# SECTION 2: FINANCIAL ECONOMICS

# Introduction

These five papers are sucked into a field containing company finance and stock markets. True, a free-standing Selden paper would probably be attracted in some other direction (Chapter 16). But the focus of the other four papers is compelling; one is tempted to interpret Selden rather plastically, transmogrifying the characteristics of 'his' price-paths − relative to different monetary regimes − into remarks about differential inventory-profit sequences, interest-rate paths, real-growth paths, etc., all importantly affecting stock markets, all encompassed within the full reach of the neo-quantity theory of money accepted by Selden.

It is not surprising that so distinguished an authority on stock-market regulation as Irwin Friend should be writing about stock markets (Chapter 17), as indeed he was asked to do. And of course, the turbulent, erratic behaviour of stock markets in recent years, together and not accidentally with that of the authorities, would hardly have sucked in Friend: he has always been there. So Friend's paper, despite its specificity, is in an important sense less ephemeral than those of Burstein (Chapter 13), Wallich and Mains (Chapter 14) or Pepper and Wood (Chapter 15). The latter three have been gripped by the dramas which have been played out on the world's boardrooms and bourses since the accession of Dr Burns, probably merely accidentally coincidentally. Friend centres on several themes in resource allocation and information networks. Indeed, in the end the differences between such scholars as Friend and George Benston will have to be resolved through generally price-theoretic techniques; monetary economics are not at the fore. After all, does not the *disclosure* debate reduce to something like this: Presumably all agree that, if capital markets are not *efficient* − so that, somehow, the apparent incentives of managements not to disclose various information or simply to lie, together with the incentives to form rings manipulating trading by acquiring and exerting temporary monopoly power, fomenting illusions, etc., do not become blanked out − then regulatory intervention can be beneficial. Friend concludes that in fact these forces do not become blanked out.

Efficient-market hypotheses have been formulated relative to solid empirical testing procedures. To this extent the debate has been stimulating and healthy. Still, the efficient-market hypothesis does recall the black box: *how* does all this looming chicanery get blanked out? Certainly, significant non-cooperation must thus be implied so that insider-trading gets placed in a better light.

151

Pepper and Wood develop two main directions. The first, clear from their title, leads to a natural intersection with Selden. The second concerns the company-finance/stock-market nexus and covers much ground common to Burstein and Wallich and Mains as well. All three papers treat a possibly vicious circle on which battered share prices and financiers running for cover force companies into short borrowing until balance-sheet deterioration may lead to massive real contractionary impulses as firms might have to cling to what liquidity they have left. Wallich and Mains offer evidence that such vicious circles — much abetted by deterioration in real earnings — have developed and have been exacerbated by inflation. Pepper and Wood suggest that exogenous real contractionary impulses in the company sector might lead to anti-damping consequences. But Burstein suggests that this is unlikely to be the case and in fact argues that the financial economy is probably inherently heavily damped, albeit vulnerable to erratic behaviour by discretionary monetary authorities.

Burstein, starting from Keynesian stipulations, and Pepper and Wood, starting from modified monetarist stipulations, arrive at substantially the same — monetary-ruled-rooted or at least secularly, not rheostatically, based — monetary policy. To this extent the *laissez-faire* counter-revolution limned in the Introduction to Part II, Section 1, looks the more viable. There appears to be something in the air suggesting that the immense complexity of economic processes, reduced to a certain order only by quite recent mathematical-economics developments, is more distinctly seen to be likely to swamp out still necessarily feeble official efforts to acquire, process, ingest and respond optimally to the immense volume of necessary information. As economic theorists have come to understand economic systems better, they seem on the whole to have become more timorous. They have seemingly begun to turn against incessant intervention in roughly competitive economies.

# 13 Monetary Policy, the Stock Market and the Real Economy: A Keynesian Conspectus

M. L. BURSTEIN

## Summary

Pieces of theory, quite completely described below, are arranged so that the emergent structure is quite strictly Keynesian. Thus we concentrate on changes in interest rates *cum* the unsatisfied fringe of borrowers as transmitters of central-banking actions. Indeed, real balance effects are eschewed; we tacitly adopt my earlier Burden of the Money Supply argument concerning the essentially zero-sum implications for net real wealth of purely financial assets, whether from a global or microeconomic standpoint.[1]

It is then argued that time-series of data generated by this admittedly largely implicit system, in so far as they exhibited cyclical behaviour or were capable of 'explosion', would become damped at least so long as the time-path of the monetary base or 'M' or what have you, call this $m(t)$, obeyed a rule such as

$$m_t = m^0 e^{\alpha t} \tag{1}$$

But discretionary monetary policy could activate latent anti-damping properties, especially if official errors occurred near turning-points in the 'real' cycle.

So my Keynesian conspectus leads up to a view of optimal monetary policy not different in essentials from that of the monetarists. Blessed is the Peacemaker?

The material is arranged as follows:

1. SHORT-RATE AND THE BOURSE
1.1 How misguided monetary authorities can seriously exacerbate potential difficulties imbedded in this relationship.
1.2 Transmission from the Bourse to the 'Real Economy'.

2. LATENT ANTI-DAMPING POTENTIALS

2.1 A latent anti-damping potential: Induced Balance Sheet Deterioration.

2.2 Fisher's Theory *cum* Discretionary Monetary Policy

3. NOTE ABOUT 'HISTORICAL' TIME

4. LATENT DAMPING FEATURES

4.1 The essentially damping properties of a sensible Rule

4.2 'Finance' a la Keynes/*Treatise cum* D. H. Robertson

4.3 Disintermediation

4.3.1. How the 'disintermediation' damping feature can have anti-damping effects if officials acting with discretion act incorrectly.

## 1. Short-Rate and the Bourse[2]

In a world of certainty — whatever that can mean in the historical time of this paper[3] — there is obvious linkage between share prices and long-rate whilst that between share prices and short-rate flows only from the ways in which long- and short-rate relate. Under *uncertainty* any Keynesian sees things very differently. Thus, consider a stock deemed by a transactor to be fundamentally undervalued. This stock, *J*, may be sold short by him at $t = \tau$. He may come to believe that the forces which have already depressed the stock will become exacerbated soon, perhaps only for a few weeks. Long enough.

It is easy to see how short-rate comes in, but it is hard to select an illustration. The interface of subjective probability and frictions (e.g. transactions costs), together with search, make possible many models, each as (in) valid *a priori* as the other. For our purposes a simple illustration suffices, an illustration which obviously is a version of the Keynesian speculative motive for holding short-assets:

In the current state of the world I anticipate that the action defined by holding a quantum of short-assets *cum* a quantum of *J* over a short interval (not defining here the sequel) has an expected subjective rate of return, $\rho^*$.

There exists, relative to $\rho^*$, a state $\alpha$ such that $\Delta\rho > 0$ and a state $\beta$ such that the inequality is weakly reversed:

$$\Pr(\Delta\rho > 0) = \Pr(\alpha)$$

$$\Pr(\Delta\rho \leq 0) = \Pr(\beta) = 1 - \Pr(\alpha)$$

Converting the discussion into one of proportions and denoting the short-asset holding as *s*, the initial portfolio is

$$[(1 - s)^*, s^*]$$

Now we specify that the profitability of the pure strategy, $s = 1$, is to increase, that short-rate is to increase. It is easy to show that an $N-M$ rational trader would plan to sell stock and to buy short-assets. And it is easy to imagine how, in Wall Street, such a process could lead to fear supplanting greed. The expected profitability of holding shares could cumulatively decay, both absolutely and relative to a short-asset strategy.

If a misguided central banker used his discretion to promote substantially higher short-rate just when business confidence was eroding, then the bear market of 1974, and worse, could follow. Thus the transmission from short-rate to the bourse under uncertainty.

1.2. There are a number of well-recognised channels for *transmission of stock-market impulses to the 'real economy'*, including:
  1. *Effects on subjective costs of capital and the sequel of these effects.* A company with a p/e of 4 which expects a multiple of 10 under consensually tranquil conditions has to surrender $0·60 of subjective net worth for each dollar of fresh equity capital. Such a prospect will lead to distortion of equity/debt ratios and to aborting of investment plans.[4]
  2. *Wealth effects of changes in market values of equity holdings.* The seemingly obvious properties of this point must become subject to some qualifications in so far as shares have purely financial elements and in so far as Burden of the Money Supply arguments hold.
  3. *Induced pressures on the bourse* as equity sales are forced by deterioration of collateral values. Collateral values will be pushed below minimum-ratio requirements in the train of the initial deterioration in the bourse.
  4. *Interest rates will rise further as firms move into debt finance* (cf. Section 2.1 below).

## 2. Latent Anti-damping Potentials

2.1. *Balance-sheet deterioration.* It is obvious that declining profitability, if prolonged, will lead to deteriorated balance sheets, sooner or later themselves clogs on investment: various projects will become unprofitable as risk-premia requirements of potential investors in or lenders to companies become more exigent.

A more interesting case flows directly from declining stock prices, independently of ongoing company profitability. We have seen how reluctant companies will be to float shares in bear markets relative to stable internal states of long-run expectation. So debt will increase relative to equity, as these are reckoned in conventional accounting. And if a strongly inflationary episode, requiring substantial increments of finance of working capital for example, should coincide with a bear market, another twist will be imparted to the growth of debt both absolutely and relative to equity. So it would become still harder to float new equity issues. And indeed, as prudent limits on balance-sheet ratios would begin to bind (as constraints of this sort would become active), the propensity to invest could begin to fall very substantially.

2.2. *The Fisher theory*[5] *cum discretionary monetary policy.* Of course, positive inflationary expectations will impart an upward push to interest rates. And Irving Fisher's distinction between real and nominal rates of interest, albeit highly subjective in its roots, is useful enough. But is is not at all clear that, over the reaches of time pertinent to the adjustment processes of this paper, interest-rate movements will reflect what in any case are highly varied, often inchoate, expectational states with any great precision. Indeed it *is* clear that suppliers of capital are little able to impose their inflation expectations upon the market. Financial institutions are restricted by law and circumstances to financial assets — and claims to shares and real estate have proved to be uncertain inflation hedges. Households have a bit more freedom in this regard: they can increase their investments in consumer durables relative to their financial assets. But household response is in fact quite restricted too: it is difficult in life to rearrange one's portfolio of consumer durables without affecting one's consumption pattern; consumer durable holdings, treated as pure investment, have dreadful liquidity properties and are subject to erratic price behaviour even when price quotations can be obtained in a timely manner.[6]

So any dynamic of practical interest supporting the Fisher—Fama proposition will have to be rooted in *demand* for capital. But a substantial literature is emerging showing how is it that inflationary environments typically do not permit companies to maintain unimpaired or improved 'real' profitability.[7] Some of the explanation is found in the structure of taxation: progressivity develops in a money-illusory way. Another part is in politics: price controls seem inevitable at least some of the time during a serious inflationary episode, as does a savage squeeze or two.[8] Non-uniform inflation tends to increase subjective uncertainty, clogging the propensity to invest. Nor does correct economic reasoning permit one to assert that just because firms might expect their rate of return on fresh tranches of funds devoted to fixed capital to rise if interest rates were stable under inflationary conditions, they would massively increase planned investment outlays: the aggregate marginal efficiency of capital function might be quite interest-inelastic. Indeed it would seem that the only profit component maintaining lock-step with inflation is *inventory profit* (*stock profit* in the British locution). And while these profits are validly such, the inflationary process generating them increases the industrial finance requirement at least $1:1$ with inventory profit,[9,10] so that indeed upward pressure is imposed upon interest rates in this connection relative to the clearly relaxing effects on interest rates which would flow from the reduced finance requirement ordinarily associated with increased profits. Furthermore, speculation in

inventory investment fits neatly into the Fisher theory. There is no doubt
that the spectacular growth in demand for credit in 1973—4 partly reflected inventory speculation and flowed from inflationary expectations.[11]
But even the inventory-speculative motivation is based on postulation
either of collective irrationality or collective inability to *learn*. Thus by
now it is clear that inventory-accumulation binges, leading to the inventory/
sales ratios which are excessive unless it is believed that commodity-price
inflation will continue, also lead to inventory recessions. Rather than go
for inventory profits — and, later, inventory losses and severe balance-
sheer deterioration — companies could be expected, as they learn about
the economy's interactive logic, not to engage in inventory speculation,
devoting their borrowing capacity to secularly profitable ends instead.
So we have yet another example of the triviality, if not counter-productive-
ness, of general-equilibrium/macroeconomic models based on universal
price-taking instead of price-quoting.[12] And we are led towards focusing
upon the role of *conjectural interdependence* as it may underlie macroeconomic theory.

Strict adherence to the Fisher—Fama theory led to serious misunderstanding of the historically very high interest rates of the summer of
1974.[13] If one viewed the rate increments as incremental inflation premia
then he would not be disturbed as, for too long, the Federal Reserve
were not disturbed — or so it seems.

Of course, excessive commitment to the Fisher—Fama theory could encourage excessive monetary ease. Authorities might interpret dramatic
rate falls as mostly reflecting a consensus that inflation rates were to fall
rather than as reflecting stronger expansion of the monetary base together
with reversal of disintermediation.

So discretionary Fisher—Fama central bankers could, in the metaphor
of an American statesman, become loose cannon(s) on the Policy deck,
more than fulfilling their 'latent anti-damping potential'. They could
easily come to regard the interest-rate effects of their erratic monetary
expansion policies as being comprised of a tranquil real-rate and a volatile inflation-expectation premium.[14]

### 3. Remarks About Historical Time

It has become commonplace for theorists to distinguish between notional
(logical, meta-) time and historical time in dealing with any economic
process without an indefinitely short half-life. In monetary economics,
analyses working in the former sort of time cast up numerous invariance
propositions (although corresponding processes are unobservable in historical, i.e. calendar, time). But historical-time analyses, such as this one,
almost always depict shifts in monetary policy as affecting interest rates,
etc., in ways which break up invariance of the state of the 'real' economy
to nominally defined parameters. And indeed such analyses must strictly

probably be detached altogether from equilibrium analysis: the structure
of the system becomes dependent upon the system's behaviour in historical time, behaviour which cannot be entirely specified now. We are led
into Karl Popper's famous theorem.

#### 4. Latent Damping Features

4.1. *The essentially damping properties of a rule such as* $M_t = M^0 e^{\alpha t}$. One
must not pretend to a false rigour. The theorising of this paper is too
implicit to permit one properly to *prove* this proposition. So I shall but
offer a modest suggestion:

> The predominant property of the processes taken up here, in turn
> selected for their seeming empirical significance, has been one of
> endogenous, i.e. spontaneous, damping. This means that recessionary
> episodes tend automatically to lead to cheaper money and boom
> episodes to dearer money, relative to some steady rate of monetary
> expansion. So, if the nexi of this paper are closed up with a rule like
> the one above, one has reason to believe that the upshot will be highly
> damped processes.

4.2. *Finance.* I have long been fascinated by 'finance' in the sense of the
*Treatise* and by the related exchanges of Keynes and Dennis Robertson.
This has been partly because the discussion poses the possibility of anti-
damping behaviour: as a recession develops, excess demand for loans con-
ceivably could cumulatively increase. However, the following 'fixprice'
model suggests that 'finance' will not lead to anti-damping, thus invoking
the odd ambiance of Robertson's *Banking Policy and the Price Level.*
    Consider a unit reduction in autonomous expenditure and its associated
multiplier, $\lambda$. Then consider

$$\Pi = f(y) \qquad f'(y) > 0 \tag{2}$$

Evaluate $f'(y_\tau)$,

$$\Delta\Pi = f'(y_\tau)\Delta y^{15} \tag{3}$$

Tacitly shifting from time-dimensionality to non-time-dimensionality
(i.e. to cumulants), perhaps by converting to a period analysis, carefully
defining the periods relative to units thus far employed, the change in the
industrial finance requirement is

$$-\Delta A + k(\Delta\Pi)$$

where $k$ = the retention rate; $\Delta\Pi$ will be negative and is being measured
absolutely. So the condition for a reduction in autonomous expenditure
leading to a reduction in the industrial finance requirement (or an increase

leading to an increase) is

$$1 > f'(y)\lambda k \tag{4}$$

This condition would appear easily to be met, to the extent that empirical work can be matched with the theory of this paper. Thus an incremental profit share of $0{\cdot}3$ would be on the high side, as would a multiplier of $2{\cdot}5$: $(0{\cdot}3)(2{\cdot}5) = 0{\cdot}75$, for $k = 1$!

Now necessarily verging upon abandonment of fixprice, consider *in-ability to accomplish intended reductions in autonomous expenditure, say via inventory decumulation*. We continue to treat $\Delta A$ as a datum, now an *ex-post* datum. But we shall assume that some sort of price-cutting behaviour transpires so that the finance requirement of industry is to increase by the quantified factor $\xi$.[16]

### 4.3. *Disintermediation.*[17] Stipulate that sector A's liabilities comprise the economy's only reserve asset,[18] save for A's reserves. Assume that A-reserves take the form of an asset (liability) supplied by the authorities exclusively to A. Centre on A's sight liabilities (e.g. demand deposits) versus A's longer-term liabilities. Assume uniform reserve requirements. Claims on sector B are all for term.

It is obvious that isolated transfers from A-deposits to B-deposits do not put the A-sector into global imbalance.[19] It is just as obvious that the member of A, bank $a_j$, might become imbalanced because of such a transfer; but for A = $(a_j, a_k)$, bank $a_k$ must then experience an equal and opposite impulse.

Isolated transfers from the B-sector to the A-sector deplete B-reserves whilst not increasing the liquidity of A.[20] Such *disintermediation* leads to excess supply in credit markets as B-institutions seek to restore their liquidity.[21]

### 4.3.1. *Damping versus anti-damping effects, depending upon the extent to which discretionary officials may act incorrectly relative to full data.* Except to the extent that B-institutions might be specialised to supplying credit to sector C, able to rely on no other type of creditor — so that contraction in B could bankrupt C with disastrous chain-reaction effects — the disintermediation force, or, for that matter, the opposite force, i.e. enhanced intermediation, works as a dampening agent in a more or less *laissez-faire* specification of the system. Noting that B deposit rates tend to be rigid, as do yields on B investments, disintermediation will tend to develop during booms and to reverse itself (i.e. transform itself into enhanced intermediation) during recessions, certainly to the extent that we accept eq. (3) and related arguments.

Now consider a discretionary central-bank regime. Such a regime might squeeze the banking sector (A) at just the wrong time, say at a downward turning-point in the business cycle. So disintermediation might be provoked at just the point when — under a *laissez-faire* regime — increased intermediation would have been easing credit conditions. *Cf. 1974!* And if the authorities adhered to 'Fisher–Fama', they would be able to insulate themselves from reception of any signal that this is what is happening: the received signal would say that inflation premia are widening. In the same way, discretionary Fisher–Fama authorities[22] might continue to expand the A reserve base at rates above secular norms at and after an upward turning-point in the real cycle. *Voir summer 1975?* Increased intermediation would be provoked at just the time when, naturally, there would be some degree of disintermediation, dampening down developing inflationary pressures. And the authorities, pleased that inflation premia were falling in efficient credit markets, might be induced further to accelerate expansion of the monetary base: the data would simply feed their complacency.

### Notes

1. Cf. M. L. Burstein, *Economic Theory* (London: Wiley, 1968) chap. 13, esp. pp. 292–3.
2. Cf. M. L. Burstein, *Money* (Cambridge, Mass.: Schenkman 1963) pp. 495–6.
3. Cf. Section 3 below. Also Burstein, *Economic Theory*, pp. 29–31, esp. the discussion at p. 30 concerning 'I today am not I tomorrow'.
4. A secular-growth-rate expectation cannot rigorously be defined independently of the terms on which the firm expects to be able to raise capital.

   *Pace* many commentators, a high multiple does not mean a low cost of capital: everything hinges upon expectations of earnings growth (decay). Or consider a firm belonging to a group subject to a discount factor of 10 per cent per annum on expected earnings. The management anticipates a secular growth rate in earnings per share of 8 per cent per annum. But the market accords a p/e of 10. As the management sees it, the market is discounting the right-hand term of the expected (by management) earnings cumulant, *infra*, by something like 30 per cent, thus reducing the right-hand term's present value to zero. The management will not float fresh shares. It might withdraw from the capital market, abandoning investment schemes. Or it might push debt finance further, submitting to further balance-sheet deterioration.

$$(n + 1)E(0) + \sum_{1}^{n} [(0 \cdot 08)(E(0))] \, (1 \cdot 08)^t \quad n \to \infty$$

Share price $(t = 0) = (10) \, [E(0)]$ .

5. Cf. Irving Fisher, *The Theory of Interest* (New York: Kelley & Millman, 1954) chap. 19. This edition originally came out in 1930 and the book's earliest version was *Appreciation and Interest* (1896!). Fisher himself could not obtain from data more than qualitative support for his hypothesis that observed interest rates were composed of a quite stable 'real' part and a quite volatile inflation-premium part:

   'We have found evidence . . . with both bond yields and short-term interest rates that price changes do, generally and perceptibly, affect the interest rate in the direction indicated by the *a priori* theory. But since forethought is imperfect, the effects are smaller than the theory requires and lag behind price movements, in some periods, very greatly. When the effects of price changes upon interest rates are *distributed* over several years, we have found remarkably high coefficients of correlation . . . ' (op. cit., p. 451).

And so was an industry born. So was the *distributed lag* set among economists who knew what to do with it. Indeed, not a single proposition has been falsified by data since this singular concept was donated to the profession.

Nobody claimed anything more about the empirical underpinnings of the Fisher theory until recently, when Eugene Fama reported that:

> 'the results presented here indicate that, at least during the 1953—1971 period, there are definite relationships between nominal interest rates and rates of inflation subsequently observed. Moreover, during this period the bill market seems to be efficient in the sense that nominal interest rates summarize all the information about future inflation rates that is in time-series of past inflation rates. Finally . . . expected real returns on bills seem to be constant during the period.'
>
> Eugene F. Fama, 'Short-Term Interest Rates as Predictors of Inflation', American Economic Review, LXV (3) (June 1975) 269, at pp. 269—70.

The Fisher theory indeed has a certain plausibility. One cannot be shocked that a given set of data handled in a certain way does not falsify the theory. But it is not clear that the Fisher theory really is tractable to statistical test: a surrogate expectations function is not morphologically the same as the set of expectations $E_j$ when $j$ indexes the expectations of traders 1, 2, . . . , $n$. Furthermore, Fama really 'tests' only against the null-hypothesis, not against any explicit alternative hypothesis such as might have been constructed from Professor Tobin's remarks:

> 'Monetarists in particular have seized upon inflationary expectations as the principal source of variations of nominal interest rates. . . . The premise, usually tacit, is that the real rate moves little and slowly. The conclusion is that a rise of nominal interest rates [is] not a meaningful rise of rates in any real economic sense. . . . A correctly anticipated general inflation, *neutrally* embodied in interest rates, would not change equity values. . . . '
>
> James Tobin, 'Inflation, Interest Rates and Stock Values', *Morgan Guaranty Trust Survey* (July 1974) pp. 4—7, at pp. 5—6.

One awaits with interest 'tests' based on the wild gyrations of interest rates in 1974—5 in the United States, concomitant as these were with drastic U-turns in Federal Reserve policy.

6. For a rigorous demonstration of the inextricability of consumption and investment decisions by households, cf. M. G. Allingham and M. Morishima, Veblen Effects and Portfolio Selection', in M. Morishima *et al.*, *Theory of Demand: Real and Monetary* (Oxford: Clarendon Press, 1973) pp. 242 ff.

7. Cf. Tobin, op. cit., p. 6.

8. Ibid., p. 6.

9. In steady inflation the growth rate of the finance requirement and profits will be 1:1 so that the absolute value fo the finance requirement will be increasing.

10. Perhaps explaining the surprisingly widespread error that inventory profits are not profits. Cf. M. A. King, writing in the *Economic Journal* 1974, for a correct analysis.

11. Professor Tobin goes beyond his very sound brief when he calls inventory profits *fictitious* (op. cit., p. 4).

12. Cf. the chapter in this book by M. G. Allingham, extending his 'Equilibrium and Stability', *Econometrica*, XLII (4) (July 1974).
13. Cf. Tobin, op. cit., esp. p. 7.
14. It seems to me that, if the Federal Reserve had persisted in its (Fisher–Fama) squeeze into 1975, the financial texture of the American economy would have been ruptured by the end of spring 1975.
15. A fuller and more proper analysis would consider a cumulant of profit change over an interval, $\int f'(y)dy$.
16. As a fastidious analyst gets pushed into $n$-market discussion, as he will in anything like a serious macroeconomic study, he will be forced to complicate and hence to some extent to obscure the simple lines of the text's analysis. So in order to maintain the clarity of the text and to indicate the directions of a more thoroughgoing analysis, I append the note below. Observe that we strictly avoid any *Treatise*-like definitional tangle concerning the relationship of profit to investment.

To the extent that price-cutting has occurred, the household sector's real income will have increased so that their savings will have increased, meaning that there will have been generated an endogenous increase in the supply of finance. So we have already been driven from exclusive treatment of industrial finance towards household finance. And it would not be long before the theme of dishoarding (of cash) would emerge so that we would enter the heartland of the now ancient Keynes–Robertson discussion.

Picking up all these themes, an extended version of (4), giving the condition for direct and indirect effects of a reduction in autonomous expenditure in the industrial sector on net excess demand for finance leading to augmented excess supply of finance (still ignoring the official sector) is

$$1 > f'(y_T)\lambda k + \xi - \omega + s\lambda - \epsilon \tag{5}$$

where the fresh symbols and their meanings are:

$\omega$   indicating the increment to household savings implicit in the discussion of the second paragraph of this note and related textual discussion;
$s$   where $s$ is a relationship between household saving and net national product (albeit not strictly a propensity to save for obvious reasons) so that a first approximation to the (negative) effect on this source of finance is $s\lambda$;
$\epsilon$   induced cash disgorgement.

Of course, the 'model' is not explicit. The various differentials must be put into coherent relationship if the analysis is to be rigorous.
17. Cf. Burstein, *Economic Theory*, Chap. 13.
18. A *reserve asset* is thus being defined as a claim (necessarily against somebody and hence somebody's liability) which might be said to be in an absorbing state: the act of encashment of such a claim yields up such a claim. Compare presentation of a Bank of England note for redemption.
19. Except to the extent that the upshot may find an increase in the sight-liability component of A's balance sheet, perhaps to a level violating prudential constraints. It is evident from the text that the *reserve asset* definition applies to A, not to component $a_j$.
20. Except to the extent that the structure of A-liabilities becomes longer so that $a_j$ is more liquid. Cf. note 19.
21. The analysis is intensely Keynesian. It is the reserve asset (liability) property of bank paper, not any monetary property, which produces our result. And outcomes are measured in terms of effects on credit conditions, not M-magnitudes.

22. I suspect that Professor Fama is opposed to discretionary monetary authority. The text's point is that the *mélange* of doctrine which some say has been accumulated by Dr Burns, but which in any case could be accumulated by one or another discretionary authority, described in the text, has disastrous potential whilst a system governed by a rule would, in this Keynesian conspectus, tend to behave quite properly.

# 14 Equity Values in Periods of Inflation

HENRY C. WALLICH and NORMAN E. MAINS

*The analysis and conclusions are those of the authors and do not necessarily indicate concurrence by other members of the research staffs, by the Board of Governors, or by the Federal Reserve Banks.*

## 1. Introduction

Despite dramatic increase in share prices during the first half of 1975, nominal stock prices have returned only to 1964 levels; real stock prices are substantially lower.

This paper will attempt to show that the lack of growth in nominal stock prices reflects (1) a widespread deterioration in the quality of reported profits by American corporations, and (2) an inability of these corporations adequately to increase their equity capital either internally or externally. The paper is organised as follows. Section 2 presents the nominal and real rates of return for long-run equity ownership over the last fifty years and shows that, despite the stress on performance, the most recent ten-year period, 1965–74, has been one of the poorest periods for equity ownership in the last half-century. Section 3 will show that this widespread lack of growth in both nominal and real equity prices reflects the inability of America corporations to maintain robust operating profits, although reported profits have shown sizeable increases. This, in turn, has forced corporations to rely on external sources of funds to finance their investment outlays, largely high-cost debt. The difficulty experienced by corporations in increasing their equity capital through retained earnings has been further aggravated by the record level of both short- and long-term interest rates in recent years. Section 4 discusses the changing pattern of both debt and equity ownership in recent years and suggests that traditional net purchasers of equities may have shifted their preferences to other assets. This section also suggests that the corporate bond market has contributed to the 'two-tier' market for corporate equities: the highest-rated corporations have greater access to funds in the public debt markets and are able to borrow money at significantly lower costs. Finally, Section 5 discusses the implications of these events for capital formation.

164

## 2. Nominal and Real Rates of Return, 1926—74

Several years ago Fisher and Lorie (1968) published a comprehensive study
of the average annual rates of return that were hypothetically earned by investing in all common stocks listed on the New York Stock Exchange over
the 1926—65 period. Among its most important results was the conclusion
that, on average, owners of equities earned approximately 9·2 per cent over
the entire period. However, Fisher and Lorie's results were expressed as
nominal rates of return and ignored the impact of changes in purchasing
power due to rising and falling prices. Since the last fifty years encompasses
periods of significant inflation and deflation, it is worth seeing the impact
of these price changes by focusing on the real rates of return.

Using Standard and Poor's 500 Stock Index as a broadly-based measure
of stock price movements, Table 1 presents the nominal and real average
annual rates of return that were earned over each successive ten-year period
beginning in 1926 (1926—35) and ending in 1965 (1965—74). The first row
shows, for example, that an investor's nominal rate of return was, on average, 5·9 per cent over the 1926—35 period. (This return is, of course, a hypo-
thetical result since it ignores all brokerage costs and assumes that all dividends were reinvested at the end of each year during the period.) These
nominal rates of return show that the poorest ten-year period was 1929—38,
a period during which each dollar invested would have been worth slightly
less than 94 cents ten years later. With the exception of this one ten-year
period, however, investing in common stocks always resulted in a positive
nominal rate of return provided the investor was willing to maintain his or
her holdings for the entire ten-year period. The nominal returns also show
that the most recent ten-year period, 1965—74, was one of the poorest over
the entire period, since an investor achieved an average annual return of
only 1·2 per cent. Even if the period is lengthened to include the advance
in stock prices in early 1975, the average annual return is increased to only
4·0 per cent.

A strikingly different picture is presented by the real rates of return,
however. The real returns were estimated by adjusting each year's nominal
increase or decrease in stock prices by the change in consumer prices (on a
December-to-December basis), and wide differences result when a ten-year
period was characterised by large changes in the overall level of prices. The
1930s was, for example, a period of generally declining common stock
prices. But consumer prices also declined dramatically during 1930, 1931
and 1932, and consequently the ten-year average annual *real* rates of return
that include this three-year period are all positive. Likewise, the rapid rise
in common stock prices during the Second World War was accompanied by
a rapid price inflation resulting in relatively low *real* rates of return. The
most dramatic result in Table 1 is, however, the most recent ten-year period,
1965—74. Its average annual nominal rate of return, 1·2 per cent, reduces
to a negative real return of —4·1 per cent owing to the rapid rise in consumer

TABLE 1

*Average Annual Nominal and Real Rates of Return*
(ten-year holding periods, 1926—74)

| Ten-year period | Average annual rate of return | | Ten-year period | Average annual rate of return | |
|---|---|---|---|---|---|
| | Nominal | Real | | Nominal | Real |
| | (per cent) | | | (per cent) | |
| 1926—35 | 5·9 | 10·4 | 1946—55 | 16·2 | 8·3 |
| 1927—36 | 7·9 | 12·2 | 1947—56 | 17·9 | 14·4 |
| 1928—37 | 0·3 | 3·9 | 1948—57 | 15·9 | 13·4 |
| 1929—38 | —0·6 | 3·3 | 1949—58 | 19·4 | 17·5 |
| 1930—39 | 0·1 | 4·6 | 1950—59 | 18·8 | 16·7 |
| 1931—40 | 1·8 | 4·4 | 1951—60 | 15·8 | 13·6 |
| 1932—41 | 6·2 | 4·0 | 1952—61 | 16·1 | 14·5 |
| 1933—42 | 9·1 | 3·5 | 1953—62 | 13·1 | 11·7 |
| 1934—43 | 7·0 | 1·7 | 1954—63 | 15·6 | 14·1 |
| 1935—44 | 9·1 | 4·6 | 1955—64 | 12·6 | 8·8 |
| 1936—45 | 8·2 | 4·1 | 1956—65 | 10·9 | 9·2 |
| 1937—46 | 4·3 | —3·8 | 1957—66 | 9·0 | 7·2 |
| 1938—47 | 9·3 | —0·2 | 1958—67 | 12·6 | 10·9 |
| 1939—48 | 7·0 | —3·4 | 1959—68 | 9·8 | 7·9 |
| 1940—49 | 8·9 | —1·9 | 1960—69 | 7·7 | 5·3 |
| 1941—50 | 13·0 | 2·1 | 1961—70 | 8·0 | 5·1 |
| 1942—51 | 16·8 | 6·9 | 1962—71 | 6·9 | 3·7 |
| 1943—52 | 16·6 | 8·3 | 1963—72 | 8·1 | 6·3 |
| 1944—53 | 13·9 | 5·9 | 1964—73 | 5·9 | 1·9 |
| 1945—54 | 16·6 | 8·4 | 1965—74 | 1·2 | —4·1 |

| | | *Nominal* | *Real* |
|---|---|---|---|
| Mean | | 10·1 | 6·6 |
| Standard deviation | | 5·4 | 5·4 |
| Maximum | | 19·4 | 17·5 |
| Minimum | | —0·6 | —4·1 |

prices, the lowest ten-year average over the entire 49-year period. Extending the period to include the rapid rise in stock prices in early 1975 increases the real return to only —1·5 per cent.

The real rates of return clearly demonstrate the sizeable impact of purchasing-power changes on the historical nominal rates of return achieved through equity investment. It is somewhat surprising, then, that almost all the rigorous empirical studies of capital market equilibrium in recent years have ignored the sizeable differences that have existed between nominal and real rates of return. It seems reasonable to suggest, for example, that some of the principal results of the capital asset pricing model need to be closely re-examined. In addition, the relationship between inflation and equity values must be more clearly understood. Lintner (1973) notes that relatively little rigorous theoretical and empirical work has been directed at this important issue, although the topic has begun to be re-examined.

Cagan (1974) recently published an important work considering whether common stocks have provided a hedge against inflation in major industrialised countries. Using broadly-based stock price indices, he concludes that equities *have* been an effective hedge in the long run. Cagan emphasises, however, that the values of common stocks during and after inflationary episodes may take ten or more years to 'catch up', regaining their long-run relationship.

### 3. Profits, Interest Rates and Common Stock Prices

Since economic theory postulates that the value of an ownership claim such as a share of common stock is the capitalised value of its expected stream of dividends discounted by an appropriate rate of interest, it implies that fluctuations in economic activity, interest rates and corporate profits interact to produce fluctuations in the levels of stock prices (and vice versa). The relationship between these variables has been investigated recently by Moore (1975). Using the eight growth cycles identified by Mintz (1974) for the American economy during the 1948—70 period, Moore shows that 'no cyclical swing in the [stock] market occurred without an accompanying swing in the growth cycle, [and] only one growth cycle downswing occurred, that of 1951—2, without a cyclical downswing in the market'. Moore's work emphasises the cyclical relationship between interest rates, stock prices and growth cycles, and his results show that both interest rates and stock prices appear to lead growth cycles by several months, but that the exact length of these leads is highly variable.

The strong cyclical relationship between common stock prices and growth cycles probably explains some of the large gyrations that often occur when a corporation announces quarterly earnings that are slightly different than the 'market' was expecting. While these movements are sometimes justified by the impressive empirical and theoretical literature which has shown that American capital markets are highly efficient, it is nevertheless very unnerving for many investors, both unsophisticated and sophisticated, to see large price changes due only to fractional changes in earnings. These price movements have surely been exacerbated by the 'performance consciousness' that has permeated both the equity and bond markets in recent years. Performance evaluation periods are considerably shorter today than they were a few years ago, and more and more information is now available documenting the performance records of competing professional portfolio managers. However, minor interruptions in earnings streams due to unforeseen adverse developments, even those lasting as long as a year or two, should not necessarily cause such abrupt price changes unless the corporation's *long-run* earning capability is impaired. Thus, some of these wide price movements suggest that too much weight is being given to short-run developments. It should also be noted that a number of both economic and political events have occurred in recent years that have depressed stock prices. Since theory suggests that stock prices will decline whenever expected returns move lower or uncertainty increases, the recent decline in equity values is not wholly surprising. However, the magnitude of this decline seems less easy to rationalise in the light of the resilience that our economic and political system has demonstrated in coping with these unexpected events.

Since Moore's work clearly indentifies that a cyclical relationship exists between stock prices and corporate profits, it may seem somewhat surprising that current stock prices are only at levels first reached in 1964, since total reported corporate profits have more than doubled over the same period. But just as it was demonstrated that a wide difference has existed between nominal and real rates of return in recent years, the inflation's impact on corporate balance sheets has also produced a wide gap between reported and actual profits.

A corporation can generate funds to support its activities in three ways: (1) its basic operations can produce revenues greater than out-of-pocket expenses; (2) it can borrow additional money; or (3) it can liquidate real or financial assets that were previously accumulated. The ability to produce profits from its basic operations is, however, its fundamental strength, since additional borrowings or liquidations of assets are not a limitless source of funds to any corporation. It seems reasonable, then, that the value of a corporation must ultimately rest on its ability to earn profits from its basic operations. Therefore, a contributing factor to the lack of growth in equity values in recent years has been the realisation by investors that while reported profits have been increasing, the quality of these profits has been declining.

The illusory nature of reported corporate profits in recent years can be easily demonstrated. Table 2 presents the annual total profits reported by American corporations. Total profits were reported to be $140·7 billion in 1974, and this represents a sixfold increase over the 1946 total of $24·6 billion. In addition, year-to-year increases in total reported profits were recorded in 19 of the 28 periods, with declines in only nine periods. These totals include, however, profits earned by financial institutions (including the Federal Reserve System) and repatriated profits earned by foreign subsidiaries, initially accounting for only 10 per cent of total profits, but steadily increasing so that they have recently accounted for more than 20 per cent of the total. The rest-of-world profits were especially large during 1974, at $9·9 billion, owing in part to the foreign profits of the American-based multinational oil companies. One can focus on the profits of the domestic non-financial corporations and the basis for their profit-tax computations, excluding foreign and financial profits from the totals. The United States taxed these profits at a 48 per cent rate in recent years, but tax payments were influenced by such items as investment tax credits so that 1974's tax payments show an overall effective tax rate of approximately 41 per cent.

TABLE 2

Corporate Profits and Retained Earnings, 1946–74
($ billion)

| Year | Total reported corporate profits | Financial and rest of world | Domestic non-financial corporate profits | Profit taxes | Dividends | Retained earnings | Inventory valuation adjustment | Retained earnings and I.V.A. | Capital consumption allowances | Internal cash generation |
|---|---|---|---|---|---|---|---|---|---|---|
| 1946 | 24·6 | 2·6 | 22·0 | 8·6 | 5·1 | 8·3 | -5·3 | 3·0 | 4·6 | 7·6 |
| 1947 | 31·5 | 2·4 | 29·1 | 10·0 | 5·9 | 12·4 | -5·9 | 6·5 | 5·7 | 12·2 |
| 1948 | 35·2 | 3·4 | 31·8 | 11·9 | 6·5 | 13·4 | -2·2 | 11·2 | 6·9 | 18·1 |
| 1949 | 28·9 | 4·0 | 24·9 | 9·5 | 6·5 | 8·9 | 1·9 | 10·8 | 7·8 | 18·6 |
| 1950 | 42·6 | 4·1 | 38·5 | 16·7 | 7·9 | 13·8 | -5·0 | 8·8 | 8·6 | 17·4 |
| 1951 | 43·9 | 5·8 | 39·1 | 21·0 | 7·8 | 10·3 | -1·2 | 9·1 | 10·1 | 19·2 |
| 1952 | 38·9 | 5·1 | 33·8 | 17·8 | 7·8 | 8·1 | 1·0 | 9·1 | 11·3 | 20·4 |
| 1953 | 40·6 | 5·7 | 34·9 | 18·5 | 8·0 | 8·4 | -1·0 | 7·4 | 12·9 | 20·3 |
| 1954 | 38·3 | 6·2 | 32·1 | 15·7 | 8·2 | 8·1 | -0·3 | 7·8 | 14·7 | 22·5 |
| 1955 | 48·6 | 6·6 | 42·0 | 19·8 | 9·4 | 12·8 | -1·7 | 11·1 | 17·1 | 28·2 |
| 1956 | 48·8 | 7·0 | 41·8 | 19·8 | 10·1 | 11·9 | -2·7 | 9·2 | 18·5 | 27·7 |
| 1957 | 47·2 | 7·4 | 39·8 | 18·9 | 10·4 | 10·5 | -1·5 | 9·0 | 20·4 | 29·4 |
| 1958 | 41·4 | 7·7 | 33·7 | 16·3 | 10·2 | 7·3 | -0·3 | 7·0 | 21·5 | 28·5 |
| 1959 | 52·1 | 8·9 | 43·2 | 20·8 | 10·9 | 11·6 | -0·5 | 11·1 | 23·0 | 34·1 |
| 1960 | 49·7 | 9·6 | 40·1 | 19·5 | 11·6 | 9·0 | 0·2 | 9·2 | 24·3 | 33·5 |
| 1961 | 50·3 | 10·0 | 40·3 | 19·8 | 11·6 | 8·9 | -0·1 | 8·8 | 25·6 | 34·4 |
| 1962 | 55·4 | 10·7 | 44·7 | 20·9 | 12·8 | 11·1 | 0·3 | 11·4 | 29·3 | 40·7 |
| 1963 | 59·4 | 10·3 | 49·1 | 22·9 | 14·3 | 11·9 | -0·5 | 11·4 | 31·0 | 42·4 |
| 1964 | 66·8 | 11·0 | 55·8 | 24·4 | 15·0 | 16·5 | -0·5 | 16·0 | 32·9 | 48·9 |
| 1965 | 77·8 | 12·0 | 65·8 | 27·6 | 16·9 | 21·3 | -1·7 | 19·6 | 35·4 | 55·0 |
| 1966 | 84·2 | 13·0 | 71·2 | 30·1 | 18·2 | 22·9 | -1·8 | 21·1 | 38·4 | 59·5 |
| 1967 | 79·8 | 13·6 | 66·2 | 28·4 | 18·9 | 18·9 | -1·1 | 17·8 | 41·7 | 59·5 |
| 1968 | 87·6 | 15·2 | 72·4 | 34·0 | 20·9 | 17·5 | -3·3 | 14·2 | 45·4 | 59·6 |
| 1969 | 84·9 | 16·9 | 68·0 | 33·7 | 20·7 | 13·6 | -5·1 | 8·5 | 50·1 | 58·6 |
| 1970 | 74·0 | 18·3 | 55·7 | 27·6 | 20·0 | 8·1 | -4·8 | 3·3 | 54·0 | 57·3 |
| 1971 | 85·6 | 20·4 | 63·2 | 29·8 | 20·2 | 13·2 | -4·9 | 8·3 | 58·2 | 66·5 |
| 1972 | 99·2 | 22·9 | 76·3 | 33·4 | 22·2 | 20·8 | -7·0 | 13·8 | 63·6 | 77·4 |
| 1973 | 122·7 | 26·9 | 95·8 | 40·7 | 23·7 | 31·3 | -17·6 | 13·7 | 68·1 | 81·8 |
| 1974 | 140·7 | 30·6 | 110·1 | 45·6 | 30·7 | 33·9 | -35·1 | -1·2 | 73·2 | 72·0 |

Table 2 also shows that dividend payments have been quite steady over the years, reflecting the reluctance of most corporations to lower their regular dividend payments when profits decline. Subtracting both taxes and dividends from reported profits yields up *reported* retained earnings. Reported retained earnings have registered a less impressive record of growth than total profits in the post-Second World War era, rising from $8·3 billion in 1946 to $33·9 billion in 1974.

It is well known that reported profits include inventory gains (or losses) caused by corporations increasing (or decreasing) the values of their inventories relative to changes in price levels. Table 2 shows that inventory profits were sizeable in the inflationary episodes shortly after the Second World War, accounting for almost half of reported retained earnings in 1947, and particularly large again in recent years. Inventory profits contribute to a corporation's tax liability, but do not generate, relative to the inflationary process, 'free cash'. They represent capital gains on assets which when liquidated must be wholly or partially replaced if the firm is to continue to do business. Deducting these amounts from the reported retained earnings results in a measure of retained earnings from operations more sensitive to corporate finance requirements. This measure of corporate profitability shows increases in only thirteen years since the Second World War, declines in thirteen years, and no change in two years. An inspection of these data for recent years, however, shows that corporate earnings, net of inventory profits, peaked at $21·1 billion in 1966 and have not since approached this level; such earnings were only $3·3 billion in 1970, and, more surprisingly, they were actually negative during 1974.

Since corporate earnings net of inventory profits measure the operating cash flow generated from internal operations, these amounts plus *reported* capital consumption allowances are the total internal funds available to the corporations to support their capital expenditures. Obviously corporations must finance their capital expenditures either through internal funds, external borrowings, or the liquidations of previously acquired real or financial assets. And so inflationary effects understate the finance requirements of corporations and capital consumption allowances also are understated: these totals are based on historical rather than replacement costs. The understatement of reported capital consumption allowances can be offset, of course, by changes in the tax laws; although depreciation rules have been altered several times in recent years, Nordhaus (1974) has recently concluded that economic depreciation in 1973 was $2·3 billion greater than reported capital consumption allowances so that corporate profits were overstated by this same amount.

The overall importance of both inventory valuation adjustments and economic versus reported depreciation is that retained earnings are a smaller *source* of funds to corporations than their reported figures would seem to indicate. And since corporations have reported almost uninterrupted increases in their total annual *uses* of funds over the last thirty years (total physical investment plus net acquisitions of financial assets), the difference between total *uses* and internal *sources* has been an increasing reliance on external sources of funds, particularly credit market borrowings.

Using Flow-of-Funds data, Table 3 presents the annual net funds raised in markets by domestic non-financial corporations since 1946. These data show that a significant upward movement began in 1965 and that the total has increased on a year-to-year basis in each of the successive years. It is no coincidence, of course, that the inflation rate has increased markedly since 1965. And while non-financial corporations have been net *acquirers* of financial assets in every year except 1946, their growth has *not* kept pace with the increase in real assets: the corporate liquidity position has been deteriorating. In addition, the external sources of funds have been largely credit market borrowings, not new equity share issues. Approximately one-fourth of total physical investment was financed by credit market borrowings in earlier years. This amount has risen to approximately one-half in the more recent years. A more detailed composition of these borrowings is presented in Table 4. It shows that these external sources of funds have largely been corporate bonds and bank loans, new equity issues contributing sizeable amounts in only two recent years, 1971 and 1972. The small amount of new equity capital in earlier years was supplemented, of course, by retained earnings, but Table 2 demonstrates that this *source* of funds has been greatly reduced in recent years. Finally, the last two columns in Table 4 show that non-financial corporations maintained a reasonable balance between their additions to equity — net new stock issues plus reported retained earnings — and funds raised in the capital markets until the mid-1960s. During the last ten years, however, new addition of equity capital (including the retention of profits) has totalled only $164·9 billion, while new capital market debt has totalled $382·4 billion. This shift towards debt financing by corporations in the earlier years would seem to have been a logical profit-maximising response to the emergence of inflationary expectations together with the tax deductibility of interest payments. Whether the shift was indeed due to such expectations is moot: events have not resulted in what might have been expected, increasing profits and higher share prices. Increased reliance on borrowed funds simply has resulted in a reduction in the relative importance of equity in corporate balance sheets.

Valuing fixed assets and inventories at current or replacement prices (book-value data are not readily available) and financial assets at par or book value, Table 5 shows the erosion of equity in the balance sheets for domestic non-financial corporations over the ten-year period 1965—74. The same table also shows the relationship between equity and total assets using the market value of domestic non-financial corporate equities. This measure shows a much greater deterioration, owing to the lack of growth in share prices over the period. Finally, a comparison of the balance-sheet (adjusted for price-level changes) equity totals and the market valuation of these ownership claims highlights the pronounced decline in stock market prices

*Sources and Uses of Funds of Domestic Non-financial Corporations, 1946–74*
($ billion)

| Year | Total internal funds | Net funds raised in markets | Total | Net acquisition of financial assets | Total physical investment | Discrepancy | Credit market borrowing ÷ Total physical investment (per cent) |
|---|---|---|---|---|---|---|---|
| 1946 | 7·8 | 6·8 | 14·6 | −5·0 | 17·9 | 1·7 | 32·2 |
| 1947 | 12·6 | 8·6 | 21·2 | 2·6 | 17·2 | 1·4 | 43·8 |
| 1948 | 18·7 | 6·3 | 25·0 | 1·7 | 20·2 | 3·1 | 26·2 |
| 1949 | 19·1 | 3·2 | 22·3 | 6·2 | 15·2 | 0·9 | 12·8 |
| 1950 | 17·9 | 7·2 | 25·1 | 0·4 | 24·0 | 0·7 | 24·5 |
| 1951 | 19·9 | 10·0 | 29·9 | 1·8 | 29·8 | −1·7 | 27·2 |
| 1952 | 21·1 | 9·2 | 30·3 | 5·8 | 24·3 | 0·2 | 28·6 |
| 1953 | 21·1 | 5·6 | 26·7 | 1·6 | 24·5 | 0·4 | 16·0 |
| 1954 | 23·3 | 6·3 | 29·6 | 5·7 | 21·5 | 0·4 | 22·4 |
| 1955 | 29·2 | 10·3 | 39·5 | 3·5 | 31·3 | 2·4 | 27·0 |
| 1956 | 28·9 | 12·9 | 41·8 | 1·5 | 35·7 | 4·7 | 29·8 |
| 1957 | 30·6 | 12·0 | 42·6 | 4·6 | 34·5 | 4·6 | 28·1 |
| 1958 | 29·5 | 10·6 | 40·1 | 9·6 | 27·0 | 3·5 | 32·0 |
| 1959 | 35·0 | 12·6 | 47·6 | 6·6 | 36·7 | 3·5 | 28·7 |
| 1960 | 34·4 | 11·9 | 46·3 | 1·6 | 38·7 | 4·3 | 27·0 |
| 1961 | 35·6 | 12·3 | 47·9 | 6·5 | 36·3 | 6·0 | 27·7 |
| 1962 | 41·8 | 12·5 | 54·3 | 6·2 | 43·6 | 5·1 | 27·6 |
| 1963 | 43·9 | 12·1 | 56·0 | 6·2 | 45·2 | 4·5 | 28·2 |
| 1964 | 50·5 | 14·5 | 65·0 | 6·0 | 51·6 | 4·6 | 25·6 |
| 1965 | 56·6 | 20·4 | 77·0 | 5·9 | 62·3 | 7·4 | 32·8 |
| 1966 | 61·2 | 25·3 | 86·5 | 1·8 | 76·5 | 8·8 | 31·4 |
| 1967 | 61·5 | 29·6 | 91·1 | 13·9 | 71·4 | 8·2 | 31·1 |
| 1968 | 61·6 | 31·5 | 93·1 | 8·5 | 75·0 | 5·8 | 42·3 |
| 1969 | 60·7 | 38·9 | 99·6 | 10·0 | 83·7 | 9·6 | 42·4 |
| 1970 | 59·4 | 39·5 | 98·9 | 8·2 | 84·0 | 5·9 | 40·2 |
| 1971 | 68·0 | 46·8 | 114·8 | 17·4 | 87·2 | 6·7 | 40·7 |
| 1972 | 78·7 | 55·3 | 134·0 | 16·8 | 102·5 | 10·2 | 43·3 |
| 1973 | 84·6 | 67·2 | 151·8 | 16·5 | 121·5 | 14·7 | 49·2 |
| 1974 | 81·4 | 74·7 | 156·1 | 17·3 | 125·8 | 13·0 | 56·6 |

Source: *Flow-of-Funds*, Board of Governors of the Federal Reserve System.

TABLE 4

*External Sources of Funds for Domestic Non-financial Corporations, 1946–74*
($ billion)

| Year | Total net funds raised in markets | Net new equity issue | Corporate bonds | Mortgages | Bank loans n.e.c. | Other | Reported retained earnings plus net new equity | Net Funds raised in the capital markets |
|---|---|---|---|---|---|---|---|---|
| 1946 | 6·8 | 1·0 | 1·0 | 1·5 | 3·5 | -0·2 | 4·0 | 5·8 |
| 1947 | 8·6 | 1·1 | 2·8 | 1·6 | 3·2 | -0·1 | 7·6 | 7·5 |
| 1948 | 6·3 | 1·0 | 4·3 | 1·1 | -0·1 | 1·0 | 12·5 | 5·3 |
| 1949 | 3·2 | 1·3 | 2·9 | 0·9 | -1·8 | -0·1 | 12·1 | 1·9 |
| 1950 | 7·2 | 1·3 | 1·6 | 0·9 | 3·3 | 0·1 | 10·6 | 5·9 |
| 1951 | 10·1 | 1·8 | 3·3 | 0·8 | 3·8 | 0·3 | 11·4 | 8·1 |
| 1952 | 9·2 | 2·3 | 4·7 | 0·9 | 0·8 | 0·5 | 10·8 | 6·9 |
| 1953 | 5·6 | 1·7 | 3·4 | 0·9 | -0·5 | 0·1 | 8·9 | 3·9 |
| 1954 | 6·3 | 1·5 | 3·5 | 1·6 | -0·6 | 0·3 | 9·3 | 4·8 |
| 1955 | 10·3 | 1·8 | 2·8 | 1·8 | 3·9 | – | 13·9 | 8·5 |
| 1956 | 12·9 | 2·2 | 3·6 | 1·6 | 5·2 | 0·3 | 11·4 | 10·7 |
| 1957 | 12·0 | 2·4 | 6·3 | 1·6 | 1·1 | 0·6 | 9·4 | 9·7 |
| 1958 | 10·6 | 1·9 | 5·7 | 2·9 | -0·3 | 0·4 | 13·0 | 8·6 |
| 1959 | 12·6 | 2·1 | 3·0 | 3·0 | 4·0 | 0·5 | 11·3 | 10·5 |
| 1960 | 11·9 | 1·5 | 3·5 | 2·5 | 2·2 | 2·2 | 10·3 | 10·4 |
| 1961 | 12·3 | 2·2 | 4·6 | 4·0 | 0·7 | 0·8 | 13·6 | 10·1 |
| 1962 | 12·5 | 0·4 | 4·6 | 4·5 | 2·9 | 0·1 | 11·8 | 12·0 |
| 1963 | 12·1 | -0·6 | 3·9 | 4·9 | 3·6 | 0·3 | 10·8 | 12·7 |
| 1964 | 14·5 | 1·3 | 4·0 | 3·6 | 4·5 | 1·1 | 17·3 | 13·2 |
| 1965 | 20·4 | – | 5·4 | 3·9 | 10·5 | 0·6 | 19·6 | 20·4 |
| 1966 | 25·3 | 1·3 | 10·2 | 4·2 | 8·3 | 1·3 | 22·4 | 24·0 |
| 1967 | 29·6 | 2·4 | 14·7 | 4·5 | 6·6 | 1·4 | 20·2 | 27·2 |
| 1968 | 31·5 | -0·2 | 12·9 | 5·7 | 9·6 | 3·5 | 14·0 | 31·7 |
| 1969 | 38·9 | 3·4 | 12·0 | 4·6 | 11·8 | 7·1 | 11·9 | 34·5 |
| 1970 | 39·5 | 5·7 | 19·8 | 5·2 | 5·6 | 3·2 | 9·0 | 33·8 |
| 1971 | 46·8 | 11·4 | 18·9 | 11·4 | 4·4 | 0·7 | 19·7 | 35·4 |
| 1972 | 55·3 | 10·9 | 12·7 | 15·6 | 13·5 | 2·6 | 24·7 | 44·4 |
| 1973 | 67·2 | 7·4 | 10·9 | 16·1 | 30·6 | 2·2 | 21·1 | 59·7 |
| 1974 | 74·7 | 3·5 | 20·6 | 10·8 | 27·5 | 12·3 | 2·3 | 71·3 |

Source: *Flow-of-Funds*, Board of Governors of the Federal Reserve System.

TABLE 5

Corporate Capital Structure, 1965–74
($ billion at year-end)

| Year | Domestic non-financial corporations | | | | Market value of corporate equities | | | | |
|---|---|---|---|---|---|---|---|---|---|
| | Total assets (1) | Total liabilities^b (2) | Equity (3) | Col.(3) ÷ Col.(1) | All corporations (4) | Financial and foreign (estimated)^c (5) | Domestic non-financial (6) | Col. (6) ÷ Col.(1) | Col. (6) ÷ Col.(3) |
| 1965 | 752·7 | 348·9 | 403·8 | 0·54 | 713·7 | 160·0 | 553·7 | 0·74 | 1·37 |
| 1966 | 821·0 | 383·9 | 437·1 | 0·53 | 647·8 | 143·6 | 504·2 | 0·61 | 1·15 |
| 1967 | 886·2 | 414·7 | 471·5 | 0·53 | 824·8 | 172·2 | 652·7 | 0·74 | 1·38 |
| 1968 | 972·8 | 466·6 | 506·3 | 0·52 | 975·0 | 234·3 | 730·6 | 0·75 | 1·44 |
| 1969 | 1,072·1 | 520·7 | 551·4 | 0·51 | 859·4 | 219·4 | 640·0 | 0·60 | 1·16 |
| 1970 | 1,154·0 | 559·6 | 594·3 | 0·51 | 852·9 | 209·8 | 643·1 | 0·56 | 1·08 |
| 1971 | 1,244·9 | 600·4 | 644·5 | 0·52 | 989·5 | 242·6 | 746·9 | 0·60 | 1·16 |
| 1972 | 1,364·2 | 658·6 | 705·6 | 0·52 | 1,163·2 | 278·0 | 885·2 | 0·64 | 1·25 |
| 1973 | 1,509·2 | 743·8 | 765·5 | 0·51 | 921·4 | 219·1 | 702·3 | 0·47 | 0·92 |
| 1974 | 1,722·7 | 846·7 | 876·0 | 0·51 | 661·9 | 161·0 | 500·9 | 0·29 | 0·57 |

^aFixed assets and inventories are valued at current prices in the balance sheet after deducting depreciation on a current-cost double-declining balance basis. Financial assets valued at par at book value.
^bLiabilities valued at par or book value. Valuing these claims at market would probably lower the totals somewhat, particularly in the most recent years.
^cFlow-of-Funds staff estimate.
Source: Flow-of-Funds, Board of Governors of the Federal Reserve System.

in 1973 and 1974. The last column in the table shows that equities were selling at sizeable discounts below their adjusted book values in both those years.

The ability of corporations to carry this increased debt burden has also been adversely affected both by their declining liquidity positions and by the relatively high cost of the borrowings. Table 6 (overleaf) presents two measures of liquidity for domestic non-financial corporations over the 1946–74 period: (1) the ratio of liquid assets to short-term debt; and (2) the ratio of liquid assets to total liabilities. Both these measures show the overall decline of corporate liquidity throughout the period. Liquid assets were approximately two-thirds of short-term liabilities immediately after the Second World War; they have declined to slightly more than one-fifth at the end of 1974. Likewise, the ratio of liquid assets to total liabilities has declined steadily from 41·6 per cent in 1946 to 13·3 per cent in 1974. Moreover, the composition of these liquid assets has shifted from demand deposits and U.S. Treasury securities towards higher-yielding, but less liquid, commercial paper, State and local government securities and security repurchase agreements (R.P.s).

The enormous amount of net debt issuance has also been expensive. Domestic non-financial corporations have issued approximately $120 billion of long-term debt in the last five years with an average annual interest cost of approximately 8¼ per cent. Retirements of long-term debt over this same period were approximately $35 billion, but these issues also had an average interest cost that was significantly lower than the new issues. This sizeable increase in debt service expense has been particularly burdensome for companies which traditionally maintain high debt-to-equity ratios. Such costs for electric utilities and communication companies, for example, have surely contributed to their inability since 1969 to achieve positive reported retained earnings plus I.V.A. While the higher interest expense burden has been partly offset by the concomitant shifting within liquid assets to higher-yielding obligations, net interest paid by non-financial corporations totalled $22·9 billion in 1974, an amount sharply higher than the $5·1 billion figure ten years earlier and the $12·7 billion total in 1969.

## 4. Stock and Bond Ownership Patterns

Section 3 endeavoured to show that the escalating pace of inflation in recent years has resulted in both a deterioration in the quality of corporate profits and a dramatic substitution of high-cost debt for equity capital in corporate balance sheets. In addition, Table 1 suggested that these events have had market recognition: both nominal and real rates of return for equity ownership have been significantly below their normal levels. And the low rates of return shown in Table 1 probably understate the full impact of the decline in stock prices in recent years. The S&P 500 is a value-weighted index in which only ten stocks have accounted for approximately one-third

TABLE 6

*Liquidity Ratios of Domestic Non-financial Corporations, 1946—74*

| Year | Liquid assets[a] to short-term debt[b] | Liquid assets to total liabilities | Year | Liquid assets[a] to short-term debt[b] | Liquid assets to total liabilities |
|------|------|------|------|------|------|
| 1946 | 72·5 | 41·6 | 1961 | 41·2 | 22·4 |
| 1947 | 63·6 | 37·4 | 1962 | 41·0 | 22·1 |
| 1948 | 62·1 | 35·4 | 1963 | 40·5 | 22·0 |
| 1949 | 72·8 | 38·7 | 1964 | 37·8 | 20·8 |
| 1950 | 59·6 | 35·5 | 1965 | 34·2 | 19·4 |
| 1951 | 55·6 | 33·9 | 1966 | 29·3 | 16·7 |
| 1952 | 55·4 | 32·4 | 1967 | 29·8 | 16·6 |
| 1953 | 57·4 | 32·7 | 1968 | 29·1 | 16·4 |
| 1954 | 58·3 | 32·0 | 1969 | 26·2 | 15·2 |
| 1955 | 53·7 | 31·1 | 1970 | 24·2 | 14·0 |
| 1956 | 45·6 | 26·5 | 1971 | 27·4 | 14·8 |
| 1957 | 44·5 | 25·0 | 1972 | 26·2 | 14·1 |
| 1958 | 46·2 | 25·0 | 1973 | 24·2 | 13·5 |
| 1959 | 45·8 | 25·3 | 1974 | 22·9 | 13·3 |
| 1960 | 40·7 | 22·3 |  |  |  |

[a] Liquid assets include demand deposits and currency, time deposits, U.S. government securities, State and local obligations, commercial paper, and security R.P.s.
[b] Short-term debt includes all liabilities except corporate bonds and mortgages.
Source: *Flow-of-Funds*, Board of Governors of the Federal Reserve System.

of its movements in recent years. Broader measures of the stock market, such as an unweighted index of all stocks listed on the New York Stock Exchange, show an even more pronounced decline. The divergence between the prices of larger versus smaller companies has produced a segmentation in the market that has been popularly referred to as the 'two-tier' market. A two-tier market is one in which the prices and price/earnings ratios of some stocks are significantly above those of others. It seems reasonable to suggest that a factor contributing to this 'two-tier' phenomenon has been the deterioration of internal sources of funds and the substitution of external borrowing.[1]

A corporation's ability to borrow both short- and long-term funds is a function of the market's perception of its credit-worthiness; both the availability and cost funds depends on a company's credit standing in the market. Since the upward movement in interest rates over the last few years has been accompanied by a widening of the spreads between higher- and lower-rated obligations, borrowing has been significantly more expensive for lower-rated corporations. Indeed, the limited amount of available funds has been rationed among borrowers. Credit rationing became particularly acute during 1974 as investors became increasingly wary about the ability of many corporations to meet their contractual obligations. Such companies found their financing alternatives greatly diminished, since they were denied access to the public credit markets at the same time that the market values of many of their stocks were selling at sizeable discounts below norms based on say earnings or yields.

The allocative characteristics of the public credit markets are demonstrated in Table 7. The table presents the annual gross volumes over the 1969–74 period for publicly offered credit obligations disaggregated by both bond ratings (Moody's) and maturities. These data show that the volume of lower-rated bond issues diminishes when long-term interest rates move to significantly higher levels as they did in 1970 and again in 1974. As yields move higher and yield spreads widen, many industrial corporations become reluctant to sell their obligations at the prevailing rates and instead elect to postpone or cancel planned investments. Electric and gas utilities, on the other hand, are unable to postpone financings as easily; they have steadily growing demands and must refund maturing obligations much more often owing to their high debt/equity ratios.

Another feature of the credit-rationing process occurring when yields move higher and spreads widen is a shortening of maturities. The maturity data presented in Table 8 show that medium maturity obligations – those maturing in less than twenty years – increased in 1970, 1972, and again in 1974, and a large portion of these medium maturity obligations carry lower ratings, particularly A and Baa. The credit markets became so restrictive in 1974 that only \$1·4 billion of issues rated Baa or less were sold, mostly by utility companies.

And there has been a pronounced downward trend in bond ratings over the six-year period. Decreases have outnumbered increases by almost a 2:1 ratio, and only 56 corporations have managed to maintain their Aaa ratings (Moody's) as of late April 1975. Table 4 also shows that non-financial corporations borrowed approximately \$30 billion from commercial banks in both 1973 and 1974, appreciably larger than the \$8·8 billion average between 1965 and 1972. This increase is largely due, of course, to the inability of corporations to gain more permanent financing through either credit or new enquiry issues. Indeed, the shortening in 1974 of the average maturity of corporate debt occurred when an inverted yield curve made short-term borrowing more expensive than long-term debt.

The large amounts of debt issued by corporations in the past few years have been largely purchased by insurance companies and pension funds; Table 8 shows that these intermediaries have been large net purchasers in each of the last fifteen years. Households, including personal trusts managed by bank trust departments and non-profit organisations, were also large net purchasers in the 1967–72 period, but they were net purchasers of only \$1·1 billion in 1973 and were net sellers of \$2·3 billion in 1974.

The same table also shows that the net purchases of equities by insurance companies and pension funds totalled almost \$115 billion over the fifteen-

TABLE 7

*Gross Corporate Bond Offerings, 1969–74*
(\$ billion)

| Year | Total | Moody's bond rating | | | | Maturity | | | Rating changes (Moody's) | |
|------|-------|---------------------|---|----------------|-----------|---------------------------|-------------|---------------------|-----------|-----------|
| | | *Aaa and Aa* | *A* | *Baa and below* | *Not rated* | *Less than 10 years*[a] | *10–19 years* | *20 years or more* | *Increases* | *Decreases* |
| 1969 | 12·7 | 5·2 | 2·9 | 2·8 | 1·8 | 1·9 | 0·4 | 10·4 | 11 | 20 |
| 1970 | 25·4 | 12·1 | 8·2 | 2·6 | 2·5 | 5·6 | 0·8 | 19·0 | 15 | 21 |
| 1971 | 24·9 | 11·0 | 5·2 | 3·7 | 5·0 | 1·8 | 3·0 | 20·1 | 14 | 29 |
| 1972 | 18·4 | 7·5 | 3·3 | 1·7 | 5·9 | 4·6 | 0·9 | 12·9 | 19 | 25 |
| 1973 | 13·6 | 7·5 | 3·5 | 0·6 | 2·0 | 1·0 | 0·3 | 12·6 | 21 | 27 |
| 1974 | 25·3 | 14·5 | 7·4 | 1·4 | 2·0 | 7·3 | 2·8 | 15·2 | 39 | 70 |

[a]Includes serial bond issues.

TABLE 8

Net Acquisitions of Corporate Securities, 1960–74
($ billion)

| Year | Net purchases of corporate equities | | | | | Net purchases of corporate and foreign bonds | | | | |
|------|------------|-----------------------|----------------------------------|------------|-----------|------------|-----------------------|----------------------------------|------------|-----------|
| | Households | Open-end inv. cos. | Insurance cos. and pension funds | Foreigners | All other | Households | Open-end inv. cos. | Insurance cos. and pension funds | Foreigners | All other |
| 1960 | –0.4 | 0.8 | 2.6 | 0.2 | — | 0.6 | 0.2 | 4.8 | 0.1 | –0.1 |
| 1961 | 0.4 | 1.3 | 3.1 | 0.3 | — | 0.1 | 0.3 | 5.5 | — | –0.3 |
| 1962 | –2.1 | 0.9 | 3.1 | 0.1 | 0.3 | –0.1 | | 5.9 | — | 0.1 |
| 1963 | –2.9 | 0.8 | 2.8 | 0.2 | 0.4 | — | 0.2 | 6.4 | 0.1 | –0.1 |
| 1964 | –0.2 | 0.8 | 3.1 | –0.3 | 0.2 | 0.1 | 0.4 | 6.5 | 0.2 | –0.1 |
| 1965 | –2.2 | 1.3 | 4.3 | –0.4 | 0.5 | 1.0 | 0.4 | 7.2 | –0.1 | 0.1 |
| 1966 | –0.9 | 1.0 | 4.8 | –0.3 | 0.2 | 2.0 | 0.4 | 8.4 | 0.6 | 0.4 |
| 1967 | –4.3 | 1.9 | 6.6 | 0.7 | 0.6 | 4.6 | — | 9.4 | –0.1 | 3.3 |
| 1968 | –6.5 | 2.5 | 8.1 | 2.1 | 0.2 | 4.7 | 0.4 | 8.3 | 0.6 | 1.5 |
| 1969 | –3.8 | 1.7 | 9.9 | 1.6 | 0.6 | 6.6 | 0.2 | 6.5 | –0.1 | 0.7 |
| 1970 | –1.7 | 1.2 | 9.7 | 0.7 | 0.5 | 10.7 | 0.7 | 9.6 | 0.7 | 2.1 |
| 1971 | –5.3 | 0.4 | 18.2 | 0.8 | 0.7 | 9.3 | 0.6 | 9.3 | 0.3 | 5.3 |
| 1972 | –5.4 | –1.8 | 17.0 | 2.3 | 0.8 | 5.2 | 0.2 | 10.8 | 0.1 | 3.9 |
| 1973 | –8.2 | –2.3 | 14.9 | 2.8 | 0.8 | 1.1 | –0.9 | 12.4 | 0.1 | –0.2 |
| 1974 | –1.0 | –0.5 | 6.6 | 0.4 | 0.4 | –2.3 | –0.4 | 22.4 | 1.4 | 2.2 |

Source: *Flow-of-Funds*, Board of Governors of the Federal Reserve System.

year period 1960–74. Since net new share issues (Table 4) during the same period totalled only $50 billion, the sizeable net *sales* of the household sector ($44·5 billion) suggest that individuals sold a large portion of their direct share holdings to other investors, presumably partially to diversify their holdings and to realise capital gains. But institutions primarily displayed strong preferences for issues of larger companies listed on the New York Stock Exchange. This predilection is evident in the major holdings of bank trust departments. The fifty largest holdings of Federally chartered banks with equity assets of at least $75 billion had a total market value at year-end 1974 of almost $44 billion, or about one-half of their total equity holdings. These same fifty companies account for approximately 30 per cent of the total market value of all corporate equities (year-end 1974). The debt securities of 19 of the 50 corporations were rated by Moody's or Fitch as Aaa, 17 as Aa, and only 4 as A or below, whole 10 were not rated. As a group, these 50 corporations had an average price/earnings ratio approximately twice that for all stocks listed on the New York Stock Exchange, a relationship that has been maintained in all the last four years. Finally, the sharp decline in net purchases of common stocks by insurance companies and pension funds in 1974 may reflect a fundamental reappraisal of equity investment by many of these institutional investors in favour of more conservative instruments such as United States government obligations and corporate bonds.

## 5. Implications for Capital Formation

Sections 3 and 4 have focused on the high levels of debt financing undertaken by American non-financial corporations in recent years. Internal sources of funds have become eroded, the pronounced decline in share values has greatly increased the cost of external equity financing, and the reliance on debt financing has resulted in an increasingly leveraged corporate capital structure.

The shift towards debt financing was originally a strategy intended to increase share values when credit was readily available, internal sources of funds were robust, and share prices had displayed a pattern of relatively steady growth. The emergence of persistant and augmented price inflation greatly altered the picture. The 'gains' from inflation, in the form of higher replacement values of inventories and fixed assets, have accrued in illiquid form, creating tax burdens. The inflation has undermined profits. High interest rates have in part offset the benefits from a declining real value of debt. Inflation appears, in short, to have done major damage to corporate capital structures and capital values through a variety of interacting mechanisms, with consequent damage to the productivity and growth potential of the American economy.

## Note

1. Professor Friend held in the discussion (23 June 1975) that the 'two-tier' market was of very long standing. [Eds.]

## References

Cagan, P. (1974). 'Common Stock Values and Inflation. The Historical Record of Many Countries', *N.B.E.R. Supplement* (Mar.).

Fisher, L. and Lorie, J. H. (1968). Rates of Return on Investments in Common Stocks: The Year-By-Year Record, 1926–65', *Journal of Business*, XLI (3) (1968) 291–316.

Lintner, J. (1973). 'Inflation and Common Stock Prices in a Cyclical Context', *53rd Annual Report*, N.B.E.R. (Sept.) pp. 23–36.

Mintz, I. (1974). 'Dating United States Growth Cycles', *Explorations in Economic Research*, N.B.E.R. (Summer) pp. 1–113.

Moore, G. H. (1975). 'Stock Prices and the Business Cycle', *Journal of Portfolio Management*, I (3) 59–64.

Nordhaus, W. D. (1974). 'The Falling Share of Profits', *Brookings Papers on Economic Activity*, No. 1, pp. 169–218.

# 15 'Keynesian' and 'Monetarist' Indicators of the U.K. Economy

GORDON T. PEPPER and GEOFFREY E. WOOD

## 1. Introduction

There is a long-running dispute between 'Keynesians' and 'monetarists' as to what variable or set of variables best indicates the stance of the government's macroeconomic policy. 'Keynesians' differ among themselves but would agree that fiscal policy is of predominant importance, and that its stance can be measured by some weighted version of the public-sector borrowing requirement, while 'monetarists', although also differing among themselves, would lay paramount stress on monetary policy and use the behaviour of one (or more) of the monetary aggregates as an indicator of the stance of that policy. Behind these two positions lie both theoretical differences and differences over empirical magnitudes. It is not our intention to survey those here; surveys already exist and there is in any case no conclusive view of either position which can be used as the basis of a survey. A survey of this area is inevitably a contentious rather than a synthesising exercise. None the less, we do attempt a partial synthesis. We attempt to show that a fully worked-out 'Keynesian' interpretation and a similarly thorough 'monetarist' interpretation of the stance of macroeconomic policy in the United Kingdom would be close to each other in their conclusions. The argument may be summarised by saying that, because of the nature of the money supply process in the United Kingdom, the conclusions of the two types of analysis are inevitably closely linked, and further, we shall argue that, irrespective of one's theoretical position, the stance of macroeconomic policy in the United Kingdom is at the moment best indicated by the behaviour of the monetary aggregates.

## 2. The Search for Indicators

Economic data are not available the moment events happen. Some series, such as unemployment, are available quickly. Other series, such as stock-building and industrial production, appear after substantial delay, and are subject to frequent and major revision. A case for paying close attention to financial data can be made on these statistical grounds alone; relative to most economic data, they are published both quickly and, in general, reasonably close to their final form.

## 3. The Interpretation of the Monetary Aggregates

Two objections are frequently encountered to the monetary aggregates as indicators. The first is that there is an embarrassment of riches; there are too many aggregates. (In our view, there are actually too few; it would be useful to have a personal/corporate sector division of $M_1$ and, also, an $M_2$ series, i.e. $M_3$ minus certificates of deposit and 'wholesale' deposits.) The second is that their usefulness as an indicator depends on the disputed stability of a function. We first consider these objections.

There are two monetary aggregates, $M_1$ and $M_3$, in the United Kingdom. $M_1$ is defined as notes and coin in circulation with the public plus sterling current accounts held within the private sector, and $M_3$ is defined as all deposits held with the United Kingdom banking sector by United Kingdom residents in the public and private sectors, plus notes and coin.[1] Loosely speaking, $M_1$ is non-interest-bearing money and $M_3$ is that plus interest-bearing money. Both series are published monthly, a month in arrears, by the Bank of England. One sometimes finds that these two series are growing at very different rates. We believe that $M_1$ *is* an indicator of what is occurring, but we do not regard the indication as confirmed until $M_1$ and $M_3$ are unanimous. The arguments and evidence for this position run as follows.

We have carried out a detailed comparison of the monthly changes in $M_1$ with those of $M_3$ since the official data for $M_1$ commenced. Sometimes the two series have fluctuated together; on other occasions they have fluctuated in opposite directions. *The deciding factor appears to be interest rates.* $M_1$ is affected quickly by any sharp change in the level of interest rates. An increase encourages people to switch money from their current accounts into their deposit accounts to obtain interest on the latter. Such transactions reduce $M_1$. When rates of interest stabilise, the underlying rate of growth of $M_1$ resumes. If rates of interest fall, there may be some rebound in $M_1$. Fig. 2 illustrates this general pattern. It compares the monthly change in $M_1$ with the rate of interest on three-month certificates of deposit, the latter being inverted so that the two series tend to fluctuate in the same direction.

The first reduction in $M_1$ which occurred in the month to mid-January 1972 was not, in fact, due to interest rates; it was associated with a similar downward fluctuation in $M_3$. Otherwise Fig. 2 confirms that whenever there has been a sharp rise in interest rates, there has tended to be an immediate reduction in the growth of $M_1$. The second reduction in $M_1$, a fall of £68 million in the month to late July 1972, was associated with a rise in the

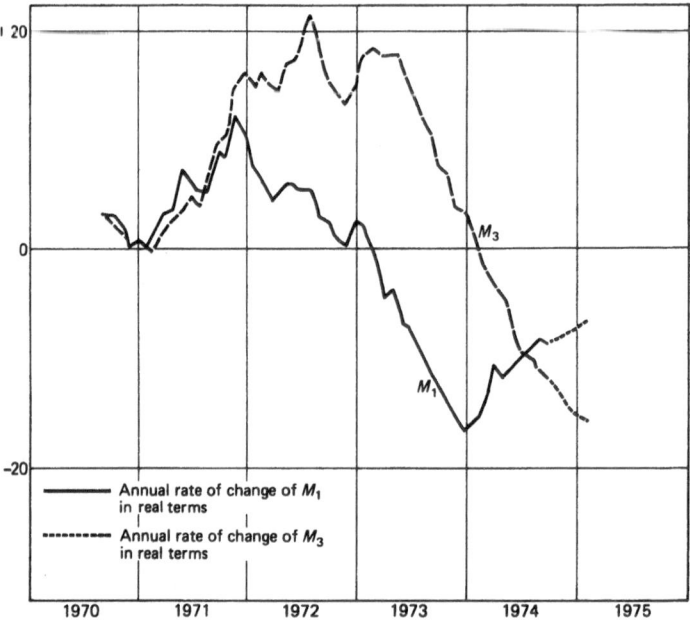

Fig. 1

interest rates on three-month C.D.s from 5 per cent to $8\frac{1}{2}$ per cent over the period from early June to late July 1972. Subsequently, when interest rates declined slightly, the growth of $M_1$ recovered. The third reduction in $M_1$, a fall of £101 million in the month to mid-January 1973, was associated with the rise in interest rates from $7\frac{1}{2}$ per cent at the end of October 1972 to 12 per cent at the beginning of March 1973. On this occasion the recovery in $M_1$ led the decline in interest rates. On the fourth occasion a big decline in $M_1$ (£506 million) in the three months between mid-July and mid-October 1973 was associated with a rapid rise in interest rates from just over 8 per cent at the end of June to $14\frac{1}{2}$ per cent at the end of August 1973. This response in $M_1$ was sharpened by press pbblicity; building societies were losing deposits to the banks and the resulting press comment publicised the height of bank interest rates. On 11 September 1973 the Bank of England introduced a $9\frac{1}{2}$ per cent limit on the rate of interest that the banks were allowed to offer on deposits of £10,000 or less. This restriction probably dampened the effect of interest rates on $M_1$, but Fig. 2 suggests that there was some reduction in $M_1$ associated with the rise in interest rates at the end of 1973. Since then, swings in $M_1$ appear to have been less dramatic, but the general relationship with interest rates holds.

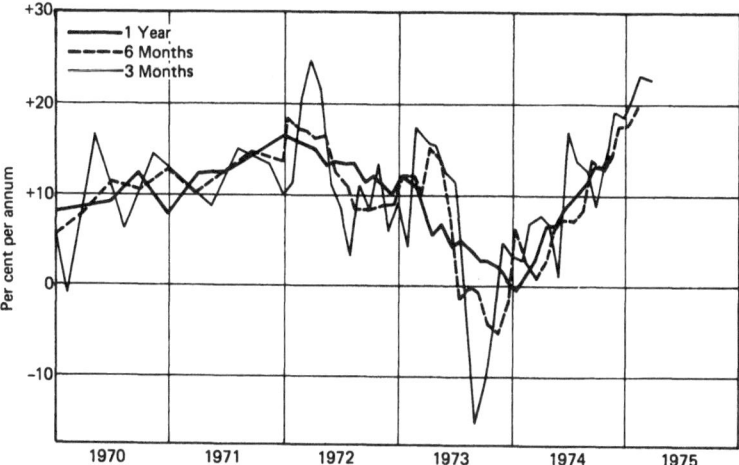

Fig. 2

The effect on $M_3$ of sharp changes in interest rates has tended to be opposite to that on $M_1$. Switching from current accounts into deposit accounts does not affect $M_3$: $M_3$ includes both current and deposit accounts. But $M_3$ is affected by changes in interest-rate relatives that influence round-tripping[2] and other arbitrage transactions.[3] Bank lending rates usually lag when deposit rates are rising sharply. $M_3$ is increased if people borrow from banks in order to obtain an arbitrage profit from investment in certificates of deposit. $M_3$ has tended to move directly with relative interest rates. However, the pattern is not as clear as that for $M_1$.

Fig. 1 shows that interest-rate changes have caused fluctuations in the monthly data for $M_1$ and $M_3$ in the way just described. In particular, round-tripping transactions were responsible for the triple peaks in the growth of $M_3$ which are shown in that graph. As for $M_1$, the sharp increase in the level of interest rates, starting in June 1972, accelerated its downswing. We conclude that fluctuations in $M_1$ relative to $M_3$, caused by sharp changes in interest rates, explain the lead of $M_1$ over $M_3$ shown in Fig. 1.

### 4. Real or Nominal Money?

We have so far used *real* rather than *nominal* monetary magnitudes. We regard real monetary growth as the appropriate indicator, though *not* the appropriate policy target.

It is most important to distinguish between the money supply as an indicator of the likely course of future economic activity and pressure on capital markets and as a policy target. For the former use, in the United

Kingdom the real-terms statistic is a more efficient leading indicator than the money-terms statistic. But the nominal statistic should be the policy target. Brittan (1975) commented on the incorrect use of the real terms statistic as a policy target as follows:

> This means (*a*) that any change or temporary upsurge of the price level gets built into the system by monetary policy and (*b*) ignores the fact, evident in all major historical inflations, that the faster prices rise, the lower the real money balances people will wish to hold. At the height of the German hyperinflation after World War 1, Dr Schacht's predecessor at the Reichsbank reassured people with the thought that the real value of the money supply was a twentieth of what it was in 1913.

In past economic cycles in the United Kingdom, movements in velocity of circulation have acted as a buffer. When the money supply has been squeezed, velocity has increased. During periods of monetary ease, the velocity of circulation has declined. Velocity variability underlies the notoriously long and variable time-lags between a change in the growth of the money supply and a change in economic activity. That variability is also responsible for its being difficult to quantify with precision the impact of changes in the growth of the money supply on economic activity. Nevertheless, in past economic cycles the velocity of circulation has never varied sufficiently to *reverse* the impact of changes in the real money stock on economic activity. During hyperinflations, on the other hand, movements in the velocity of circulation became destabilising, more than offsetting changes in the nominal quantity of money.

At what level of inflation does the money supply become an unreliable indicator? At what stage does the velocity of circulation become more important? Two classic studies of hyperinflation are by Bresciani-Turroni (1937) and Brown (1955). Bresciani-Turroni sums up the German experience as follows:

> Examining the monetary events which occurred in Germany, we may, I believe, come to these conclusions: (*a*) in an early stage, which was the longest, monetary depreciation was mainly in proportion to the quantity of paper money; (*b*) in the next period, that is from the summer of 1921 to the summer of 1922, the influence of the new notes issued was intensified by the increase in the velocity of circulation.

Brown (1955) in chap. 8, 'Hyperinflation and the Flight from Cash', reviews the experience of several countries. His general conclusion is as follows: 'The general "flight from cash" in such countries [as have experienced hyperinflation] is hard to start; there is no evidence that it has ever started until prices have doubled in six months or less.' The current rate of inflation in the United Kingdom (July 1975) is on that evidence below the level at which a 'flight from cash' is likely.

Besides the technical difficulties just considered, there is a more fundamental difficulty. The aggregates are meaningful only if a stable demand function for money can be identified. We have not ourselves carried out detailed econometric research on the demand for money, but have relied on the substantial amount of work recently carried out in the United Kingdom by the Bank of England and various academic economists.[4] Although there are differences of view, one position is clearly rejected by all this work; the demand for money is not a completely unstable function, shifting about from day to day. Several papers have been published by the Bank of England (1970, 1972, 1974) reporting on estimated demand for money functions. The first two of these showed a convergence on a stable function, with a real income elasticity of demand for $M_3$ of about 1·5. The most recent paper suggests that, following Competition and Credit Control, there has been a shift in this function. Against the belief that there has been a shift, one finds Artis and Lewis (1974) who argue that, when properly allowing for the own-rate of money, the function has been stable through C.C.C., and Hamburger (1974) who found that, when allowing for the openness of the United Kingdom economy, the function was stable from 1963 to 1971 (the end of his data period). But even if one accepts that the function has shifted, it is important to recognise the very limited significance of the latest Bank of England work for the use of monetary aggregates. Its upshot is *not* that the function is chronically unstable, but only that it shifts from time to time in response to structural changes.

We now proceed to argue that monetary aggregates are a good indicator of the stance of macroeconomic policy. The argument is approached via a discussion of some of the channels of influence of monetary policy.

## 5. A Channel of Monetary Influence

There is clear evidence from the United States (Modigliani, 1971) that changes in wealth — in particular in stock prices — have a large and significant impact on private-sector consumption expenditure. We have analysed the relationship (in the United Kingdom) between the behaviour of the monetary aggregates and the level of both gilt-edged stock and equity prices. We first briefly set out a survey of the 'conventional' relationship between the monetary aggregates and gilts prices and then at greater length develop an argument which our work has led us to think is of considerable importance. This relationship leads to flow-of-funds analysis, and thus to the reconciliation we are attempting.

The relationship between the business cycle and cyclical changes in the level of interest rates is well established. Rates of interest rise during an upswing of the business cycle and fall during a downswing of the business cycle. The peak in interest rates lags the peak of an economic recession. (This is described in detail in Cagan, 1971).

The usual explanation for the cyclical variation in *long-term* interest rates can be summarised as variation in price inflation. Inflation affects the level of interest rates because investors attempt to maintain the real return on their investment, i.e. if inflation accelerates, rates of interest rise in money terms and vice versa if inflation decelerates. During an upswing in the business cycle, price inflation accelerates; it decelerates during a downswing. Like interest rates, price inflation lags the business cycle, for various reasons. First, there is a lag before changes in wholesale input prices are reflected in wholesale output prices which are then reflected in retail prices. Second, wage claims and awards have in the past been based on price increases in the previous year rather than on current and expected price increases. Third, productivity gains vary according to the stage of the economic cycle. During the early stages of a business upswing, productivity gains are abnormally high because spare industrial capacity is being absorbed; during the early stage of a downswing, productivity gains are usually negligible. Because both price inflation and rates of interest lag the economic cycle, cyclical changes in interest rates tend to be correlated with cyclical changes in price inflation.

So far only domestic economic factors inducing interest-rate movements have been considered. There is a close connection between the domestic economic cycle and the behaviour of the current account of the United Kingdom's balance of payments. In periods of expansion of domestic demand, exports are diverted to home markets and additional imports are sucked in to satisfy domestic demand, and vice versa in a recession. Also important is the cycle in stocks of industrial raw materials. During the early stages of a recovery in aggregate demand, stocks tend to be run down. Later in the economic cycle, stocks tend to be built up, not only to replace the earlier fall but also to bring them into line with the new higher level of production. The peak of the stockbuilding cycle tends to be about two-thirds of the way up the business cycle. During the downswing of a business cycle, corresponding destocking occurs. The effect on the monthly figures for international trade can be very important. During the downswing of an economic cycle, the improvement in the trade figures encourages the gilt-edged market and vice versa during rhe upswing.

The last few economic cycles in the United Kingdom have tended to be approximately in phase with the international economic cycle, which is mainly dependent on the United States. There can be leads or lags, but a cyclical fall in domestic interest rates usually occurs against a background of a cyclical fall in international interest rates.

Our research led us to a very different balance of emphasis. Fiscal and monetary squeezes tend to be implemented at cyclical peaks: monetary stringency ensures that there is insufficient demand for gilt-edged stock for the gilt-edged market to anticipate the coming fall in interest rates. Correspondingly, at troughs one is likely to see additional public expenditure and reduced taxation. But in a recession low confidence levels, hence weak marginal propensities to spend, will cause these injections to produce excess supply of funds and hence lower interest rates.

A second reason for the lag of interest rates is the lag of credit demand. In the early stages of an economic downswing, just after the peak of a boom, there is usually substantial involuntary demand for credit because of three factors. First, there is a profits squeeze at that stage of the economic cycle. Second, there will tend to be involuntary accumulation of stocks of finished goods, which must be financed. Third, in the preceding boom capital investment projects will have been authorised; because of long gestation periods of major projects there is a long delay before the cost of financing such projects tapers off.

Flow-of-funds research indicates that an extremely important force towards lower interest rates is the flow of funds within the banking sector. The involuntary loan demand just described sooner or later subsides, leaving sluggish voluntary loan demand (because of the recession) as the dominant factor. The banks start to experience a slack demand for loans. Further, before the economy can recover from a recession, the growth of the money supply must recover. An expansion in the money supply is primarily a growth in bank deposits. Given surplus funds which must be invested somewhere and the climate of falling interest rates characteristic of this phase of the cycle, the banks will buy gilt-edged stocks.

Fig. 3 shows the close connection between the flow of funds in the banking sector and the changes in the banks' holdings of gilt-edged stock. The dashed line, which represents the change in the banks' gilt-edged holdings, shows the data only for the London Clearing Banks. (Only for

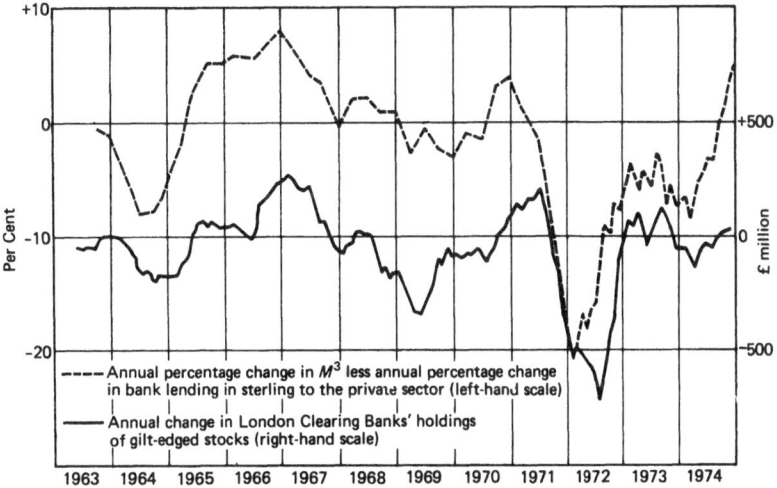

Fig. 3

this part of the banking sector is the data available monthly.) The relationship between the two lines demonstrates clearly that the flow of funds in the banking sector has a powerful influence on the banks' gilt-edged holdings. (We have investigated variations in special deposits. If Fig. 3 is adjusted for such changes, the relationship still holds.)

A similar analysis applies to equity prices at turning-points. In a previous paper, Pepper and Thomas (1973) showed that, over a run of data since 1927, a monetary expansion led to an upturn in the level of equity prices, which reinforces the monetary effect on expenditures of the movement in gilt-edged prices and thus strengthens the monetary assistance given to the fiscal expansion.

## 6. Sectoral Flows of Funds

We now show that changes in the financial position of the public sector, due to fiscal changes, affect the financial position and thus expenditure decisions of other sectors; and the relationship between these changing financial positions and the behaviour of the monetary aggregates is then set out.

The economy is for the present purpose divided into three sectors: the public, overseas and private sectors. The private sector can be further broken down: persons; industrial and commercial companies; banks and other financial institutions. Fig. 4 illustrates the close relationship between the financial *surplus* of industrial and commercial companies and the financial deficit of the combined public and overseas sectors. It will be seen that

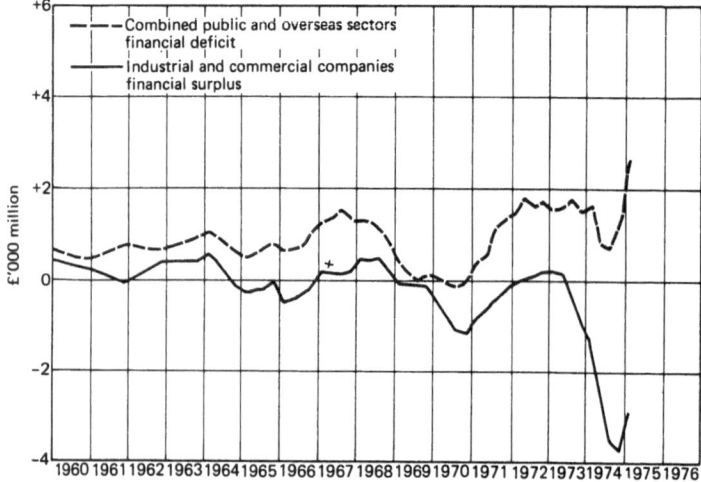

Fig. 4

the two series fluctuate together. In particular, if the combined public and overseas sectors swing into financial surplus, industrial and commercial companies are forced into financial deficit (because the other components of the private sector can more quickly adjust to maintain balance).

One of the ways in which industrial and commercial companies react when forced into financial deficit is to attempt to restore their financial position by reducing capital formation and stockbuilding. Inevitably, however, there is a time-lag before they are able to achieve this retrenchment. During the three cycles since 1960 the time-lag has averaged six quarters for stockbuilding, and eight quarters for capital formation because of the latter's long gestation period. The relationships are illustrated in Figs. 5 and 6. Both graphs show the financial surplus of industrial and

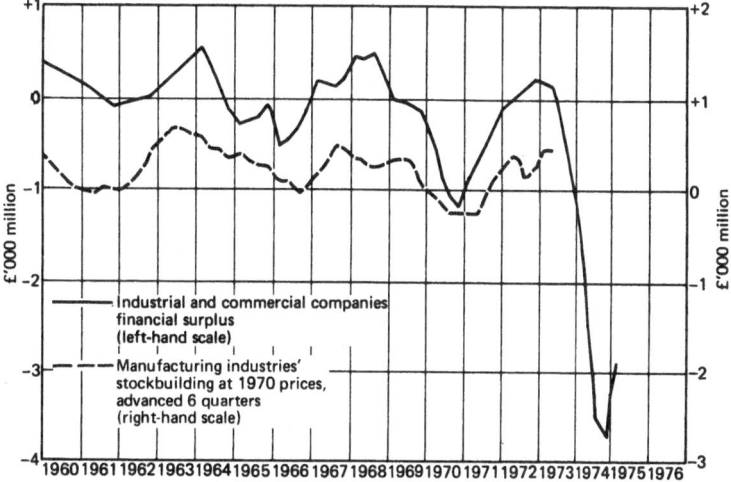

Fig. 5

commercial companies. Fig. 5 also shows manufacturing industries' stockbuilding in real terms, with the plots advanced six quarters, and Fig. 6 also shows manufacturing industries' gross fixed capital formation, in real terms, with the plots advanced eight quarters. The graphs show that the lagged series fluctuate together. (The financial position of industrial and commercial companies is of course not the only factor influencing capital formation and stockbuilding.)

The financial positions of both the public and overseas sectors themselves alter as a result of the changing pressures in the economy. As economic activity declines, the deficit of the public sector increases. In the United Kingdom the effect on the balance of payments is also of great importance. In many ways the balance of payments operates like a safety-

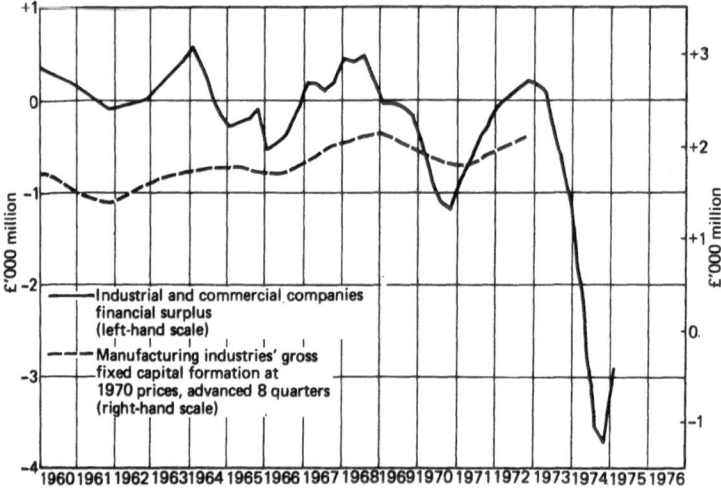

Fig. 6

valve for the economy. When excessive pressure is allowed to build up within the domestic economy, the balance of payments will swing into substantial deficit. When the pressure dissipates, so will the balance of payments deficit. If there is slack in the domestic economy, the balance of payments will tend towards surplus. Again, there is a time-lag before the balance of payments responds. Fig. 7 shows the financial deficit of the

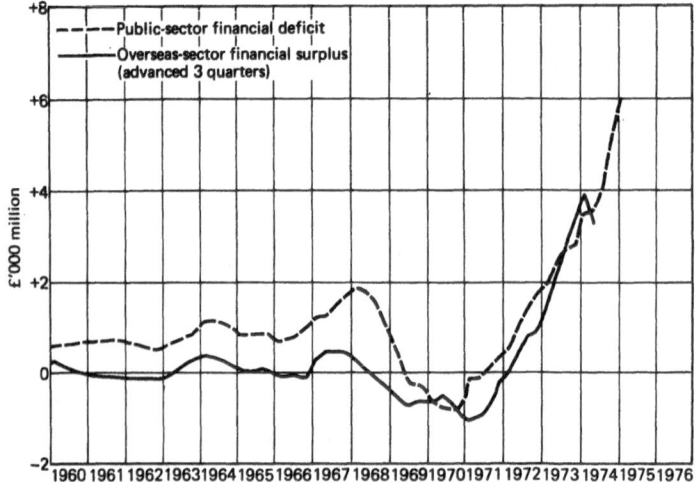

Fig. 7

public sector together with the financial surplus of the overseas sector, with the plots of the latter series advanced three quarters. It will be seen that the lagged series have fluctuated roughly together since 1960 — hence the conclusion of Robert Nield and Wynne Godley at Cambridge that the public-sector financial surplus determines the balance of payments.[5]

The relationship of the corporate sector's financial position to the money supply is now shown. This will make explicit the relationship of fiscal pressures on the corporate sector to the behaviour of the monetary aggregates. Before doing so, it is worth noting in passing that, given a stable relationship between the public-sector deficit and the behaviour of the monetary aggregates, one thus arrives at the monetarist approach to the balance of payments: a public-sector deficit leads, via a monetary expansion, to an overseas-sector surplus.

It must of course be stressed that, although Figs 4–7 appear to illustrate close relationships between the lagged series, the post-1960 period is too recent for the relationships to be securely established. In particular, the time-lags are almost certainly not constant.

## 7. Relationship of the sectoral financial positions to changes in $M_3$

Factors influencing the supply of money are traditionally analysed under the following format:

> Growth of the money supply ($M_3$)
> > equals
> Public-sector borrowing requirement
> > less
> Private-sector acquisition of public-sector debt
> > less
> Finance raised from overseas by the public and banking sectors
> > plus
> Bank lending to the private sector
> > less
> Net growth in non-deposit liabilities of the banking sector.

The flow-of-funds approach suggests that it might be better to focus attention on the financial deficit of the public sector rather than the public-sector borrowing requirement. The financial deficit differs from the borrowing requirement in that it excludes financial capital account items, which do not place a *direct* claim on real resources. The relationship can be seen as follows:

> Public-sector current account deficit
> > plus
> Public-sector capital formation and stockbuilding
> > equals

Public-sector financial deficit
       plus
Public-sector net acquisition of financial assets
       equals
Public-sector borrowing requirement.

The transactions of the overseas sector can be broken down on exactly the same lines as those of the public sector. The financial surplus of the overseas sector consists almost entirely of the balance-of-payments deficit on current account. The financial transactions which are excluded from the overseas sector's financial surplus but which are included in any analysis of the supply of money are private-sector capital account items and the balancing item of the balance of payments.

This approach suggests that it might be better to group the factors influencing the supply of money under three headings — financial deficits, bank lending, and transactions in financial assets — with the first expected to have the most direct and quick impact on the economy and the last the slowest impact:

Growth of the money supply ($M_3$)
       equals
Financial deficits of the public and overseas sectors
       plus
Bank lending to the private sector
       plus
Transactions in financial assets.

Quarterly data according to the above classification are available since 1963. Fig. 8 shows the annual rates of change.

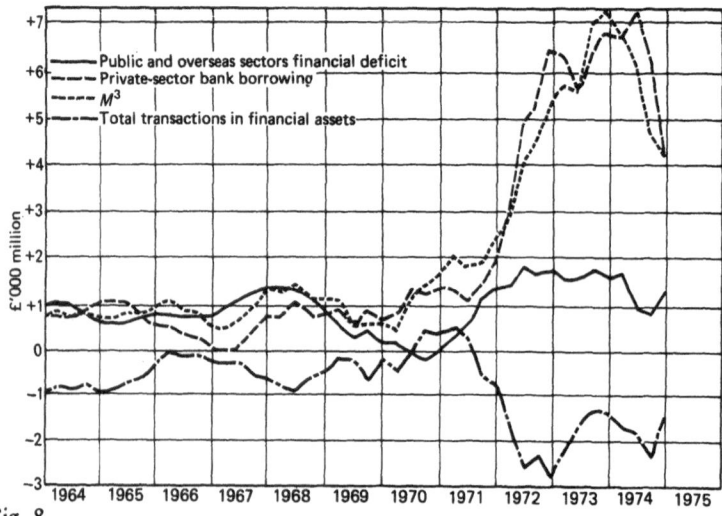

Fig. 8

From the graph it would appear that cyclical changes in the financial deficit of the public and overseas sectors, in $M_3$ and in bank lending tend to occur together, but cyclical changes in financial transactions are in counter-phase. In other words, there has been a clear relationship between direct fiscal pressures (as identified in the flow-of-funds classification) and $M_3$. If there are no major distortions (such as massive 'round-tripping') in bank lending, there is a close relationship between cyclical changes in $M_3$ and those in the financial deficit of the combined public and overseas sectors (see Fig. 9). This is because bank lending and financial transactions tend to offset each other. It must be stressed that these patterns are not definitely established; data are available only for ten years, some of which are distorted by C.C.C.

Fig. 9

Fig. 9 compares fluctuations in the growth of $M_3$ with the financial deficit of the combined public and overseas sector. It is interesting to compare the turning-points of the two series. $M_3$ appears to lag at the peak turning-points, at the end of 1965, at the end of 1967 and, more recently, at the end of 1973. $M_3$ also lagged at the 1966 trough turning-point, but led at the 1970 trough turning-point. The main explanation for the lags in all cases appears to be the behaviour of private-sector borrowing from the banks. Such borrowing increases $M_3$ but it does not affect the financial deficit of the public and overseas sectors. At the peak turning-points of the economy, loan demand tends to be strong, and therefore the downturn in $M_3$ is postponed. As far as the trough turning-points are concerned, in 1970 industrial and commercial companies were in substantial financial deficit and as a result required substantial accommodation from their banks — the increase in the bank loans appears to have been responsible for the upswing in $M_3$ leading that in the financial deficit of the public and overseas sectors. A similar pattern did not occur in 1966, probably because industrial and commercial companies had only a small financial deficit and therefore did not need substantial accommodation from their banks. As a general rule, there has been a close relationship between the public and overseas deficits, which represent demand pressures on the economy, and the behaviour of $M_3$.

The close relationship between the monetary aggregates and the balance of 'Keynesian' pressures also emerges by another route, to which attention has been drawn by Fand (1970).

## 8. The Role of the Government Budget Constraint

The government has to raise the money it spends; the sources are taxation, debt sales and monetary expansion. This is approximately captured[6] in the expression:

$$dM/dt + dB/dt = P(G - T\{Y\})  \qquad (1)$$

where $M$ is the nominal stock of outside money, $B$ is the nominal stock of interest-bearing debt, $P$ the price level, $G$ real government expenditure, and $T$ real tax revenue as a function of income, $Y$.

That expression is not complete; interest has to be paid on the outstanding stock of debt, so the complete expression should be written:

$$dM/dt + \frac{1}{r}(dB/dt) = P\{G + B - T(Y) + B\}  \qquad (2)$$

where it is assumed that all bonds are perpetuities paying £1 per year. Total interest charges[7] are therefore $B$, where $B$ is the number of bonds, $B/r$ their total nominal value and interest payments are taxable. Note that the left-hand side includes only $1/r (dB/dt)$ and excludes $d(B/r)/dt$; i.e. we include the change in the number of bonds, evaluated at current market price, and exclude as not relevant for the government's revenue the change in the value of the initial stock.

Eq. (2) captures an essential feature of government financing. This can best be seen by rewriting it as follows:

$$dM/dt = G + B - T - \frac{1}{r}(dB/dt)  \qquad (3)$$

That is to say, one cannot increase the stock of high-powered money without either deficit spending or bond retirement. In the extreme case where bond retirement is ruled out, deficit spending necessarily implies an equivalent expansion in the stock of high-powered money. In the words of Fand (1970): 'Deficits (surpluses) are usually associated with acceleration (deceleration) in money stock growth, and it is therefore possible for fiscalists and monetarists to cite the same evidence to support their respective views.'

In terms of Eq. (3), he concludes that while of course $1/r$ $(dB/dt)$ is not constrained to zero, it is in general of little quantitative significance compared to $G + B - T$.

A weighted, standardised, full-employment surplus is the appropriate 'Keynesian' indicator of the stance of macroeconomic policy. Such complexity is necessary for three reasons. Because tax revenue varies with income, it is necessary to eliminate the effect of variations in national income on the budget; hence the need to calculate the budgetary position at a constant employment level. The budget has to be weighted to take account of the balanced budget theorem and it has to be standardised to allow for the effect of the different amounts by which different kinds of income vary over the cycle. These matters, and the further complexity introduced by inflation, are discussed by Hansen (1969). Such a number would not be simple to compute, and its value is (as Blinder and Solow, 1974, show) very sensitive to the econometric model used, as indeed are the associated multipliers. Interpretation of the stance of policy based on such a number would certainly be more contentious than an interpretation based on the behaviour of the money supply.

## 9. Summary and Conclusions

The behaviour of the monetary aggregates is dominated in the United Kingdom by the stance of fiscal policy. In general, therefore, 'Keynesians' and 'monetarists' should not be too far apart in their assessment of the stance of macroeconomic policy. Indeed, we would argue that, irrespective of one's theoretical view, the behaviour of the monetary aggregates is a good indicator of the stance of fiscal policy and, at the moment, by far the best indicator for the United Kingdom which is available reasonably quickly. There should at least be agreement among economists on what is the stance of policy at any time.

### Acknowledgements

The authors are very greatly indebted to Mr R. L. Thomas of W. Greenwell & Co. both for his valuable statistical assistance and for his detailed criticisms. Also to the editors for invaluable editorial advice.

## Notes

1. The Bank of England changed the basis of U.K. banking statistics in May 1975. The new reporting system distinguishes between sight and time deposits. Sight deposits are defined as current accounts plus interest-bearing overnight deposits and call money. The new definition of $M_1$ is notes and coin in circulation with the public plus sterling sight deposits of the private sector.
2. i.e. arbitrating between bank loans and C.D.s to take advantage of the higher rate payable on C.D.s than is charged on bank loans.
3. e.g. so called 'soft arbitrating', the selling of Treasury bills and local authority deposits to buy C.D.s, which is a switch from public liabilities to banking liabilities.
4. We are indebted to Mr T. C. Mills of Warwick University for an invaluable discussion of this work.
5. A very clear written statement of their views, and the transcript of an oral defence of these views, can be found in the New Cambridge Policy Group report.
6. See, for example, Christ (1968).
7. The reader is left to supply correct flow-rate interpretations.

## References

Artis, M. J. and Lewis, M. K. (1974). 'The Demand for Money: Stable or Unstable', *The Banker*, CXXIV(572).

Bank of England (1970). 'The Importance of Money', *Bank of England Quarterly Bulletin* (June).

Bank of England (1972). 'The Demand for Money in the U.K.', *Bank of England Quarterly Bulletin* (Mar.).

Bank of England (1974). 'The Demand for Money in the U.K.: Experience since 1971', *Bank of England Quarterly Bulletin* (Sept.).

Blinder, A. S. and Solow, R. M. (1974). 'Analytical Foundations of Fiscal Policy', in *The Economics of Public Finance* (Washington, D.C.: Brookings Institution).

Bresciani-Turroni, C. (1937). *The Economics of Inflation: A Study of Currency Depreciation in Post-war Germany, 1914–1923* (London: Allen & Unwin).

Brittan, S. (1975). 'Economic Viewpoint', *Financial Times*, 23 Jan.

Brown, A. J. (1955). *The Great Inflation, 1939–1951* (London: Oxford Univ. Press).

Cagan, P. W. (1971). 'Changes in the Cyclical Behaviour of Interest Rates', in *Essays on Interest Rates*, vol. II, ed. J. M. Guttentag and P. W. Cagan (New York: National Bureau of Economic Research).

Christ, C. F. (1968). 'A Simple Macro-economic Model with a Government Budget Restraint', *Journal of Public Economics*, LXXVI (Jan–Feb.).

Fand, D. I. (1970). 'A Monetarist Model of the Monetary Process', *Journal of Finance*, XXXV (May).

Hamburger, M. J. (1974). 'The Demand for Money in an Open Economy: Germany and the U.K.', Federal Reserve Bank of New York Research Paper No. 7405 (Apr.).

Hansen, B. (1969). *Fiscal Policy in Seven Countries, 1955–1965* (Paris: O.E.C.D.).

Modigliani, F. (1971). 'Monetary Policy and Consumption: Linkages via Interest Rates and Wealth Effect in the F.M.P. Model' in *Consumer Spending and Monetary Policy*, Federal Reserve Bank of Boston Conference Series.

New Cambridge Policy Group Ninth Report from the Public Expenditure Committee of the House of Commons, *Public Expenditure, Inflation, and the Balance of Payments* (H.C. 328).

Pepper, G. T. and Thomas, R. L. (1973). 'Cyclical Changes in the Level of the Equity and Gilt-Edged Markets', *Journal of the Institute of Actuaries*, XCIX/3 (414).

# 16 Money and Inflation: Some International Comparisons

## RICHARD T. SELDEN

### I

It is defensible that a capital market symposium should include a paper that says nothing about capital markets *per se*, focusing instead on the inflationary environment in which capital markets have been operating for a generation or more. Lenin is supposed to have expressed the view that debauchment of currency is the surest way of undermining the social order — a sentiment that has been echoed by John Kenneth Galbraith, among others.[1] Neither Lenin nor Galbraith provided a detailed rationale for their hypothesis. One can surmise, however, that they may have had in mind the disruptive consequences of inflationary shocks on capital markets.

In this paper I shall accept as axiomatic both the notion that inflation has adverse consequences on capital markets, especially if the rate of inflation is highly variable, and the broader view that inflation has unsettling political repercussions. Moreover, I shall ignore the obvious feedback that exists between weak political systems and the fostering of inflation through unsound economic policies.

If one accepts these premises, then it becomes a matter of great urgency for the defenders of liberal society to have a correct understanding of the nature of the inflation problem and ways of overcoming it. These topics have scarcely been neglected in recent years, but controversy does not seem to be abating. Nor have policy-makers yet learned how to deal effectively with the problem.

My aim in this paper is to extract a few lessons about inflation and its control by comparing the experiences of several high-income countries. The countries chosen for study — Belgium, Britain, Canada, the Netherlands, Sweden and the United States — differ significantly in (1) the degree of inflation experienced over the last quarter-century, (2) the degree of external exposure, and (3) the types of strategies adopted in fighting inflation. Yet they are similar enough in basic institutions to permit valid comparisons.

### II

Social scientists are notorious for letting their preconceptions determine their 'findings'. It seems only fair to begin this discussion by listing some of my own biases or preconceptions on the subject of inflation.

In my judgement a substantial inflation cannot persist for more than a few months without a roughly commensurate growth in money per unit of output. Moreover, I believe that all governments — and certainly those of the countries under discussion here — have the means to prevent the monetary expansion that is needed for inflation to continue, and to do so without incurring costs that would be too high in relation to the benefits achieved. In short, I am a monetarist.

Possibly I am not unlike the hero of Thornton Wilder's novel, *The Bridge of San Luis Rey*.[2] This pious Franciscan, Brother Juniper, sought to buttress his belief in God's beneficence by searching for the divine intent when a suspension bridge suddenly collapsed early in the eighteenth century in Peru, hurling five hapless victims to their deaths. Despite the unpromising material with which he had to work — a casual observer would not have regarded any of the victims as 'ready' for death — Brother Juniper never really doubted that God's love would eventually be revealed if he dug deeply enough into the victims' histories.

Just so, I regard every new episode of inflation as an opportunity for a further 'test of faith'. Not all the episodes discussed here have been easy for a monetarist to understand. Still, my faith in the basic validity of the monetarist view of inflation remains intact.

## III

What *is* the monetarist model of inflation? Several varieties have appeared in the literature.[3] Probably the best way of indicating the main points that they have in common is to use the exchange identity as an analytic framework:

$$MV \equiv PO \tag{1}$$

where $M$ is the average money stock outstanding during some period, $V$ is the velocity of circulation or turnover rate of $M$, $P$ is a price index of currently produced goods and services, and $O$ is a measure of aggregate real income, such as real G.N.P. For present purposes it will be convenient to work with proportionate rates of change (in lower-case letters) rather than with levels of these variables. So in place of (1) we can write

$$m + v \equiv p + o \tag{2}$$

$$m \equiv dM/M; v \equiv dV/V; \text{etc.} \tag{2a}$$

$$p_t \equiv m_t + v_t - o_t \tag{3}$$

where the subscripts remind us that the identity holds only if all changes are measured over the same time-interval. It is worth noting that the validity of the identity is entirely unrelated to the length of the time-span selected for analysis; weeks are just as appropriate as decades, from this point of view.

By itself, of course, an identity such as (3) says nothing about the causes of inflation. To convert (3) into a theory of inflation we must add assumptions about the behaviour of the variables. Monetarist theories of inflation include three essential assumptions. First, monetarists assert that the rate of monetary growth, $m$, is controllable by the monetary authorities, certainly over periods of a quarter or longer and probably over shorter periods as well, and without violent consequences for credit markets. If we let $m_{o,t}$ represent the policy-determined rate of monetary growth in period $t$, then we can convert (3) into

$$p_t = m_{o,t} + v_t - o_t \tag{4}$$

which is no longer an identity.

Second, monetarists hold that both $v$ and $o$ are well-determined variables that are fairly stable over the long run, except for deviations associated with business cycles. The rate of output growth in the long run reflects demographic trends and the gradual improvement of productivity. Neither of these is likely to experience sudden erratic movements. The trend of velocity also appears to be quite dependable, reflecting mainly the impact of such slow-changing variables as per capita real income, the technology and costs of cash management, the development of money substitutes and, of course, the general level of interest rates. As Marshall would have put it, *natura non facit saltum.*[4] The cyclical variations in $v$ and $o$ are at times substantial. However, there is a strong positive correlation between them, with the result that they tend to offset each other, leaving only a minor net (positive) contribution of these two variables to cyclical movements in $p$.

Monetarists recognise that $v$ and $o$ are also subject from time to time to fairly sizeable shorter-term variations. These can arise from all sorts of causes. Examples are the poor grain harvests of 1971–2 and the Arab oil embargo of 1973–4. Similarly, a war scare such as occurred at the outset of the Korean War in 1950 can have a strong though temporary effect on $v$. In all these instances the disturbances cited exerted upward pressure on $p$. Obviously, disturbances of a deflationary nature also can – and do – occur. From a monetarist point of view the important point about these short-run disturbances is that they tell us little about the causes of inflationary trends measured over periods of two or three years or even longer.

The foregoing remarks boil down to an assertion by monetarists that the rate of inflation, measured over periods sufficiently long to wipe out the transitory effects of essentially random movements in $v$ and $o$, will be closely approximated by the rate of monetary growth plus a constant. Thus we can write

$$p_t^L = \alpha + m_{o,t}^L \tag{5}$$

where the superscripts denote that the rates of inflation and monetary expansion are long-run rates rather than the annualised month-to-month or quarter-to-quarter rates that figure so prominently in public discussions, and $\alpha$ is constant representing the net contribution of the rates of change in $V$ and $O$ to the rate of inflation.

A third basic assumption – actually, a set of assumptions – pertains to the relationships between $m$ and $v$ and $m$ and $o$. From what has already been said it should be clear that monetarists deny the existence of any lasting impact of $m$ on either $v$ or $o$. During the first few months or quarters following a change in $m$, however, there is ordinarily an offsetting change in $v$. In the more familiar terminology of the day, there are lags in the effects of monetary policy. The length of these lags is still a matter of dispute, but most economists, monetarists and non-monetarists alike, would probably agree that the full effect of a monetary disturbance typically is not achieved in less than two years.[5]

This 'velocity lag' implies a delay in the response of nominal income to a change in $m$, and consequently a delayed price response as well. However, there is a further sort of price delay. As nominal income begins to respond to a change in $m$, the increment in income consists initially primarily of a change in $o$ rather than in $p$. It may take a year or more before this temporary output effect is superseded by price effects.

The practical import is that we must modify eq. (5) to allow for monetary lags. Moreover, we should expect these lags to be quite long since they represent a combination of the familiar lag of nominal income behind monetary changes and a lag of prices behind output. Undoubtedly some kind of distributed lag specification would most accurately describe the true economic structure. For present purposes, however, we can simply write

$$p_t^L = \alpha + m_{o,t-n}^L \qquad (6)$$

where $n$ can be regarded as the average value of some lag distribution, in the sense that half of the price effects can be expected to occur by $n$ quarters following a change in $m$.

In summary, I interpret monetarist models of inflation as resting on three basic assumptions: first, that the monetary authorities have firm control of the money stock and its rate of growth; second, that the main determinant of the rate of inflation, over periods sufficiently long to minimise the effects of more or less random disturbances to velocity and output, is the rate of monetary growth; and third, that there are substantial lags between variations in the rate of monetary growth and the associated price responses. Eq. (6) embodies these assumptions. It will be the basis of most of the empirical work reported below.

## IV

Before considering the experiences of the various countries, I shall anticipate two methodological objections. First, it will be argued by some critics that studying individual countries, with the possible exception of the United States, is unsound since inflation is a global phenomenon.[6] This objection is not without merit. It may well be that a small and highly exposed country like the Netherlands, which exports about half its gross domestic product, will find it difficult to achieve a substantially lower inflation rate than those of its principal trade partners, especially if it insists on stable exchange rates. 'Efficient market' theorists like Robert Mundell and Arthur Laffer appear to maintain that even the United States, with an exports to G.D.P. ratio of only 5 per cent, cannot be analysed correctly apart from the rest of the world. They contend that equivalent goods will sell at essentially the same real prices everywhere. Hence a devaluation of the dollar will provide a prompt and roughly proportional upward thrust on most United States prices, regardless of whether the items actually enter into trade.[7]

External inflationary impulses clearly exist. However, it is also clear that countries differ widely in rates and timing of inflation. In addition, the transmission mechanisms of external impulses are likely to differ from country to country. To understand these differences it is essential to focus on the experience of individual countries.

A second kind of objection is that inflation must be studied in the context of an elaborate general equilibrium model, rather than by simple regressions of prices on money. In principle, I readily concede the validity and importance of this objection. It is generally accepted, for example, that there are feedback mechanisms whereby inflation calls forth monetary expansion, reflecting either an accommodative central bank or a variety of other linkages. To the extent that causality runs from prices to money as well as from money to prices, a single-equation approach may result in biased estimates of the responsiveness of the price level to the rate of monetary growth. However, this paper does not aim to provide accurate estimates of parameters. Rather, the intention is to scan a broad sweep of evidence to determine the extent of its conformity to the monetarist model.

## V

Let us begin by looking at the inflation 'league tables' within the O.E.C.D. Table 1 shows inflation rates for individual countries as well as weighted rates for all O.E.C.D. countries and European members since 1961. The most striking feature of the table is the progressive acceleration of inflation since the early 1960s, and especially since 1971. With few exceptions this has been true in all countries, in each succeeding time-period.

In general, the experience of the six countries surveyed in this paper has paralleled that of other O.E.C.D. countries. However, there have been some noteworthy differences among them. During the early 1960s three of the six — Canada, the United States and Belgium — had relatively little inflation, while the other three — Britain, Sweden and the Netherlands — had above-

TABLE I

*Inflation Rates, O.E.C.D. Countries, 1961—74*
(Percentage change, at annual rate)

| Country | Consumer price index | | | | | G.D.P. deflator |
| | 1961—71 | 1966—71 | 1972 | 1973 | 12 months to Sept. 1974 | 1966—71 |
|---|---|---|---|---|---|---|
| Belgium | 3·4 | 3·5 | 5·5 | 10·4 | 15·6 | 4·0 |
| Britain | 4·6 | 5·7 | 7·1 | 9·2 | 17·1 | 5·6 |
| Canada | 2·9 | 3·7 | 4·8 | 7·6 | 10·9 | 3·8 |
| Netherlands | 4·8 | 5·3 | 7·8 | 8·0 | 10·3 | 5·3 |
| Sweden | 4·6 | 4·6 | 6·0 | 6·7 | 9·8 | 4·8 |
| United States | 3·1 | 4·5 | 3·3 | 6·2 | 12·1 | 4·4 |
| Australia | 2·8 | 3·7 | 5·8 | 9·5 | 16·3[a] | 4·6 |
| Austria | 3·7 | 3·8 | 6·3 | 7·6 | 10·1 | 3·8 |
| Denmark | 6·1 | 6·3 | 6·6 | 9·3 | 16·7 | 5·7 |
| Finland | 5·4 | 5·3 | 7·4 | 11·4 | 17·8 | 5·9 |
| France | 4·3 | 4·9 | 5·9 | 7·3 | 14·8 | 5·2 |
| Germany | 3·0 | 3·0 | 5·5 | 6·9 | 7·3 | 4·2 |
| Greece | 2·2 | 2·1 | 4·4 | 15·5 | 24·9 | 2·5 |
| Iceland | 12·0 | 12·0 | 9·7 | 20·6 | 41·4[a] | 13·4 |
| Ireland | 5·4 | 6·5 | 8·7 | 11·4 | 17·9[a] | 7·1 |
| Italy | 4·2 | 3·4 | 5·7 | 10·8 | 23·2 | 4·4 |
| Japan | 5·9 | 5·7 | 4·5 | 11·7 | 23·8 | 4·7 |
| Luxembourg | 3·0 | 3·3 | 5·2 | 6·1 | 10·6 | 5·1 |
| Norway | 4·9 | 5·5 | 7·2 | 7·5 | 10·3 | 5·7 |
| Portugal | 5·5 | 7·8 | 10·7 | 12·9 | 31·1 | 3·8 |
| Spain | 6·8 | 5·4 | 8·3 | 11·4 | 15·2 | 5·5 |
| Switzerland | 3·8 | 3·8 | 6·7 | 8·7 | 11·3 | 5·1 |
| Turkey | 7·4 | 10·0 | 15·5 | 14·0 | 25·5[a] | 7·7 |
| O.E.C.D. Total | 3·7 | n.a. | 4·7 | 7·7 | 14·1 | n.a. |
| O.E.C.D. Europe | 4·2 | n.a. | 6·5 | 8·7 | 14·7 | n.a. |
| E.E.C. | 4·0 | n.a. | 6·2 | 8·3 | 14·5 | n.a. |

[a]To latest month; September data not available.

Sources: Consumer prices, *O.E.C.D. Outlook*; G.D.P. deflator, *O.E.C.D. Economic Surveys*, B.L.E.U., July 1974.

average inflation rates. During 1966—72 Belgium and Canada continued to have relatively good records. The United States began to become a rapid inflator in the late 1960s and early 1970s. Its improvement in 1972 proved to be a brief interlude, attributable, as we shall see, almost entirely to the controls of the Nixon Administration's Phases I and II. Belgium, too, suddenly became a rapid inflator after 1972. In 1973 it had the worst inflation among the six, and in 1974 the second worst, after Britain. Sweden, a country that had a rather poor price record in the 1950s and 1960s, has experienced a marked relative improvement in the 1970s. Indeed, in the most recent period, Sweden's 9·8 per cent inflation rate was bettered only by Germany's rate of 7·3 per cent, among the twenty-three countries included in the table. Only Britain, among the six, has consistently been a high inflator.

## VI

Additional price data are displayed in Fig. 1, which shows quarter-to-quarter percentage changes in consumer prices in each of the six countries from 1950 to 1974, along with similar changes in the stock of money. Both series have been seasonally adjusted and smoothed by use of centred three-term averages. It is immediately apparent that prices (the broken lines in the chart) are much less volatile than money. The extreme example is Canada, whose quarterly price movements have followed very closely those of the United States, both in amplitude and timing. The timing of Canada's monetary growth has also corresponded closely to that of the United States, but the amplitudes of its monetary changes have been huge in comparison with those of the other countries, and especially in comparison with the United States. This is an expected result, given the similarity of Canada and the United States, the high degree of integration of the two economies, and the generally stable exchange rate that has existed between the United States dollar and the Canadian dollar. Efficient market considerations assure that Canadian and United States prices will keep close pace with one another, and the ease of short-term capital flows between the two countries, coupled with the Bank of Canada's exchange-rate policy, has meant that the Bank of Canada has usually harmonised its monetary policies with those of the Federal Reserve in order to avoid excessive swings in Canadian interest rates. However, to a lesser degree the sluggishness of prices relative to money exists in the other five countries as well.

Of greater interest is the relationship — or rather the lack of one — between monetary growth rates and inflation in the short run. Although it is clear that the severe inflations of recent years have been associated in every country with the fastest monetary expansions of the entire quarter-century covered by the chart, it is also clear that in most of the countries there is only a weak correspondence between phases of monetary and price changes, even if one makes allowance for the existence of monetary lags (or leads). The United States appears to be the signal exception. The period of declining monetary growth in the United States in 1952–3, for example, was followed by moderating inflation through mid-1955. The monetary acceleration of 1954–5 corresponds to a price acceleration in 1956–8, and the monetary slowdown of 1956–7 foretold a calming of inflation for several years beginning in 1958. The rapid rise in $M$ in 1965 and 1967–9 was once

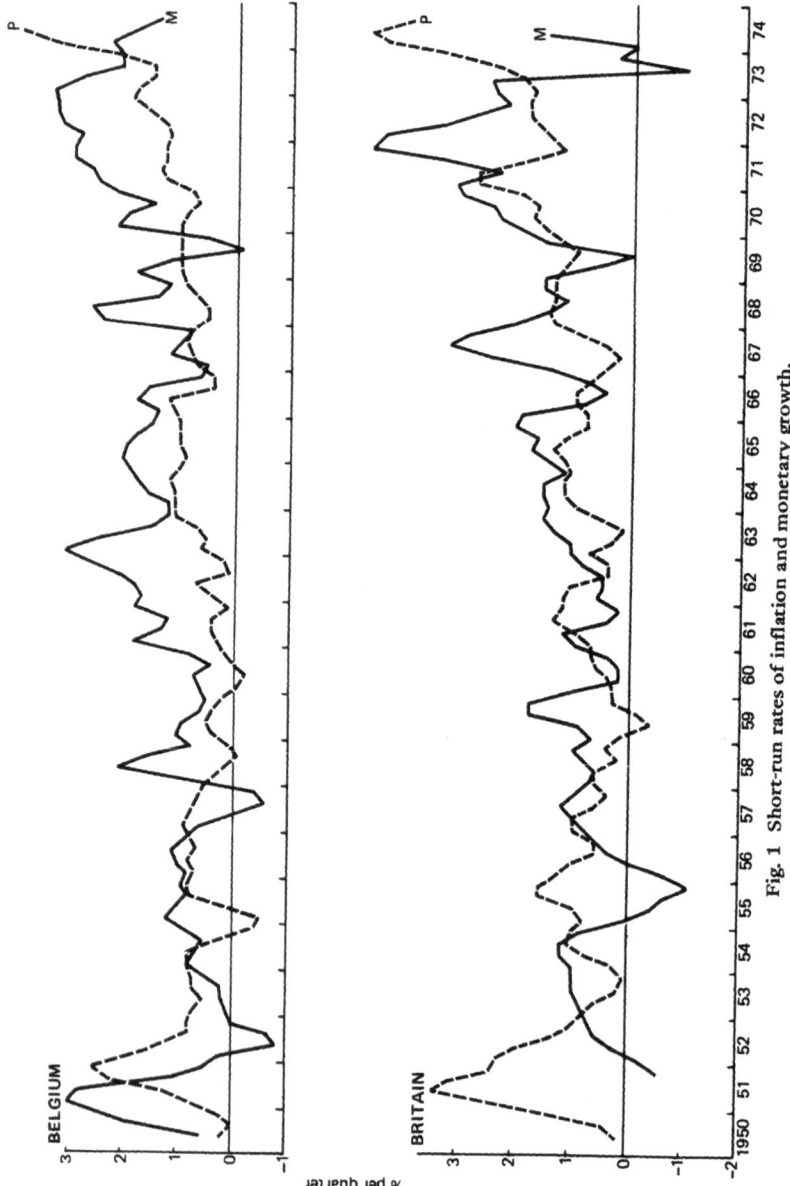

Fig. 1　Short-run rates of inflation and monetary growth.

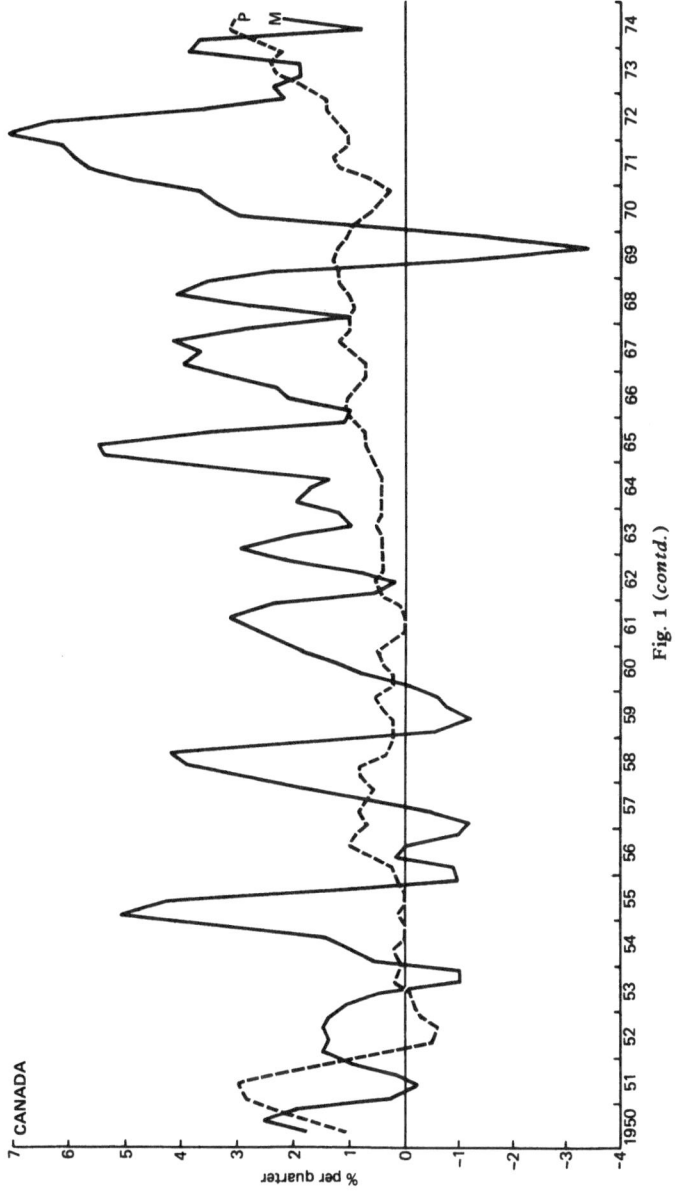

Fig. 1 (*contd.*)

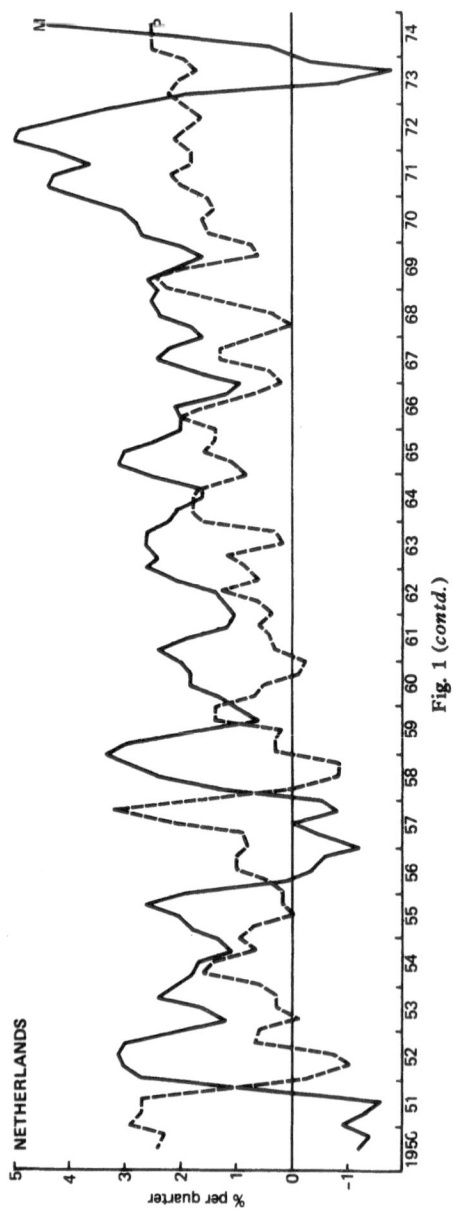

Fig. 1 (*contd.*)

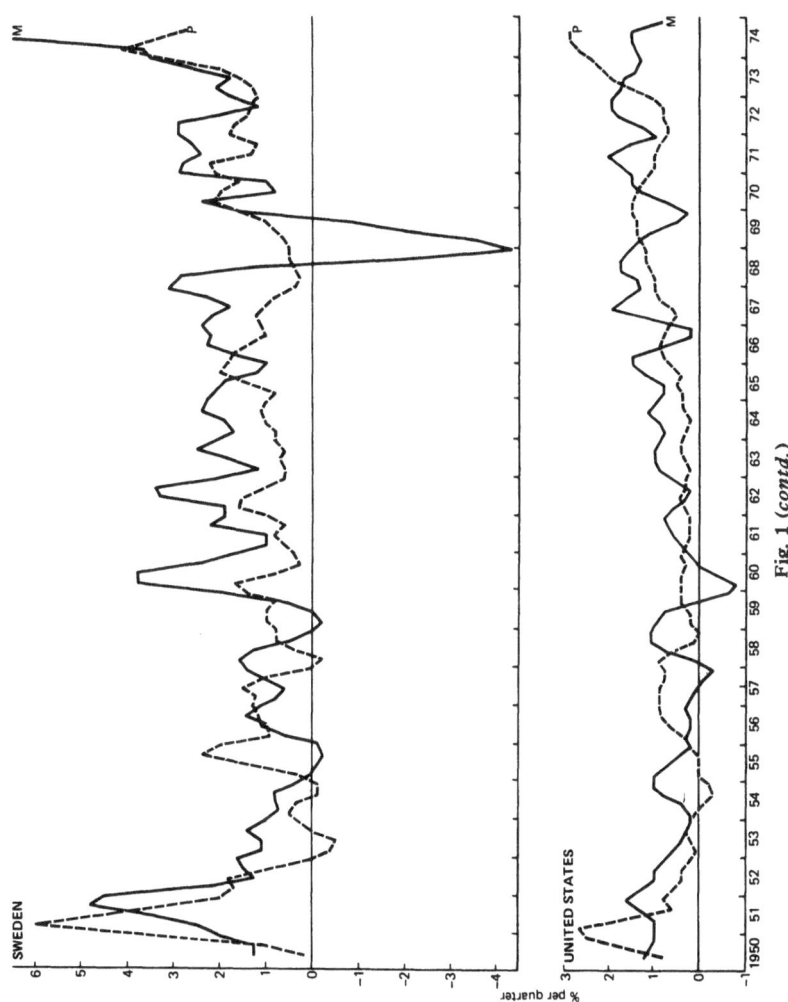

Fig. 1 (*contd.*)

again accompanied by a steady build-up of inflation from 1967 until early 1970. The restraint of 1969 has its counterpart in declining rates of inflation throughout 1970–1, and the adoption of easy money throughout most of the period since 1970 was followed by a renewed price explosion in 1973–4. However, the consistency between the two series is far from perfect. The monetary speed-up of 1958–9, for example, has no counterpart in the price series.

These impressions are confirmed by the regression results reported in Table 2. For each country quarterly percentage change in $P$ was regressed on quarterly percentage change in $M$ with discrete leads and lags extending from $t + 8$ to $t - 16$. The table shows the highest $R^2$ obtained, together with the lead or lag which produced this $R^2$. For the United States, $R^2$ was a respectable 0·38 when monetary growth seven quarters earlier was the regressor. Among the other countries, Sweden and Britain had fairly high $R^2$s (0·26 and 0·25), but without any lead or lag in the British case and a three-quarter *lead* in the case of Sweden. The Netherlands had a low maximum $R^2$ of only 0·13, again with a lead in place of the expected monetary lag.

TABLE 2

*Regressions of Quarterly Percentage Changes in*
*P on M, Six Countries*

| Country | Maximum $R^2$ | Number of quarters lead (+) or lag (−) in M |
|---|---|---|
| Belgium | 0·10 | −5 |
| Britain | 0·25 | 0 |
| Canada | 0·13 | −4 |
| Netherlands | 0·13 | +4 |
| Sweden | 0·26 | +3 |
| United States | 0·38 | −7 |

Mention should be made of another set of results that is not reported in Table 2. For the United States I regressed real G.N.P. on $M$ (both in percentage changes) in the same fashion as the price regressions. $R^2$ was maximised at 0·11 when $M$ was lagged six quarters. For $t$ through $t - 3$ the regression coefficients were positive (but not significant). They were negative and sometimes significant for $t - 4$ through $t - 16$. It is especially interesting that the sum of all coefficients ($t$ to $t - 16$) was strongly negative. After six quarters the sum of coefficients was close to zero, as monetarists would expect, suggesting that monetary acceleration stimulates output growth only in the very short run.

**VII**

Although the foregoing results do not provide strong support for the monetarist theory of inflation, they are not surprising to a monetarist. As was pointed out earlier, monetarists do not (or should not) purport to have a monetary explanation of price movements in the short run. The question remains: to what extent can longer-run price movements be explained by fluctuations in *M*? To explore this issue I calculated one-year, two-year, three-year and four-year percentage changes in the quarterly G.N.P. deflator (where available) and consumer prices and in narrow and broad money ($M_1$ and $M_2$), with and without seasonal adjustment. As with the regressions discussed above, discrete leads and lags were used, covering $t + 8$ through $t - 16$. Table 3 presents for each country the regression that maximised $R^2$.

Clearly, an entirely different picture emerges when the money—price relationship is studied in a long-run context. For every country it appears that monetary growth eight to sixteen quarters earlier has been a major determinant of inflation rates measured over three- or four-year time-spans. The strongest relationship was found in the United States, which had an $R^2$ of 0·86. The Netherlands and Sweden had the lowest $R^2$s, each with 0·59. Both these countries have relied quite heavily from time to time on price controls, selective credit controls, subsidies and variations in indirect taxes. The Netherlands has pioneered in the development of incomes policies. While it is doubtful that such policies can have a lasting effect on broad price indexes, they are probably capable of changing the time-path of inflation, deflecting it from its normal course and thereby weakening the correlation between *M* and *P*. This would be true especially of short-run infla-

TABLE 3

*Long-run Inflation and Monetary Growth, Six Countries*

| Country | Period | Independent variable | Quarter lags | Regression coefficients[a] | | $R^2$ |
|---------|--------|----------------------|--------------|------|----------|-------|
| | | | | M | Constant | |
| Belgium | 1958(I)−1971(IV) | $M_1$, 4-yr p.c. | 8 | 0·48 | 0·01 | 0·82 |
| | | | | (15·51) | (0·08) | |
| Britain | 1962(I)−1971(IV) | $M_3$, 4-yr p.c. | 16 | 0·56 | 1·68 | 0·78 |
| | | | | (11·61) | (7·43) | |
| Canada | 1958(I)−1971(IV) | $M_1$, 4-yr p.c. | 8 | 0·23 | 0·72 | 0·79 |
| | | | | (14·34) | (5·13) | |
| Netherlands | 1958(I)−1971(IV) | $M_1$, 4-yr p.c. | 8 | 0·41 | 0·93 | 0·59 |
| | | | | (8·78) | (2·55) | |
| Sweden | 1958(I)−1971(IV) | $M_2$, 4-yr p.c. | 15 | 0·24 | 2·53 | 0·59 |
| | | | | (8·88) | (13·72) | |
| United States | 1958(I)−1971(II) | $M_1$, 3-yr p.c. | 14 | 1·04 | 0·01 | 0·86 |
| | | | | (17·56) | (0·02) | |

[a]Figures in parentheses are *t*-statistics.

tion rates, but even three-year rates could be distorted in this way. It is interesting that four-year rates gave substantially higher $R^2$s than three-year rates for both Sweden and the Netherlands.

The difference in lags shown in the table may be related to differences in the length of collective bargaining cycles, the extent of indexation and the degree of external exposure. In both Sweden and the United States, long-term wage agreements have been quite common, at least until recently; in Belgium and the Netherlands, on the other hand, the typical duration of agreements has been one year. Unfortunately, Canada and Britain appear not to fit this pattern; Canada has many long-term contracts but short monetary lags, while long-term contracts are rare in Britain but lags are long. The two most exposed countries, Belgium and the Netherlands, have short money–price lags, while the United States, with long lags, is perhaps the least exposed economy in the world. This explanation does not help us to distinguish between short-lag Canada and long-lag Britain and Sweden, of course. Obviously much work remains to be done on these issues.

No particular significance should be attached to the fact that the coefficient on $M$ is close to unity for the United States, in contrast to the substantially lower coefficients for the other countries. Over the estimation period (1958(I) to 1971(II)), $M_1$ velocity in the United States had a pronounced upward trend which came close to matching the trend rate of growth of real G.N.P. Consequently, for that period a crude quantity theory model works well. In the future, however, the trends of velocity and output may diverge, as they have throughout much of United States history, in which case the price equation in Table 3 will no longer be valid.

## VIII

Let us take a closer look at recent price trends in the United States. Both the short-run data of Fig. 1 and the long-run data of Fig. 2 suggest that the monetary restraint of 1969–70 was beginning to bring inflation under control in 1970 and early 1971. In Fig. 1 it can be seen that the quarterly inflation rate declined steadily for several quarters after peaking in the first quarter of 1970. The restraint period was severe enough to cause a definite decline in the long-run rate of monetary growth. The actual long-run inflation rate did not decline, but at least there was a retardation in its rate of increase. However, the period of restraint was far too brief to have a lasting impact on United States inflation. By February 1970 it had become clear that a recession was under way. Accordingly, monetary policy was shifted abruptly from restraint to ease. Top priority was given to reducing unemployment. Between the first quarter of 1970 and the third quarter of 1971, $M_1$ grew at an inflationary rate of 7·3 per cent per year. By then the long-run inflation rate predicted by our United States equation had climbed back to its 1969 peak. Thus the ground that had been won so painfully was soon lost.

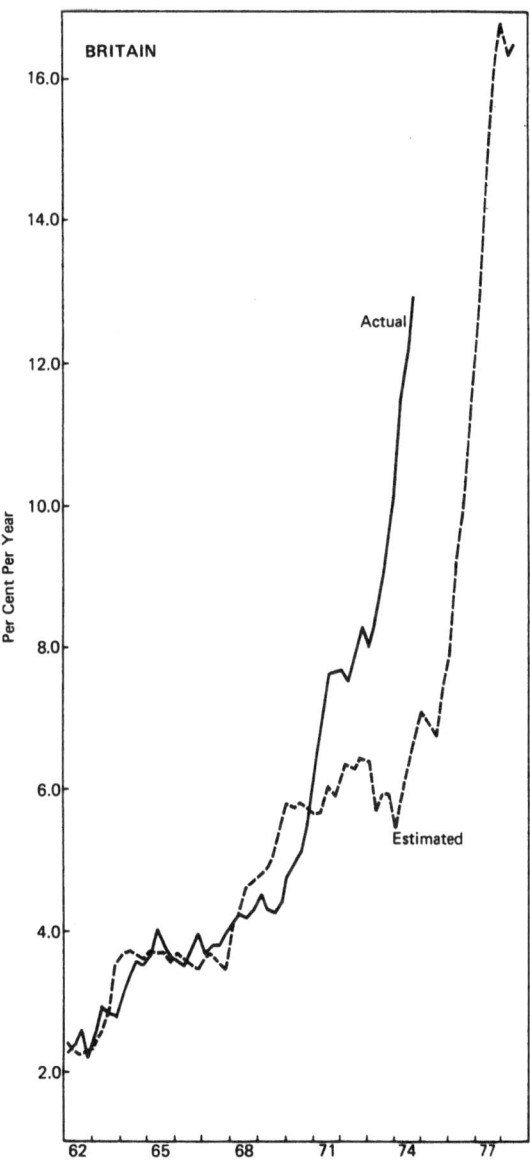

Fig. 2 Actual and estimated long-run inflation rates.

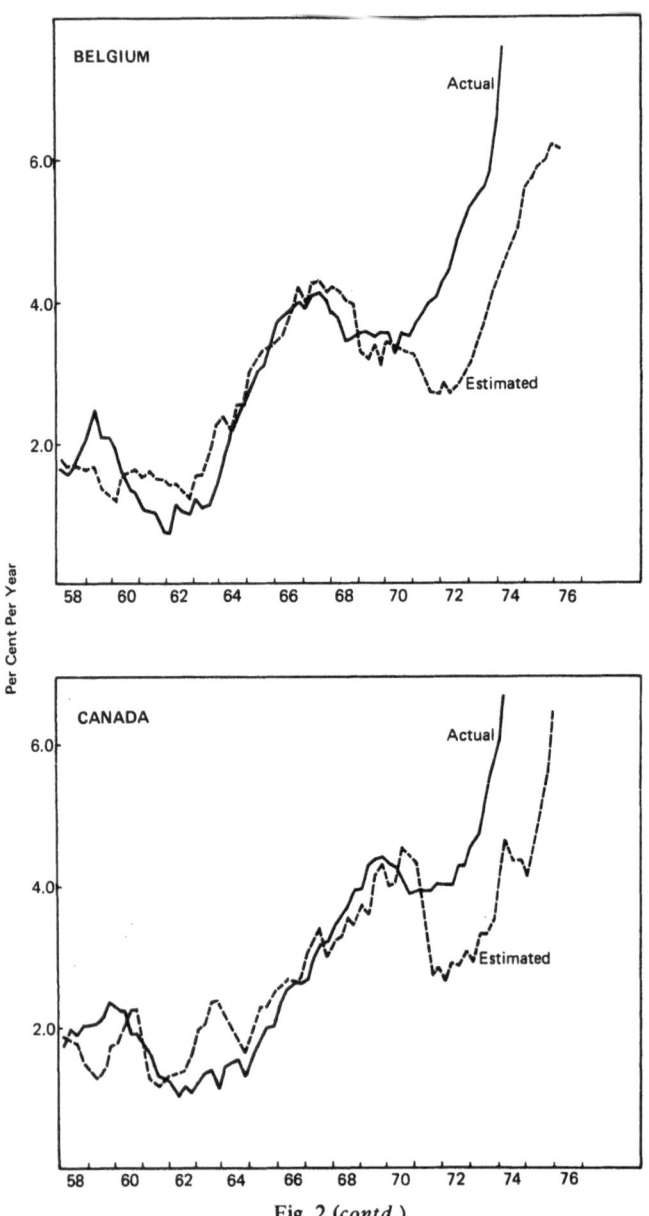

Fig. 2 (contd.)

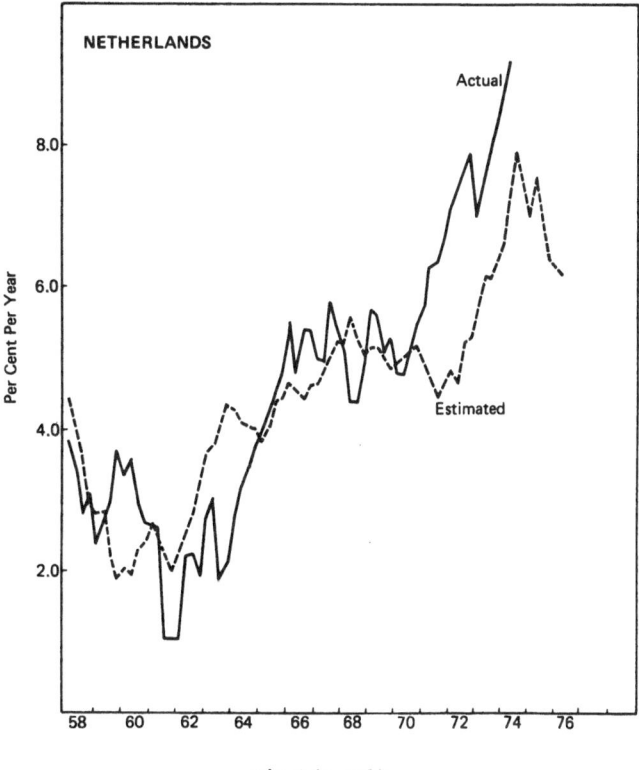

Fig. 2 (*contd.*)

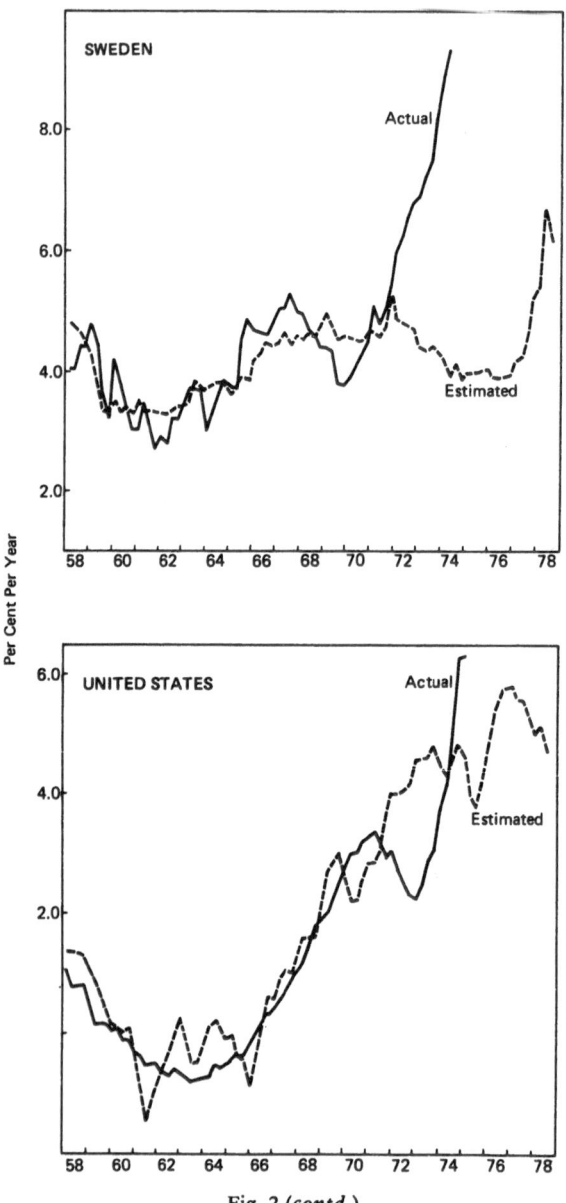

Fig. 2 (*contd.*)

By the summer of 1971 the United States balance of payments had badly deteriorated, after the aggressively easy money of the preceding year. Progress against inflation seemed to be grinding to a halt. The election was fifteen months off. President Nixon finally accepted the advice that Chairman Burns of the Federal Reserve Board and others had been pressing upon him for many months. The Phase I price–wage freeze was announced on 15 August 1971.

The 'new economic policy' made a major impact on the rate of inflation. As Fig. 2 makes clear, the rapid monetary expansion of 1967–9 caused the predicted long-run inflation rate to rise very sharply in 1971–2. But the *actual* long-run inflation rate plummeted during this controls period. By the first quarter of 1973 the predicted inflation rate was 6·6 per cent while the actual rate was only 4·3 per cent. The weakly administered control programme could not possibly hold back the pressures implied by such a huge discrepancy between actual and predicted inflation rates. Recognising this elementary truth, Mr Nixon opted – wisely, I think – for a policy of dismantling controls rather than the alternative of hiring a gigantic police force to enforce them. Not surprisingly, an extended price explosion then occurred. In order for the long-run inflation rate to attain 'equilibrium' rate of about 6·5–7 per cent based on prior monetary growth, the short-run (i.e. quarterly) inflation rate had to soar far above the long-run rate. The short-run rate got as high as 14·4 cent per year in the final quarter of 1974.

However, by the end of 1974 the actual long-run inflation rate had overshot its 'equilibrium' level. It remained about 8·4 per cent in 1975(I), compared with a predicted level of only 6·7 per cent. Various reasons could explain this overshooting. It is possible that the high inflation rates of 1973–4 made Americans much more inflation-conscious than before; many individuals feared augmented inflation in 1975. Perhaps the most common explanation is the oil crisis, which caused a 'one-time' reduction in world real G.N.P. below its trend rate of growth. A development such as this, supplemented by poor crops, could cause a discontinuity in the inflation estimation equation. However, if real G.N.P. returns to its trend rate of growth, we should expect the long-run inflation rate gradually to approach the levels predicted by the equation. By early 1977 I believe that both the long-run and short-run inflation rate in the United States will be a little under 8 per cent per year (see Fig. 2).

Note that this forecast is based solely on monetary growth that has already taken place. It does not rest on any particular assumption about the kind of monetary policy that the Federal Reserve will adopt during the business recovery which apparently began in the late spring of 1975. The consequences of the monetary policies of the spring and summer of 1975 will not, of course, bear fruit until the last years of this decade. The current political setting in the United States, I fear, is likely to force the hand of the Federal Reserve, requiring monetary growth at an unsustainable rate in 1975 and 1976. The tax cut enacted early in 1975, together with a strong likelihood of rising government expenditures, almost assures this outcome. An attempt by the Federal Reserve to compensate for excessive monetary expansion in 1975 by adopting slow monetary growth later on (after the November 1976 elections, one presumes) will probably lead to a new recession late in 1977 or 1978.

## IX

Let us turn to the other five countries. During the middle or late 1960s each country's predicted long-run inflation rate increased substantially. In Belgium the rise began in 1963; in Britain, in 1968; and in Canada, the Netherlands and Sweden, in 1965. These rises in predicted inflation came to a halt in every country in the late 1960s or early 1970s; in every country except Britain there followed a protracted interval of decline in expected inflation. The British expected long-run inflation rate paused only briefly, in 1970, then rose again in 1971–2. The British rate fell quite sharply in 1973, but this gain was more than wiped out by the end of 1974. In Belgium the decline persisted for five years, from 1967 to 1972. Canada's period of declining expected inflation was brief but sharp, extending from mid-1970 to mid-1971. In the Netherlands the decline was quite gradual but it lasted from mid-1968 through 1971. Sweden's period of decline was also lengthy and rather moderate; it began later than the others, extending from the end of 1971 through early 1976.

Actual long-run inflation rates tell a very different story. Up to 1970 or 1971 actual and expected rates of most coincided in each country. Thereafter a wide gap opened as actual long-run inflation soared far above predicted rates. And, as was noted earlier, a similar gap appeared on the United States chart after mid-1974.

How can we account for the sudden disintegration of traditional money–price relationships in all six countries in recent years? Have we entered a new economic environment in which the old rules no longer work? I think not. There are a number of conceivable explanations of the breakdown that make sense in terms of conventional theory. In every country the slopes of the predicted and actual lines are quite similar. What seems to have happened is that these countries experienced the inflation predicted for 1975–6 a year or two ahead of schedule. One way of explaining this abrupt shortening of monetary lags is to argue that a certain 'expectations threshold' was triggered by the dramatic rises in grain prices after the poor harvests of 1972 and 1973, and in oil prices after the OPEC embargo of 1973–4. This could have led to velocity rises, reflecting either a traditional 'flight from cash' or a general reluctance to enter into long-term contracts at fixed prices. Certainly there has been much wider use of escalator clauses in collective bargaining and other contracts in the last two or three years in all countries.

Another plausible explanation was mentioned in the United States discussion above — namely, that the commodity supply problems of recent years have imposed real income losses on the six countries. The estimation periods for the price equations of Table 3 ended in 1971, prior to the emergence of the supply problems. The validity of those equations for projections of future price trends depends critically, of course, on continuation into the future of past trends in velocity and real income. A once-for-all income decline would distort the equations for a few years. In particular, a decline in real income would imply an underestimation of future prices — precisely what has happened.

To my mind the above hypotheses go far towards explaining the poor performance of the price equations since 1971. It is easy to concoct other explanations, however. One is that we may have seriously underestimated rates of monetary growth in recent years by ignoring Euro-currency balances. The unexpectedly severe inflation may somehow be associated with the breakdown of the Bretton Woods system of stable but adjustable exchange rates. I am not convinced of the importance of either explanation. Euro-currencies did not suddenly blossom forth in 1971; they existed at least a decade earlier and had reached major dimensions by the mid-1960s. The transition from pegged to flexible exchange rates may have induced central banks to be less cautious in controlling monetary gorwth, but this is no explanation of why inflation has responded to monetary growth differently from the past. If it is contended that depreciation of the dollar after August 1971 contributed importantly to United States inflation, then why did not appreciation of the Belgian franc result in a slowdown of Belgian inflation? The argument seems to raise more questions than it answers.

Earlier I predicted a long-run inflation rate for the United States in the 7—8 per cent zone between mid-1975 and mid-1978. For Belgium, Canada and the Netherlands the equations of Table 3 suggest long-run inflation rates of about 6 per cent by early 1976. Since Canada's actual long-run inflation rate was about 9 per cent per year early in 1975, no drastic adjustment seems required for coincidence of predicted and actual inflation rates there. In Belgium and the Netherlands the adjustments will have to be a bit more severe since, according to the latest figures available, both countries had long-run rates of about 10 per cent per year early in 1975. Sweden is still another country that can expect a steady-state inflation rate of 6—7 per cent per year if its long-run rate of monetary growth remains at recent high levels. Because of the long lags in the Swedish equation, a reduction in the long-run monetary growth rate is not likely to eliminate the basic inflation that exists in that country before the end of the decade.

The most interesting — and ominous — case is that of Britain. It alone, among the six countries studied, failed to achieve a long-run inflation rate at least as high as its steady-state inflation rate. The latter stood at 16·5 per cent per year, based on $M_3$ growth, compared with an actual rate of 14·2 per cent in the first quarter of 1975. The British equation suggests that a long-run inflation rate less than 16 per cent is unlikely to be achieved in this decade. The most optimistic statement that can be made with regard to Britain is that its *short-run* inflation should back off from the 25 per cent per year rate that prevailed in the spring of 1975 fairly soon.[8]


# X

Anti-monetarists will not, I suspect, be impressed by the fact that long-run inflation rates, defined as percentage changes over time-spans of three or four years, are quite closely related to long-run rates of monetary growth two to four years earlier. One possible interpretation is that I have simply picked up a manifestation of the business cycle, which has usually run for three to four years in the countries examined here. Thus it could be argued that the central bank is apt to adopt an easy-money policy as unemployment rises during recessions. As recession gives way to boom, perhaps for reasons unrelated to monetary policy, inflation blossoms forth two or three years later, either because of labour-market tightness (the familiar Phillips curve analysis) or because prices, and therefore wages, are rising in the sector that competes on world markets, and this induces inflationary wage rises in the low-productivity-growth domestic sector (the Scandinavian 'Aukrust–EFO' analysis).[9] On this view, then, we have a classic case of correlation without causation. The variables that really move the system have been omitted from the analysis.

I cannot take time to spell out and respond to all the objections to the monetarist view of inflation. There is one objection, however, that seems to me to have real merit and that deserves at least brief discussion. Even if one is willing to accept, provisionally, the monetarist view, it is important to recognise that it does not carry us very far. What we need to know additionally is *why* central bankers have been creating money at highly inflationary rates.

Consider the basic identity that equates the money stock to the product of base money and a multiplier. Although I have not completed careful analyses of the data at this time, it is clear that in all six countries most of the fluctuations in $M$ in recent years are attributable to fluctuations in $B$, the base.[10] The next step is to examine the components of $B$, and especially to assess the relative importance of domestic and international disturbances. This analysis has not yet yielded definite and precise conclusions. However, it is clear that domestic credit expansion played a very important role in all six countries during the 1960s. More recently it appears that international sources of variations in $B$ (hence $M$) have been relatively much more important than before, but domestic credit continues to account for much of the growth in $B$. Moreover, it appears that central government borrowing has accounted for a sizeable share of domestic credit expansion.[11]

For the present I prefer to sidestep the issue of whether or not central banks really can control the international sources of monetary growth. The issue is irrelevant to the present discussion since the behaviour of central banks with regard to domestic credit has been inflationary, independently of international factors. Why have central banks recently permitted inflationary rates of domestic credit expansion?

Explanations of central bank behaviour fall into two broad classes. One view is that central bankers, as a class, are either poorly educated or not very bright. They have been accused, for example, of suffering from 'money market myopeia' — an inability to grasp the big picture because of preoccupation with the minutiae of the banking industry. Traditionally, central bankers have tended to come to their trade after careers in commercial banking. Thus they are not, it is argued, accustomed to thinking globally. In the frequent instances where economists have served as central bankers, it has been claimed that they studied at the wrong universities — that they have swallowed Keynesian fallacies. On a somewhat higher plane, it is said that central bankers and other policy-makers have not sufficiently appreciated the long lags in the effects of their actions.

I feel a little uncomfortable being cast in the role of defending the wisdom of central bankers as a class. Undoubtedly major blunders have been perpetrated in one country or another, from time to time. Nevertheless, I do not believe that we can explain a pervasive tendency towards inflationary monetary growth in terms of mistaken judgements by central bankers.

This brings me to the second broad class of explanations of central bank behaviour — namely, that the policies adopted by governments, especially with regard to the size of the public sector and the means of financing it, have left central banks with very limited policy options. Much nonsense has been written about the independence of central banks. In fact, the Federal Reserve Board stands almost alone among central banks in enjoying a modicum of independence, in the sense of being able, within limits, to adopt a monetary policy that is not to the government's liking. In all the other five countries the Minister of Finance has the formal power to issue instructions to the central bank — a power that may never have been used but is none the less real. But even the Federal Reserve is subject to intense political pressures, and it is fanciful to think that it has the option of refusing to finance a government deficit.

For the United States a recent study has shown that a close association has existed, at least since the early 1950s, between expansions in the money stock and growth of Federal government debt held by the Federal Reserve Banks.[12] Although I have not studied this question carefully in the other countries, I suspect that a similar relationship holds in each of them. If so, then the fundamental sources of inflation in modern societies can be traced to the great rises that have taken place in recent years in public expenditures, both absolutely and as a fraction of G.N.P., coupled with the failure of governments to finance these expenditures in a non-inflationary way. But this question needs much further study before we can be confident of the answer.

## XI

I have attempted to gain insights into the recent worldwide worsening of inflation by examining experience within six industrialised countries: Belgium, Britain, Canada, the Netherlands, Sweden and the United States. A simple model was developed, incorporating monetarist assumptions about the nature of inflation. In brief, this model asserts that the long-run rate of inflation, $p^L$, will be equal to the long-run rate of monetary growth, $m^L$, in earlier periods, plus a constant:

$$p_t^L = \alpha + m_{o,t-n}^L \tag{7}$$

In this equation, $m_o$ refers to the actual rate of monetary growth, which is assumed to be policy-determined, and the rates of change are calculated over periods of two to four years.

An examination of quarter-to-quarter rates of growth revealed only a weak relationship between money and prices. However, when growth rates in money and prices were calculated over time-spans of three or four years, in conformity with the model, a strong relationship was discovered between money and prices. In four countries — Belgium, Britain, Canada and the United States — it is possible to explain about 80 per cent of the long-run inflation rate during the 1960s by relating it solely to prior monetary growth In the Netherlands and Sweden, countries that have experimented widely with direct controls, a purely monetary model of inflation performs less well, accounting for less than 60 per cent of the actual long-run inflation rate. Lengthy lags were found in each country, ranging from eight quarters in Belgium, Canada and the Netherlands to fourteen quarters in the United States, fifteen quarters in Sweden and sixteen quarters in Britain.

The discovery of a close link between money and prices leads one to ask why central banks have been expanding money supplies at inflationary rates in recent years. A reliable answer to this question will require much additional research on the sources of monetary growth in each country. However, casual inspection of the data suggests that a major contributor to excessive monetary growth has been the sharp rise in central government expenditures, coupled with the failure of taxes to keep pace with expenditures. Ultimately, then, it appears that one must explain the forces underlying the expansion of the public sector and the means of financing it if one is to understand why we are living in an age of inflation.

### Notes

1. Where and when Lenin made this remark is not clear. The earliest reference I have come across is in J. M. Keynes, *Essays in Persuasion* (New York: Norton, 1963) p.77, in an essay that was published originally in 1919: 'Lenin is said to have declared that the best way to destroy the Capitalist System was to debauch the currency.' Keynes added his own opinion that 'Lenin was certainly right'. A recent reference appears in J. Rueff's contribution to the *Sunday Times*, 22 June 1975. Rueff quotes

Lenin with approval (without citation, however) as saying: 'To destroy the bourgeois regime, it is sufficient to corrupt its currency.'
In *The Affluent Society* (Boston: Houghton Mifflin, 1958) Galbraith states that nothing so weakens government as persistent inflation' (p. 209).

2. Thornton Wilder, *The Bridge of San Luis Rey* (New York: Boni, 1927).

3. A very incomplete listing of monetarist works on inflation would include the following: various articles by Milton Friedman, collected in his *An Economist's Protest*, 2nd ed. (Glen Ridge, N. J.: Horton, 1975), *Dollars and Deficits* (Englewood Cliffs, N.J.: Prentice-Hall, 1968) and *A Theoretical Framework for Monetary Analysis*, National Bureau of Economic Research Occasional Paper 112 (New York: Columbia Univ. Press, 1971); Phillip Cagan, *The Hydra-Headed Monster* (Washington: American Enterprise Institute, 1974); Karl Brunner *et al.*, 'Fiscal and Monetary Policies in Moderate Inflation', *Journal of Money, Credit, and Banking*, V(1), Part II (Feb. 1973); D. E. W. Laidler, 'The Current Inflation: Explanations and Policies', *National Westminster Bank Quarterly Review* (Nov. 1972) and 'The 1974 Report of the President's Council of Economic Advisors: A Critique of Past and Prospective Policies', *American Economic Review*, LXIV(5) (Sept. 1974) 535–43, and other articles cited there; and Michael Parkin, 'United Kingdom Inflation: The Policy Alternatives', *National Westminster Bank Quarterly Review* (May 1974).

4. Marshall used this sentiment – which he borrowed from Darwin – as the motto of his *Principles of Economics*, 8th ed. (London: Macmillan, 1920).

5. The literature on monetary lags has become voluminous. A useful summary and critique of literature through the mid-1960s appears in Thomas Mayer, 'The Lag in the Effect of Monetary Policy: Some Criticisms', *Western Economic Journal* (Sept. 1967). More recent contributions are examined in Michael J. Hamburger, 'The Lag in the Effect of Monetary Policy: A Survey of Recent Literature', in *Monetary Aggregates and Monetary Policy* (New York: Federal Reserve Bank of New York, 1974) and Phillip Cagan and Anna J. Schwartz, 'How Feasible is a Flexible Monetary Policy?', in Richard T. Selden (ed.), *Capitalism and Freedom: Problems and Prospects* (Charlottesville: Virginia Univ. Press, 1975).

6. The need for a global approach is stressed by the contributors to the Spring 1975 issue of the Federal Reserve Bank of San Francisco's *Business Review*, which is devoted entirely to 'World Inflation'. Also, see various contributions to a recently published conference proceedings edited by David I. Meiselman and Arthur B. Laffer, *The Phenomenon of Worldwide Inflation* (Washington: American Enterprise Institute, 1975).

7. See Arthur B. Laffer, 'The Phenomenon of Worldwide Inflation: A Study in International Market Integration', and Robert A. Mundell, 'Inflation from an International Viewpoint', both in Meiselman and Laffer, op. cit. The Laffer paper contains numerous citations to other pertinent writings. A concise statement of Laffer's views appeared in his 'The Bitter Fruits of Devaluation', *Wall Street Journal*, 10 Jan. 1974. A fuller statement, written by a non-economist, is Jude Wanniski, 'The Mundell–Laffer Hypothesis: A New View of the World Economy', *The Public Interest*, No. 39 (Spring 1975).

8. For a somewhat different monetarist assessment of the British predicament, see Michael Parkin, 'Where is Britain's Inflation Going?', *Lloyds Bank Review* (July 1975). Note that Parkin's conclusions are based on narrowly defined money in contrast to the present paper, which is based on the broader $M_3$ concept. Parkin may well be right in thinking that the narrower measure is more appropriate. As he points out, the two series have followed very different time-paths in recent years.

9. This analysis has been developed jointly in recent years by the Norwegian economist, Odd Aukrust, and three Swedish economists, G. Edgren, K. O. Faxen and C. E. Odhner (hence 'EFO'). For a discussion of this interpretation of inflation, see Assar Lindbeck, *Swedish Economic Policy* (Berkeley and Los Angeles: Univ. of California Press, 1974) pp. 157–61.

10. United States data are examined in Karl Brunner, 'Monetary Growth and Monetary Policy', *Banca Nazionale del Lavoro Quarterly Review*, No. 111 (Dec. 1974), and in Susan R. Roesch, 'The Monetary—Fiscal Mix through Mid—1976', *Federal Reserve Bank of St Louis Review* (Aug. 1975). See the July 1975 Parkin article for a very brief discussion of British data.

11. Again, see the Roesch and Parkin articles.

12. In addition to the Roesch article, see Darryl R. Francis, 'How and Why Fiscal Actions Matter to a Monetarist', *Federal Reserve Bank of St Louis Review*, LVI(5) (May 1974). For a considerably more sceptical view of the importance of fiscal policy for monetary policy, see J. A. Cacy, 'Budget Deficits and the Money Supply', *Federal Reserve Bank of Kansas City Monthly Review* (June 1975).

# 17 Economic Foundations of Stock Market Regulation

IRWIN FRIEND

## 1. Introduction

Before considering the economic impact of stock regulation in the United States, which has pioneered in this area, it is desirable to review briefly the general purposes of such regulation. The two basic aims of the original legislation — the Securities Act of 1933 and the Securities and Exchange Act of 1934 — were protection of investors and promotion of the broader public interest as this interest is affected by trading in securities. The first aim has a fairness orientation and the second an economic orientation, since the public interest in the area of securities regulation relates largely to the impact of regulation on the economic performance of securities markets.

These two aims were to be achieved largely by policies designed to require full disclosure of material facts on securities sold in the primary and secondary markets, to prevent manipulation of securities prices, to curb unfair trading practices, to maintain orderly and liquid markets, and to control 'excessive' use of credit. This listing of the main categories of policies is not intended to indicate mutually exclusive groups since there can be broad overlapping. Similarly, while some of the specific policies followed are directed primarily to either an equity or an economic objective, others are directed to both. Some apply to the market for new issues, a number to the market for outstanding issues, and still others to both.

The period subsequent to the original legislation which set up the United States Securities and Exchange Commission (S.E.C.) to implement these objectives and policies has seen that agency, both through new legislation and new regulations, greatly expand its powers and assume a much more active and direct role in the regulation of securities issuance and trading. This trend has culminated in the recently enacted Securities Act Amendment of 1975 which gives the S.E.C. substantial new powers to structure the central market system and represents another major move away from industry self-regulation.

This chapter will consider first the economic rationale of stock market regulation and second the available evidence relating to the economic impact of such regulation. I shall largely confine my attention to economic effects, though equity considerations are obviously also relevant. I shall not discuss here several peripheral areas of securities regulation, including mutual funds, holding companies, and the recent extension of corporate disclosure requirements to social policy issues.

Before considering the technical materials to follow, I should point out that it is my belief that securities legislation in the United States has had as a whole a beneficial impact on the economy totally apart from its effect in reducing inequities among different participants in the securities markets. This does not mean that the economic case for every major facet of securities legislation has been proved beyond doubt, but simply that the economic case for some major facets is rather strong and that for other facets the case for seems to be stronger than the case against.

It has always amused me that the most vociferous economic critics of securities legislation have taken the tack that the case for such legislation must rest on irrefutable evidence that it has benefited the economy, not that the evidence for should be stronger that the evidence against. I would further argue that even if this legislation, with due consideration given to the costs involved, were neutral in its effect on the economy, much of it would be desirable on equity grounds.

To summarise my own views as to the effectiveness of different facets of securities regulation, the evidence that fuller disclosure has benefited the market for new securities issues seems to me rather strong. The position that fuller disclosure has improved the market for outstanding issues seems more defensible on the basis of the available evidence than the position that it has not, though the case is not as strong as for new issues. My evaluation of the success of the policies designed to maintain orderly and liquid markets and to control 'excessive' use of credit in the stock market is that they have probably done more economic good than harm, but the case again is not very strong. The economic rationale for some specific measures taken by the S.E.C. to prevent manipulation of securities prices and to curb unfair trading practices might be questioned, without much empirical support either way, but such policies can frequently be justified on equity grounds. In the subsequent discussion of the available evidence relating to the economic impact of securities regulation, I shall present only selected highlights and refer to the literature for further support of my position.

The remainder of this paper will discuss in turn the ways in which the stock market might be expected, at least in theory, to impinge on the economy (Section 2), the economic rationale for believing that stock market regulation would favourably affect the market (Section 3), and the empirical evidence relating to the performance of such regulation in furthering its economic goals (Section 4). Parts of these sections rely heavily on earlier studies by myself and others, but new material is also presented including a brief discussion of some recent, relevant literature.

## 2. Theory of Market Impact on Economy[1]

The stock market affects the functioning of the economy in two principal ways. First, market developments may affect the national income through their influence on the aggregate propensities to consume, to save and to invest. Second, even with a given level of saving and investment, market arrangements can affect the efficiency of the allocation of investment funds. This paper will be concerned primarily with the second of these two potential influences, viz. the impact of the market on economic efficiency — the type of impact to which economists have directed most of their attention.

It might be noted here, however, that economists have given inadequate consideration to the fact that a highly volatile stock market may decrease aggregate investment by increasing the cost of capital to business enterprises[2] and may also result in substantial swings in the level of consumption and hence income through an asset effect. Thus a less volatile stock market might stimulate a higher secular level of investment and less pronounced cyclical swings in the level of consumption and income. Presumably, since all available evidence suggests that people are risk-averse, their expected utility would be increased by smaller cyclical fluctuations, perhaps even if the average level of the national income were lowered somewhat in the process.

*Concepts of market efficiency*

Economic theorists have shown that making assumptions they consider reasonable — including management acting in the stockholders' interests and the costless and immediate availability of all information to all investors — a firm's output decisions under capital market equilibrium will be optimal for all its stockholders and will also be optimal in the sense that in long-run equilibrium each firm will be operating at minimum average costs.[3] Perhaps the most common conception of an efficient market in recent studies of stock market phenomena is one in which every price fully reflects all the available information so that any new relevant information is reflected in prices extremely rapidly (and cannot be used to make abnormal returns). There are, however, a number of difficulties with this definition.

First, the market must in some fashion reflect all available information. The important question is the relevance of the information to the subsequent earnings or riskiness of the stock. How is information to be distinguished from misinformation. Second, is a market in which prices fully reflect the scanty information available as efficient as a market in which much more information is available and reflected in stock prices? In other words, what is the justification for considering the information set fixed? Third, is the efficiency of the market independent of the costs incurred? It seems desirable to have two measures of efficiency, one measuring the quality of the service rendered (sometimes referred to as 'allocational efficiency'), the other its cost (or 'operational efficiency').

Finally, even if the markets are efficient according to any reasonable definition, this would not ensure a flow of economic resources into the most productive real investment. However, efficient markets should ensure that the markets are providing the appropriate guidelines for the flow of capital.

Another approach to appraising market efficiency has been to set up two standards: (1) the extent to which short-run fluctuations in price— that is, those not matched by changes in equilibrium price — are eliminated or, alternatively, the extent to which transaction costs to the public are minimised; and (2) the success with which changes in equilibrium prices are anticipated.[4] The first of these standards may be considered to lead to an appropriate measure of the market's operational efficiency. For a given volume and quality of services, and for given factor costs, operational efficiency may be measured by, and is an inverse function of, underwriting and other flotation costs of new issues and transaction costs in public transfer of outstanding issues (including any relevant regulatory costs). The transaction costs in the transfer of outstanding issues from a public buyer to a public seller include not only two commissions but also either all or part of the bid—ask spread.

The second of these standards, which is addressed to the market's allocational efficiency, introduces all the difficulties in defining, and in attempting to measure, equilibrium price.[5] The latter is apparently taken to represent the intersection of the investors' demand schedule for a security with the amount outstanding — no matter how temporary or ill-advised retrospectively that price turns out to be. Again, no consideration is given to the market role of misinformation or of the adequacy of the information set.

Probably the most satisfactory way of evaluating the allocational efficiency of decisions made in the securities markets is to inquire whether the outcomes are the best obtainable with the information that was available at the time the decisions were made or that could have been made available at that time (with the costs involved reflected in the measurement of operational efficiency). The best outcomes would be obtained if the markets maintained equivalent rates of return and hence equivalent costs of financing on comparable investments. This quality of the markets would help to ensure that funds are channelled from savers to those users who will apply them most profitably and that portfolio shifts can be made to the mutual advantage of different investors. The efficiency of this allocation process can be assessed in retrospect by the extent to which there are variations in market return and by the extent to which these variations can be explained by differentials in risk.

While it is not too difficult to obtain a retrospective view of allocational

efficiency by analysing returns and risks associated with different investments, it is virtually impossible to tell how the outcomes compare with
the best obtainable at the time the decisions were made. Retrospective
data permit an absolute appraisal of the optimality of outcomes only with
the benefit of hindsight. Yet they do provide an indication of the departure of outcomes from *ex-post* optimality. If *ex-ante* measures of return and
risk at the beginning of a period bear little relationship to *ex-post* measures
at the end of the period, the value of the *ex-ante* magnitudes would be
quite limited.

In spite of the deficiencies in reliance on retrospective data to supply
an adequate measure of absolute market efficiency, they probably do provide a reasonably satisfactory index of relative market efficiency which
can be used to analyse the impact on efficiency of different financial developments and practices, including the impact of securities regulation.

## 3. Economic Rationale of Market Regulation

The economic justification for disclosure, which is perhaps the most basic
mechanism of securities regulation, is the belief that the provision of information to prospective investors is a necessary condition for efficient
markets. 'With full disclosure we would expect less drastic shifts in estimates of expected profitability of a given issue as a result of the greater
initial level of economic information (and, presumably, the reduction
in the possibility of surprises from this source), a greater scope for scientific investment analysis, a diminished reliance on and use of rumours, and
a reduction in the scale of manipulative practices.[6] Information is a basic
ingredient for rational economic behaviour. We would therefore expect
improved disclosure to increase allocational efficiency. Less importantly, it
might increase operational efficiency as a result of greater public knowledge concerning underwriting and other transaction costs, and the reduction in private expenses of investigation facilitated by the required disclosure of information. However, the provision of new information entails
additional costs which may offset some or all of the operational savings
referred to. Most people would also regard disclosure as enhancing equity
among different groups in the market.

The economic as well as non-economic justification of regulations
designed to prevent the more flagrant types of manipulation of securities
prices requires little explanation. Theoretically, such regulations might be
expected to improve both efficiency and equity in the capital markets,
and perhaps also general economic stability, even though empirical evidence
is required to assess whether the benefits achieved are worth the cost.
Restrictions on certain types of speculation to maintain orderly and
liquid markets and limitations on the use of securities credit are frequently
rationalised on similar grounds, but even the existence of economic benefits from such policies is not clear from theory alone and must depend on

evidence. For example, it is easy enough to use theoretical considerations to 'demonstrate' that, under plausible conditions, speculators on the average must stabilise stock prices so long as it is assumed that their activities do not affect the demand schedules of investors. This, however, is a heroic assumption and requires direct or indirect empirical verification.

## 4. Economic Performance of Market Regulation[7]

Some of the most convincing evidence on the S.E.C.'s accomplishments in the markets for new and outstanding issues is provided in the Pecora hearings,[8] two other United States Government pre-Second World War studies,[9] and the post-war S.E.C. *Special Study*,[10] with their documentation of the massive securities abuses of the earlier period and the much healthier post-S.E.C. experience. This evidence provides substantial reason for believing that the effects of disclosure and related aspects of securities legislation have been beneficial. Vast amounts of money were demonstrably lost in the pre-S.E.C. period as a result of activities which have been greatly reduced by securities legislation. These amounts would appear to dwarf any reasonable estimate of the costs of such legislation.

Stock market pools, bucket-shop operation, misuse of insider information and other types of manipulation and fraud, which frequently relied on the deliberate use of misinformation and the absence of full disclosure, were widespread in the pre-S.E.C. period, involved vast sums of money and seem less prevalent today. In the earlier period, enormous losses were absorbed by the public in excessively leveraged, highly speculative and frequently manipulated new issues of public utility holding companies, investment companies and foreign bonds, each of which was frequently sold under disclosure conditions bordering on fraud. It is undoubtedly true that a substantial share of the blame for such losses lies elsewhere, but an important share is attributable to inadequate and deliberately misleading information, and widespread violations of fiduciary responsibilities by market and corporate insiders.

The Pecora Investigation catalogued 107 issues on the New York Stock Exchange and 71 issues on the New York Curb in which members of these exchanges participated in pools in 1929. It also documented an impressive number of cases of new issue sales in the mid- to late 1920s with inadequate disclosure and disastrous results. Both the nature of the facts and statements by the investment bankers involved make it quite clear that with a modicum of disclosure of known facts these issues could not have been sold.

*Impact on new issues*

There is additional evidence in the post-war *Special Study* suggesting a beneficial effect on new issues of the full disclosure requirement under the

S.E.C. For example, during 1960–1 a law firm representing 17 issuers filed 13 Regulation A statements, which do not require full disclosure, and four registration statements which do. Eleven of the 13 Regulation A statements but none of the four registration statements became effective. Of the 11 Regulation A issues subsequently marketed, all went to a premium immediately after the offering but by November 1962 eight were no longer mentioned in the quotation sheets and three were quoted below their offering price. Through a variety of arrangements, the public money raised through these offerings were substantially siphoned off to persons affiliated with the law firm representing the 17 issuers. The *Special Study* also shows that while Regulation A issues in 1959–61 fared better than registered issues in the immediate post-offering period (up to one month after offering), they fared worse by 30 September 1962. This can be construed as suggesting that in the short run full disclosure may prevent unwarranted price rises and in the longer run ensure a closer coincidence between initial price and intrinsic value.

One of several tests of the effect of full disclosure which I carried out in the past in conjunction with Edward Herman is provided by a comparison of the market experience from 1958 to 1963 of unregistered new industrial common stock below $300,000 in size issued in 1958 with the smaller registered issues over $300,000 where both groups of stocks are adjusted by movements in the market averages.[11] Only non-rights, publicly offered, primary issues were included to maintain comparability. While this test was of rather limited scope, it pointed to a superior after-issue price performance of the registered issues. The price relatives for the registered small issues were not very different from those typically found for the larger issues, but they were appreciably better than the price relatives for the very small issues not subject to registration.

Another test of the effect of full disclosure which we carried out in connection with our criticism of a similar earlier test by George Stigler[12] is to compare the price performance relatives of comparable large new stock issues in the pre-S.E.C. 1923–8 and post-S.E.C. 1949–55 periods over a five-year period subsequent to their offering.[13] These price performance relatives were obtained by adjusting the price trends of new issues for the price trends of outstanding issues (as measured by the Standard and Poor's Industrial Index), in an attempt to eliminate the effects of general market conditions. Such a test assumes that any differences in the relation of the markets for new and outstanding issues in the two periods were mainly a reflection of the S.E.C., with the disclosure provisions for new issues likely to be particularly important.[14] The deficiencies in this assumption are obvious, but the results of this test are still of interest.

In this comparison of the 1923–8 and 1949–55 periods, we found that the price performance of new issues was inferior to that of outstanding issues, but was closer to outstanding issues in the post-S.E.C. than in the pre-S.E.C. period, suggesting an increase in allocational efficiency. The price performance of new issues relative to outstanding issues was, as a result, superior in the post-S.E.C. period. This superiority was least marked in the first year or so after the issue date, but this finding can be explained by two facts: the extensive price pegging and numerous manipulative pools in the 1920s which might be expected to be particularly active in the first year after the public sale of a new issue; and the extreme difficulty of securities valuation in the absence of full disclosure until there is some record of operating experience. In connection with the first of these two points, it might be noted that a sample of new issues which according to the Pecora hearings were subject to pool operations in the 1920s had an above-average price performance in the first year after the issue date.[15]

We extended the pre-S.E.C. and post-S.E.C. comparisons, in which we had covered the same time-period and size categories of issues used by Stigler, to include 1958 and the first half of 1959 and also to include small issues for 1923, the first half of 1928 and the first half of 1958. Again we obtained the same qualitative results when comparing the pre-S.E.C. and post-S.E.C. periods.

Another significant result of this comparison of pre-S.E.C. and post-S.E.C. price performance of new common stock issues relative to outstanding issues is that the variances of the price ratios for each of the five years after issue data were much larger in the pre-S.E.C. period. In other words, there was much less dispersion in relative price performance of new issues in the post-S.E.C. period, which is another result consistent with theoretical expectations of the effects of improved information and a reduction of manipulative activity. This again could be construed as evidence that securities legislation has improved the structure of stock prices.

In a subsequent analysis, we pointed out that another measure of performance advanced by Stigler suggested a statistically significant improvement in the structure of new issue prices from the pre-S.E.C. to post-S.E.C. periods.[16] Thus the correlation in the pre-S.E.C. period between new issue prices and prices one year later (with all new issue prices deflated by the price index for outstanding issues) seems to have been significantly lower than the average correlation for adjacent pairs of years after issue, whereas these correlations are identical (and higher) in the post-S.E.C. period.

The only comprehensive data updating the comparative performance of new and outstanding issues appear in an unpublished Ph.D. dissertation by Roger Ibbotson.[17] That study, which covers the price performance of S.E.C.-registered underwritten unseasoned common stock issued during each month of the period 1960–9 over a post-issuance five-year period through 1971, finds that after a short-lived initial premium these new issues are indistinguishable from other outstanding stock. If these results are taken at face value, they would seem to suggest the virtual disappearance in the post-S.E.C. period of the inferior performance of new issues. Thus, to the extent such data are relevant, they support an improvement in the efficiency of the new issue market in the post-S.E.C. period.

In the light of all these findings, it is not surprising that Randolph Westerfield and I stated in the June 1975 issue of *The American Economic Review* that 'We interpret the evidence of the 1933 Act as clearly favourable to disclosure'.[18] It may be useful, therefore, to consider a different evaluation of George Benston which appeared in that same issue.[19] Benston, in referring to the papers by Stigler, Herman and myself, which cover all the results summarised above except those obtained by Ibbotson, states that 'The data presented in these papers indicate an insignificant difference in the mean rate of return (relative to the market) on stocks floated in the years 1923–27 compared to flotations in the period 1949–55. However, the standard deviations of the returns are higher in the pre-Securities and Exchange Commission (S.E.C.) period, which F-W assume is favourable.' He then proceeds to attack the relevance of the standard deviations and concludes that from such evidence 'one should not interpret the evidence as clearly favourable to disclosure'.

Benston clearly states (1) that the 1923–7 and 1949–55 comparisons provide insignificant differences in mean rates of return and strongly implies (2) that these are the only relevant results available and (3) that our conclusion is exclusively or primarily based on the respective standard deviations, which do not constitute terribly relevant evidence. The first point is misleading, the second and third false.

Turning to the first point, both Stigler and Friend and Herman make two different comparisons of the pre-S.E.C. and post-S.E.C. performance of new issues. The first covered 1923–8 for the pre-S.E.C. period and included Class A stock as common, following Stigler's original procedures. The second covered 1923–7 and excluded Class A stock from common, following Stigler's revision of his original procedures when we pointed out that the original results, appropriately corrected, suggested a favourable S.E.C. effect in the new issue market.

What Benston does not point out is that for the first set of comparisons the post-S.E.C. period was superior in the performance of new issues for each of the five years tested subsequent to their offering and was significantly superior (at the 5 per cent level) for four of the five years. When the pre-S.E.C. period is terminated at 1927, which had the best relative price experience of the pre-S.E.C. years included, instead of 1928 which had the worst, *and* when Class A stock is excluded, it is true that the differences between the pre-S.E.C. and post-S.E.C. results for the five years subsequent to the offering are not statistically significant in any year, but Benston neglects to point out that the post-S.E.C. performance is superior in four of the five years. While the differences in two of the five years are quite small, they range from 6 to 17 per cent in the other three, with the post-S.E.C. results superior in these years. If 1928 is retained in the earlier period, but Class A stock still omitted, the post-S.E.C. performance of new issues in all the five years rose by from 9 to 37 per cent a year.

Moreover, even for the pre-S.E.C. comparison which is least unfavourable to Benston's position, a serial correlation measure of performance commented on earlier in this paper seems to show a statistically significant superiority of the post-S.E.C. period.[20]

Turning to the second point implied by Benston, that the 1923–7 and 1949–55 comparisons to which he refers are the only evidence in the papers cited on mean relative rates of return on new issues, I have already indicated that this view is baseless. Totally apart from the several other 1923–7 and 1923–8 comparisons to which I have just referred, and the comparison of standard deviations of returns to which Benston does refer, it may be recalled that I previously discussed five other reasonably independent statistical tests and a substantial amount of qualitative information all favourable to the efficacy of the 1983 Act disclosure requirements and all cited in the literature referred to by Benston.

The last point implied by Benston, that our favourable conclusion on 1933 Act disclosure depended basically on the comparison of standard deviations of returns in the pre-S.E.C. and post-S.E.C. periods, is thus completely incorrect. As for the relevance of such a comparison, the reduction in the variance of the new issue price ratios from the pre-S.E.C. to the post-S.E.C. periods, since it was clearly not associated with a reduction in relative return, can be regarded from the investor's viewpoint as a positive achievement of the S.E.C., making the usual assumption that investors are risk-averse. If Benston in referring to covariance effects is implying that the variance of the market portfolio has increased over this period as a result of covariance developments in the new issues markets, the available data do not support this hypothesis.[21]

### Impact on market for outstanding issues

I have noted elsewhere[22] that two tests derived from market equilibrium theory suggest an improvement in market structure from the 1920s to the period after the Second World War. Since they abstract from factors affecting return on the market as a whole, they supply some support to the thesis that changes in securities regulation may have improved efficiency in the market for outstanding stock. However, the evidence here is not very strong.

There are moreover two more recent studies which purport to provide evidence that securities regulation in the market for outstanding stock has had no significant impact on market efficiency. The first, carried out by R. R. Officer, concludes that the decline from the pre-S.E.C. to the post-S.E.C. periods in the one-year standard deviation of monthly returns on the New York Stock Exchange (N.Y.S.E.) stock as a whole was 'not attributable to the S.E.C.'. The second, by Benston, concludes that empirical evidence provides no support for the belief that the disclosure and related provisions of the Securities and Exchange Act of 1934 had any effect on the market for outstanding issues.

The conclusion by Officer, which as he notes differs from that reached in earlier analyses of the variability of returns of N.Y.S.E. stocks as a whole, is to a substantial extent dependent on an extension of the series on N.Y.S.E. average returns from the reasonably satisfactory data covering all N.Y.S.E stocks starting with January 1926 back to January 1915 on the basis of a 20-stock Dow Jones index and then back to February 1897 on the basis of a 12-stock Dow Jones index. In view of the major incomparabilities between the data before and after January 1926, and presumably the much higher quality of the Dow Jones stocks as compared to the market as a whole, the new evidence by Officer does not appear at all cogent, though he asserts that the biases introduced by these incomparabilities are relatively unimportant. Moreover, it should be noted that Officer addresses himself only to variance in the market return and not at all to variance in residual returns.

The analysis by Benston is of somewhat greater interest since it is directed specifically at measuring the impact of S.E.C.-mandated disclosure on the market for outstanding stocks on the basis of two tests of the impact of the 1934 Act disclosure. The first estimates the impact of changes in accounting data on common stock prices by deriving cross-sectional regressions in the year 1964 between changes in prices of individual stocks on the New York Stock Exchange (adjusted for movements in the market) and 'unexpected' changes in each of a number of different financial variables (net sales, cash flow, net operating income and adjusted net income). Expected changes in these financial variables were obtained from several simple auto-regressive models based on past data and then compared with subsequent published data to obtain estimates of unexpected changes. A similar but more limited analysis was carried out for 1963. Benston's second set of tests attempts to determine whether a large sample of individual N.Y.S.E. stocks which were affected by sales disclosure provisions of the 1934 Act behaved 'better' relative to the market than stocks for which sales data were already available prior to the Act.

As Westerfield and I pointed out in a comment on this analysis in the June 1975 issue of *The American Economic Review*,[23] Benston in his first set of tests does not use more than one of the unexpected changes in financial variables in any one regression. Even so, his findings point to statistically significant relations between price changes and the unexpected changes in each of these financial variables. Nevertheless, in view of what he considers the small size of the regression coefficients, he concludes that 'this evidence is not consistent with the underlying assumption, that the financial data made public are timely or relevant, on average'. There does not seem to be any justification for his willingness to dismiss out of hand the economic importance of these statistically significant results. Thus, he in effect considers irrelevant for stock prices knowledge about

changes in financial variables in spite of the fact that he finds an increase
of 100 per cent in the annual rate of net sales is associated with an increase
in price of 10·4 per cent in the month of the announcement, and that
changes in other variables are also associated with significant though pro-
portionally smaller changes in price.

Moreover, it seems clear that Benston's regressions considerably understate the usefulness of published financial statements. They do not allow
for the joint effects of unexpected changes in the different financial variables, and they make no adjustment for the substantial understatement of
the relevant regression coefficient arising from the very large random
measurement errors associated with any empirical measures of unexpected
change.

Finally, we pointed out that on the basis of independent analyses 'many
writers have concluded that published accounting profile variables can be
useful in making investment decisions and contribute to market efficiency'.
We cited two articles as examples, one by A. Martin,[24] the other by R. G.
May.[25] Benston had alleged that almost all previous empirical work relating published accounting data to stock price changes also leads to the
conclusion that the data are not useful or are redundant.

An expanded version of this paper[26] discusses at greater length the
deficiencies in both of Benston's tests and replies in detail to Benston's rejoinder[27] to the comment by Westerfield and myself. However, three
points merit mention here. First, since Benston in his rejoinder relies
heavily on the work of Nicholas J. Gonedes,[28] it is curious that Benston
did not point out the main conclusion that Gonedes reached: 'Our major
purpose was to determine whether the accounting numbers jointly reflect
new information. The results of our multivariate tests assign a high probability to the statement that the numbers do jointly provide information
pertinent to assessing equilibrium expected returns.'

Second, from the viewpoint of statistical theory and elementary logic,
perhaps the strangest point made by Benston is in response to our reference
to the 'substantial understatement of the relevant regression coefficients
arising from the very large random measurement errors associated with
any empirical measures of unexpected change'. The clear import of this
reference is that under plausible and well-known statistical assumptions
substantial random errors in an independent variable in a regression will
bias substantially downwards the absolute value of the coefficients of
that variable. As a result the impact of disclosure which Benston found
statistically significant in spite of this problem is clearly understated in
his analysis, and probably substantially. Benston's reply is that we 'should
question why the S.E.C. has done so little to reduce these errors, or even
to provide investors with some indication of their magnitude and effect'.
Nothing in Benston's analysis casts any light on the S.E.C.'s accomplishments in these areas since this would require comparable results for the
pre-S.E.C. period.

Third, turning to Benston's objections to our evaluation of the empirical evidence on the desirability of a total variability measure 'to *supplement* the analysis', he quotes or paraphrases Merton Miller and Myron Scholes (whom we also cited),[29] Michael Jensen,[30] and Eugene Fama and James MacBeth[31] to the contrary. He clearly misinterprets Miller and Scholes and Fama and MacBeth and presumably also Jensen. Miller and Scholes and Fama and MacBeth state in reasonably clear language that it is *possible*, though not proved, that the empirical data they investigate are consistent with capital asset pricing theory which implies that beta of an individual stock, if we could properly measure it, is the only relevant measure of its risk. Jensen, whom Benston quotes out of context (see rest of footnote 35, p. 367, to which Benston refers), is making the statement quoted about portfolios rather than individual securities and depends on Fama and MacBeth for its extension to individual assets. Moreover, a recent study provides convincing evidence that a high proportion of portfolios are dominated by a small number of assets so that the betas of individual assets are not adequate for determining the total variability of portfolios.[32] It is unfortunate that Benston did not examine total variability estimates.

*Impact of margin regulation*

Of the various regulatory policies which have been directed towards the maintenance of orderly markets, the one of perhaps greatest interest to the general economist is the regulation of margin trading, which originally reflected Congressional concerns about the possibly excessive use of securities credit on the economy as a whole as well as on the stock market itself. Chicago economists in the United States seem to consider this type of securities regulation as especially distasteful, presumably because it interferes with the freedom of behaviour of the beneficent speculators, substitutes selective credit controls for the free market, and has no obvious strong equity rationale.

I have indicated in an earlier paper[33] that my casual empiricism led me to the conclusion that margin requirements have probably tended to reduce stock price volatility and increase market efficiency, though such evidence is obviously not at all convincing. I also pointed out in that study that a rather comprehensive analysis of margin trading completed a little earlier,[34] which concluded that 'margin requirements have failed to achieve any of their objectives', was subject to deficiencies which when corrected appear to present a more favourable case for margin regulation.

Since that time I have seen three other studies of the effectiveness of margin regulation, two of them — one by George Douglas[35] and the other by James Largay[36] — presenting favourable evidence, the third by Officer[37] arguing that such regulation is ineffective. The Officer argument is based on two annual time-series regressions, apparently over the 1934—68 period, between each of two forms of the standard deviation of stock market return and both margin requirements and the standard deviation of industrial production. The two forms of the market return variable lead the margin requirements in one regression and follow them in the other, with the lead and lag both one year in duration. The lead form turns out to have a much higher correlation and the margin requirement variable is statistically insignificant in both, with the same negative coefficient and a $t$-value of somewhat over 1.

The Douglas analysis regresses the standard deviation of the rate of change in price both on the standard deviation of the rate of change in dividends and on margin requirements for the period 1926–60, where each observation is a sub-period of five-year length (with the exception of four years for the last) for each of 100 stocks. The coefficient of margin requirements is again negative but now highly significant which, according to the author, 'suggests that margin requirements tend to reduce price volatility'.

The Largay paper analyses the price and volume characteristics of 71 New York Stock Exchange and 38 American Stock Exchange stocks placed under special margin requirements during 1968–9. The price and volume characteristics of these stocks are explained both around the times when 100 per cent margins were imposed and, subsequently, when they were removed. The author concludes that 'The empirical results support the *a priori* hypothesis that banning the use of credit for transactions in individual issues is associated with a moderation of 'cooling off' of speculative activity in these stocks.' This conclusion is based on several key findings: imposition of 100 per cent margin was associated with the termination of the marked upward price movement and a reduction of the heavy volume of trading, both of which had typically preceded the new margin restriction. As the author notes, the N.Y.S.E. stocks actually declined in price after they were placed under this restriction. Prices of the restricted stocks generally declined preceding removal of the special margin requirements. After removal only prices of the AMEX stocks tended to rise again, though the volume of trading began to accelerate both for the N.Y.S.E. and AMEX stocks.

My own appraisal of this material is that the evidence of a favourable effect of margin regulation on at least stock market volatility is stronger than the evidence on the other side. However, this assessment may reflect my personal biases, and I would agree that the evidence is far from conclusive.

*Impact of other restrictions on trading activity*

I shall comment only briefly on the other major restrictions on trading activity effected by securities regulation apart from margin requirements, viz. restrictions on short sales, on ordinary floor trading by members of an exchange, on stock specialists' activities, and on trading by corporate insiders (officers, directors and principal stockholders) in stocks of the corporations with which they are affiliated. Since specialists are considered as having a responsibility for helping to maintain fair and orderly markets, their trading activity has not been subjected to as severe regulatory restrictions as those imposed on the other types of speculative activity.

In the paper referred to earlier,[38] I pointed out that my interpretation of the available evidence was that the trading activity of N.Y.S.E. floor traders appeared as a whole more likely to be destabilising than stabilising; the reverse was true of N.Y.S.E. specialists, and perhaps also of corporate insiders, at least in the post-S.E.C. period; the evidence on short selling was mixed; and that none of this evidence was terribly strong. I also noted that even if restrictions on insider trading did not have a favourable impact on stock market volatility and market efficiency, they might be justified on equity grounds.

Since that earlier paper, an interesting new analysis of insider trading has been published by J. F. Jaffe,[39] which indicates that three litigations which might have been expected to lead corporate insiders to expect stricter enforcement of the S.E.C. insider trading rules (specifically, S.E.C. Rule 10(B)−5) did not in fact have a statistically significant effect on the profitability and volume of insider trading. Actually, the two litigations which might have been expected to have the largest impact (the Cady, Roberts and Texas Gulf Sulphur decisions) *were* associated with drops in insider profitability, while the third (the Texas Gulf Sulphur indictment) was associated with an increase in profitability. However, the changes were not statistically significant and the volume of insider trading increased slightly after all three actions (again without statistical significance). As a result, at least these specific changes in the prospects for implementation of regulatory constraints on insider trading seemed to have very little effect on the profitability and volume of such activity.

While this new evidence is certainly relevant to the effectiveness of these three legal actions, all involving the S.E.C., it is not clear how much relevance it has for the broader effectiveness of Section 16B of the 1934 Act (relating to corporate recovery of short-term profits by insiders) and it would seem to have very little relevance for the effectiveness of Section 16A (relating to full disclosure provisions for insiders).[40] Thus, if these provisions of the 1934 Act had been extremely effective well in advance of the first of the three legal actions, i.e. the November 1961 Cady, Roberts decision, Jaffe would have obtained the results he did, but the interpretation of his results would be radically different. Given the extreme variability of stock price changes and rates of return, it would not be surprising to find apparently little effect of new evidence of stricter enforcement of the S.E.C. insider trading rules. Even prior to Cady, Roberts there were both the prospect and, I suspect, the actuality of private litigation for recovery of insider profits.

Clearly what is required for a more convincing answer to the overall effect of insider regulation is a careful comparison of pre-S.E.C. and post-S.E.C. insider behaviour from the scattered pieces of evidence available. My own reaction to a reading of the major United States government investigations of the stock market and related abuses of the 1920s cited earlier in this paper make me believe that insider abuses have declined substantially subsequent to that period, and I think that this is attributable at least in part to the disclosure provisions and restrictions imposed on insiders by the 1934 Act. A careful documentation of all such evidence would provide more relevant evidence than we now have available for assessing the effectiveness of the insider provisions of the 1934 Act.

Finally, I have not commented here on the ultimate type of interference with free market processes in the securities markets when trading in individual stocks or, on rare occasions, in the market as a whole is temporarily stopped in the face of major disruptions in the market. I have indicated elsewhere that under certain extreme circumstances (e.g. the assassination of President Kennedy) I consider such action desirable.[41]

To conclude, it is my view that securities legislation in the United States has, as a whole, benefited the stock market and the economy. However, as I have stated in the past, it is not yet clear whether some specific policies have been beneficial. Further exploration would be desirable.

### Acknowledgement

The author wishes to acknowledge the financial support of the Rodney L. White Center for Financial Research, University of Pennsylvania.

### Notes

1. Part of this discussion is based on Irwin Friend, 'The Economic Consequences of the Stock Market', *American Economic Review* (May 1972).
2. In completely efficient markets, the volatility may of course simply reflect the influence of different economic forces affecting investment risks and prospective returns.
3. See, e.g., Hayne E. Leland, 'Production Theory and the Stock Market', *Bell Journal of Economics and Management Science* (Spring 1974). See also Robert C. Merton and Marti G. Subrahmanyam, 'the Optimality of a Competitive Stock Market', ibid.
4. George Stigler, 'Public Regulation of the Securities Markets', *Journal of Business* (Apr. 1964) p. 117.
5. See Irwin Friend and Edward S. Herman, 'The S.E.C. through a Glass Darkly', *Journal of Business* (Oct. 1964) p. 399; (Jan. 1965) p. 109.
6. Ibid.
7. Part of this discussion is based on Irwin Friend, 'The S.E.C. and the Economic Performance of Securities Markets', in Henry G. Manne (ed.), *Economic Policy and the Regulation of Corporate Securities* (Washington, D.C.: American Institute for Public Policy Research, 1969).
8. *Stock Exchange Practices: Hearings before the Senate Committee on Banking and Currency*, 72d and 73d Cong., Parts 1–17 (Washington, D.C., 1933–4).

9. *Report of the Federal Trade Commission on Utility Corporations*, 70th Cong., 1st sess., Sen. Doc. 92 (Washington, D. C., 1935) esp. Parts 22, 71A, 72A and 73A; and *Report of the Securities and Exchange Commission on Investment Trusts and Investment Companies* (Washington, D.C., 1939—42).

10. *Report of Special Study of Securities Markets of the Securities and Exchange Commission* (Washington, D.C.: U.S. Government Printing Office, 1963).

11. The S.E.C. through a Glass Darkly', op. cit.

12. 'Public Regulation of the Securities Markets', op. cit.

13. 'The S.E.C. through a Glass Darkly', op. cit.

14. While the S.E.C. has effected significant increases in disclosure for both new and outstanding issues, the disclosure requirements for new issues are more extensive and started in the pre-S.E.C. period at a much lower base.

15. 'The S.E.C. through a Glass Darkly', op. cit.

16. Irwin Friend and Edward S. Herman, 'Professor Stigler on Securities Regulation: A Further Comment', *Journal of Business* (Jan. 1965); and George J. Stigler, 'Comment', *Journal of Business* (Oct. 1964).

17. Roger G. Ibbotson, 'Price Performance of Common Stock New Issues' (University of Chicago, 1973).

18. Irwin Friend and Randolph Westerfield, 'Required Disclosure and the Stock Market: Comment', *American Economic Review* (June 1974).

19. George J. Benston, 'Required Disclosure and the Stock Market: Rejoinder, ibid.

20. I shall not comment here on the appropriateness of a longer versus a shorter period for assessing the performance of new issues since Benston does not raise it, and it is fully covered in 'Professor Stigler on Securities Regulation: A Further Comment', op. cit.

21. See Irwin Friend and Marshall E. Blume, 'The Demand for Risky Assets', *American Economic Review* (Dec. 1975). The data there indicate that the standard deviation of return on New York Stock Exchange stocks as a whole was smaller in each of the decades 1942—51, 1952—61 and 1962—71 than the the decades 1922—31 and 1932—41 or than for the entire period 1872—1971 or for the periods 1926—71 for which the data are much more reliable.

22. 'The Economic Consequences of the Stock Market', op. cit.

23. 'Required Disclosure and the Stock Market: Comment', op. cit.

24. A. Martin, 'An Empirical Test of the Relevance of Accounting Information for Investment Decisions', *Journal of Accounting Research, Empirical Research in Accounting: Selected Studies, 1971.*

25. R. G. May, 'The Influence of Quarterly Earnings Announcements on Investor Decisions as Reflected in Common Stock Price Changes', ibid.

26. I. Friend, 'Economic Foundations of Stock Market Regulation', Working Paper No. 4—75 (Rodney L. White Center for Financial Research, University of Pennsylvania, 1975).

27. 'Required Disclosure and the Stock Market: Rejoinder', op. cit.

28. N. J. Gonedes, 'Capital Market Equilibrium and Annual Accounting Numbers: Empirical Evidence', *Journal of Accounting Research* (Spring 1974).

29. Merton H. Miller and Myron Scholes, 'Rates of Return in Relation to Risk: A Re-examination of Some Recent Findings', in M. C. Jensen (ed.) *Studies in the Theory of Capital Markets* (New York: Praeger, 1971).

30. Michael Jensen, 'Capital Markets: Theory and Evidence', *Bell Journal of Economics* (Autumn 1972).

31. E. F. Fama and J. MacBeth, 'Risk, Return and Equilibrium: Empirical Tests', *Journal of Political Economy* (May 1973).

32. Marshall E. Blume and Irwin Friend, 'The Asset Structure of Individual Portfolios and Some Implications for Utility Functions', *Journal of Finance* (May 1975).

33. 'The S.E.C. and the Economic Performance of Securities Markets', op. cit.

34. Thomas Gale Moore, 'Stock Market Margin Requirements', *Journal of Political Economy* (Apr. 1966).

35. George W. Douglas, 'Risk in the Equity Markets: An Empirical Appraisal of Market Efficiency', *Yale Economic Essays* (Spring 1969).

36. James A. Largay III, '100 % Margins: Combating Speculation in Individual Security Issues', *Journal of Finance*, (Sept. 1973).

37. 'The Variability of the Market Factor of the New York Stock Exchange', op. cit.

38. 'The S.E.C. and the Economic Performance of Securities Markets', op. cit.

39. J. F. Jaffe, 'The Effect of Regulation Changes on Insider Trading', *Bell Journal of Economics and Management Science* (Spring 1974).

40. Actually Cady, Roberts involved activities which did not require corporate insider disclosure.

41. 'The S.E.C. and the Economic Performance of Securities Markets', op. cit.

# Index

# Index of Persons

Adelman, M. A., 105, 118, 119
Alchian, A. A., 118, 119
Allingham, M. G., 5, 13, 32, 162
Archibald, G. C., 3, 15, 24, 27, 32, 34
Arrow, K. J., 11, 13, 26, 33, 34, 38, 42, 89, 93, 101, 102, 104, 119
Artis, M. J., 187, 198
Aukrust, O., 220, 223

Baier, K., 26, 28, 34
Barnes, I. R., 118, 119
Beazer, W. F., 4, 101
Becker, G. S., 37, 42
Benston, G., 151, 233–7, 241
Bergson, A., 101, 102
Blackorby, C., 34
Blan, P. M., 40, 43
Blinder, A. S., 197, 198
Blume, M. E., 241
Bod, P., 4, 88
Bork, R. H., 118, 119
Bowles, S., 38, 43
Bresciani-Turroni, C., 186, 198
Brittan, S., 186, 198
Brown, A. J., 186, 198
Brown, D. J., 28, 34
Brunner, K., 17, 24, 223, 224
Burns, Dr Arthur, 151, 163, 217
Burstein, M. L., 4, 15, 24, 42, 87, 101, 118, 151, 161, 163

Cacy, J. A., 224
Cagan, P., 167, 181, 187, 223
Canes, M., 87, 101
Carter, R., 28, 34
Chamberlain, G., 39, 43
Christ, C. F., 198
Churchman, G., 17, 24
Clower, R. W., 3, 15, 17, 18, 24
Coase, R. H., 103, 119
Cross, J. S., 116, 119

Dam, K. W., 119
Darmstadter, J., 101, 102

Darwin, Charles, 223
Debreu, G., 93, 102
De Chazeau, M., 114–15, 118, 119
Denison, E. F., 37, 38, 43
Diamond, P. A., 94, 102
Donaldson, D., 3, 27, 32, 33, 34
Douglas, G. W., 237–8, 242
Duchesneau, T. D., 118, 119
Duncan, O. D., 40, 43

Edgeworth, Y., 19
Edgren, G., 223
Edwards, C. D., 119
Erickson, E. W., 118, 120

Fama, E. F., 156–7, 160, 162, 237, 241
Fand, D., 196, 198
Faxen, K. O., 223
Fisher, F. M., 5, 13
Fisher, Irving, 154, 156–7, 160
Fisher, L., 165, 181
Francis, D. R., 224
Frankel, P. H., 115, 118, 119, 120
Freeman, R. B., 37, 38, 40, 42, 43
Friedman, Milton, 223
Friend, I., 151, 181, 233, 240, 241

Galbraith, J. K., 199, 223
Gantmacher, F. R., 12, 13
Gintis, H., 38, 43
Godley, W., 193
Gonedes, R. G., 236, 241
Gordon, D. F., 118, 120
Gorseline, N. E., 39, 43
Graham, D. A., 118, 120
Green, J. R., 104, 120
Griliches, Z., 3, 36, 43

Haigh, R., 113, 115, 116, 119, 120
Hamburger, M. J., 187, 198, 223
Hansen, B., 197, 198
Hare, R. M., 34
Hause, J. C., 39, 43
Herman, E., 231, 233, 240, 241

Hicks, Sir John, 17, 24, 101, 102, 118
Hirschleifer, J., 90, 101, 102
Hobbes, T., 26
Howitt, P. W., 15, 24

Ibbotson, R., 232, 233, 241

Jaffe, J. F., 239, 242
Jefferson, M., 87
Jencks, C., 38, 43
Jensen, M. C., 237, 241
Jevons, S., 19
Johnson, H. G., 15, 24, 89, 102
Jones, R., 17, 25
Jorgenson, D., 37

Kahn, A. E., 114, 118, 119
Kennedy, J. F., 240
Kennedy, M., 87, 102
Keynes, J. M. (Lord Keynes), 14, 68,
    154, 158, 163, 222
King, M. A., 162

Laffer, A. B., 223
Laidler, D. E. W., 223
Largay, J. A., 237–8, 242
Leibenstein, H., 31, 34
Leijonhufvud, A., 18, 24, 25
Leland, H. E., 101, 102, 240
Lenin, V. I., 199, 222–3
Lewis, M. K., 187, 198
Liebeler, W. J., 118, 120
Lind, R. C., 89, 101, 102
Lindbeck, A., 223
Lintner, J., 166, 181
Lipsey, R. G., 15, 24
Lorie, J. H., 165, 181

MacBeth, J., 237, 241
McKie, J. W., 118, 120
McLean, J., 113, 115–16, 119, 120
McManus, M., 11, 13
Mains, N. E., 151, 152
Manne, H. G., 240
Marshall, Alfred, 19, 25, 223
Martin, A., 236, 241
May, R. G., 236, 241
Mayer, T., 223
Meiselman, D., 223
Meltzer, A., 17, 24
Merton, R. C., 240
Mill, J. S., 19, 28, 34
Miller, M. H., 237, 241
Mills, T. C., 198
Mincer, J., 37, 43

Mintz, I., 167, 181
Mishan, E. J., 101, 102
Mitchell, E. J., 118, 120
Modigliani, F., 187, 198
Moore, G. H., 167, 168, 181
Moore, T. G., 241
Morishima, M., 162
Mundell, R. A., 223

Nagatani, K., 26, 34
Negishi, T., 5, 13
Nelson, P. R., 42, 43
Nield, R., 193
Nixon, R. M., 217
Nordhaus, W. D., 170, 181

Officer, R. R., 234–5, 237
Ohlin, B., 68
Ohner, C. E., 223
Ostroy, J., 15, 25

Parkin, M., 223, 224
Patinkin, D., 15, 25
Pecora, F., 230
Peltzman, S., 118, 120
Pepper, G. T., 151, 152, 190, 198
Perlman, M., 17, 25
Phelps, E. S., 42, 43

Ricardo, D., 19, 62
Robertson, D. H., 154, 158, 163
Roesch, S. R., 224
Rueff, J., 222

Saandmo, A., 89, 101, 102
Samuelson, P. A., 20, 25
Sargent, J. R., 87
Schacht, H., 186
Schmalensee, R., 118, 120
Scholes, M., 237, 241
Schultz, T. W., 37, 42, 43
Schwartz, A. J., 223
Selden, R. T., 151, 152, 223
Senior, N., 19
Sikora, R. J., 34
Smith, Adam, 19, 104
Solmon, L. C., 43
Solow, R. M., 197, 198
Spann, R. W., 118, 120
Spence, M., 38, 43
Spengler, J. J., 118, 120
Starr, R. M., 15, 25
Stigler, G. J., 104, 118, 120, 231, 232,
    233, 240, 241
Subrahmanyam, M. G., 240

Tardos, M., 3, 101
Taubman, P., 38, 43
Thomas, R. L., 190, 197, 198
Tobin, J., 162

Uzawa, H., 101, 102

Vernon, J. M., 118, 120
von Graaff, J. de, 101, 102

Wachtel, P., 43
Wallich, H. C., 151, 152

Walras, L., 5, 13, 19
Wanniski, J., 223
Warren-Boulton, F. R., 118, 120
Welch, F., 42, 43
Weles, R., 38, 43
Westerfield, R., 233, 235, 236, 241
Weston, J. F., 118, 120
Wilder, T., 200, 223
Winter, S., 27, 31, 32, 34
Williamson, O. E., 104, 120
Wolpin, K., 40, 43
Wood, G. E., 151, 152

# Index of Subjects

Aid (in Cambodia), 72ff
   effects on tax system, 73
   replacing domestic production, 73
Anti-damping potentials (of macro-model), 155—7

Belgium, inflation in, 206, 210, 211, 214
Black market in foreign-exchange (Cambodia), 76ff, 82—4

Cambodia, *see also* Aid, 4
   foreign aid to, 72
   foreign-exchange nexus, 4
   inflation in, 4
   stabilisation plan for, 61ff
Canada, inflation in, 207, 210, 211, 214
Chicago economists, 237
Conjectural interdependence (on Cambodian foreign-exchange market), 65—6
Correspondence principle, 12ff
*Cours minimum retenu*, 66
Credit rationing, 177

Damping (of macro-model), 158—60
Debt burden (of companies), 175
Debt financing,
   and capital formation, 180
   and share values, 180
Disclosure (of securities information), 235
Disintermediation, 159, 163

Education, 35ff
   and research/development expenditures, 36—7
   boom in, 35ff
   inequality and, 40ff
Efficacity ratio (*cf* Cambodian foreign-exchange reform), 65
Efficient-market hypotheses, 151—2, 227, 229—30
Emprunt obligatoire, le, 67ff
   and stock-flow analysis, 67—8
   and the transfer problem, 68

Exchange value (and exchange price), 74, 76
Expected demand (in non-Walrasian systems), 7

Finance,
   and stock-market prices, 152
   in sense of Keynes—Robertson, 158—9, 163
   of companies, 151
Fisher (and Fisher—Fama) theory (of interest-rate formation), 156—7, 161—2
Flow of funds analysis, 189, 190—3
   with special reference to $M_3$, 193—6
Foreign exchange,
   depreciation, 70
   fiscality of FX depreciation in Cambodia, 63ff
   import-demand properties and, 64
   model with black market, 82—4

General process analysis, 17ff
   formal modelling of, 18
   via trade intermediaries, 17—8
Government budget constraint, 196—7

Historical time, 157—8
Human capital theory, 37
   objections to in 'education' context, 38ff
   'supply' bias, 37

Inflation,
   and equity values, 164ff
   as monetary phenomenon, 15
   capitalist inflation and Hungary, 54ff
   in general competitive analysis, 15
   formal framework for in Cambodia, 62ff
   international comparisons of, 204ff, 218—20, 222
   in the U.K., 24, *see also* United Kingdom

Inflation (*cont.*)
   monetarist vs income-expenditure
      models of, 16, 19ff, 21–2
   theory of, 14ff
Insider trading, 239–40
Interdependence (of preference), 3
Interest rates,
   and flow-of-funds analysis, 188–90
   nominal, 122
Inventory (stock) profits, 162, 168, 170–1
Investment,
   and two-sector models, 89
   government, 96ff, 100–1
   in energy production under uncertainty,
      89ff
      determined in formal model, 90ff
      with stock market, 94, 99–100
      without profit motivation, 96ff


Keynesian model(s), 182
   of labour market, 121–2, 128–35
   of financial markets, 152, 153ff, 182


Liquidity,
   affected by yield spreads, 176–7
   of companies, 151–2

Margin (re stock purchase) regulations,
   237–8
Mathematical programming (in planned
   economies), 44ff
Monetarist,
   financial modelling, 152, 182
   model of inflation, 200–1
      considered, 220–1
      objections to, 202–3
Monetary aggregates, 182
   and interest rate swings, 183–5
   interpretation of relative to $M_1$ and
      $M_3$, 183ff
Monetary influences,
   via interest rates, 187
   via stock-price changes, 187
Monetary policy (discretionary vs non-
   discretionary), 155, 163
Monetary velocity, 201–2
   in (hyper)inflation, 186
   in U.K., 186
   lag in, 202
Money balances, 185ff
   'Real or Nominal?', 185
Money supply (and deficit spending,
   62–3, 75, 182, 197
Multiples (price/earnings ratios), 161

Netherlands (inflation in), 208, 210, 211,
   215
New stock issues (re regulation), 230–4

Oil, *see also* OPEC; *see also* Vertical
   integration)
   price of, 55
      and economic prospects, 137–8
      and OPEC imports, 139–41
      and OPEC reserves, 138
      anticipated price rise–of before
         Oct/1973, 136
      effect on Hungary, 55ff
      potential deflationary effects of
         rise in, 87, 126–7, 133–5
OPEC (Organisation of Petroleum
   Exporting Countries),
   analogies to wage-push, 121, 125–6
   emergence of, 87
   membership heterogeneity, 87
   output constraints, 141
   price-effects of, 116–7
   propensity to spend of, 127
   surplus revenues of, 138–9, 145–8
Ownership (in Walrasian economies), 6

Pareto-optimum, 91ff, 95, 100–1
Paternalism, 3, 26ff
   and the axiom of selfishness, 26
   and 'classical' welfare economics, 3
   and extended preferences, 28, 30ff
   and utilitarianism, 29
   versus non-paternalism, 27ff
Pigovian welfare economics (recessional?),
   87–8, 151–2
Planned economies (*see also* Planning),
   and market economies, 4, 52ff
   Hungarian example, 44
   formal model of, 47ff
      properties of, 47ff
         consumption-function, 49–50
         continuous and discrete
            variables, 50–1
         sectorial treatment, 51
   foreign trade of, 52
      domestic and internal prices re
         foreign trade of, 52
   mathematical programming of, 4, 44ff
Planning (*see also* Planned economies),
   constraint systems in, 46
   centres and sub-centres in, 46
   long-term (vs shorter-term), 45ff
Price adjustment, 3, 5ff
   and Walrasian process, 3
   in Hungarian planning, 56ff

Price adjustment (*cont.*)
  in perfect monopoly, 6
  via seller-quotation, 6
  staged p. a. as in Hungary, 59
Price controls,
  effects on U.S. money/inflation
    relationship, 212
  in energy, 97ff
Profits (*see also* Rates of return),
  and interest rates, 167ff
  and share prices, 167ff
  cyclical aspects of, 168
  quality of, 164
Public-sector borrowing requirement,
    182, 193, 194
Pure exchange (characteristics of
    Cambodian economy), 69

Rates of return (Nominal and Real), 165–7
Reform,
  of Cambodian foreign-exchange
    institutions, 64, 79ff
  of 1968 in Hungary, 53
    foreign-trade effects of '68 reform,
      53ff

Securities Exchange Act, 225
  'performance' effects of, 230ff, 234–7,
    240
Securities & Exchange Commission (S.E.C.),
    225
  'performance' effects of, 230ff, 234–7,
    240
Stability,
  and general process analysis, 20–1
  of natural vs Walrasian systems, 11ff

of perfect monopoly, 5
of Walrasian Tâtonnement, 5
Static properties (of natural vs Walrasian
    systems), 9ff
Stochastic price variation, 106, 111, 115
Stock markets (including bourses), 151
  and the real economy, 151, 155
  and short-rate, 154–5
  ownership patterns in, 175ff
  regulation of, 151, 225ff
  theory of regulation of, 227–30
Sweden (inflation in), 209, 210, 211, 216

Tâtonnement, 5

United Kingdom,
  and 'North Sea', 143–4
  and oil-price, 142–3
  inflation in, 24, 206, 210, 211, 213
  macro-economic policy, 182
United States (inflation in), 205, 209,
    210, 211, 216, 217–8

Velocity, *see* Monetary velocity
Vertical integration, 103ff
  attempts to explain, 103–5, 114–16,
    118
  costs of, 108–9
  definitions/description, 105–6
  gains from, 106–8
  in oil, 110–13
  incomplete prevalence (i.e. co-
    existence)of, 114

Wage-push (*see also* OPEC),
  distinction from OPEC effects, 125–6
  theory of and oil prices, 121, 123–5